CW00471894

Autonomy

BLOOMSBURY ETHICS SERIES

Bloomsbury Ethics is a series of books written to help students explore, engage with and master key topics in contemporary ethics and moral philosophy.

Series Editors: Thom Brooks is Reader in Law at Durham Law School. He is the founding editor of the *Journal of Moral Philosophy* and runs a popular Political Philosophy blog called The Brooks Blog.

Simon Kirchin is Senior Lecturer in Philosophy at the University of Kent, UK. He is President of the British Society for Ethical Theory and co-editor of *Arguing About Metaethics* (Routledge, 2006).

Available now:

Intuitionism, David Kaspar
Moral Realism, Kevin DeLapp
Reasons, Eric Wiland
Virtue Ethics, Nafsika Athanassoulis

Forthcoming in the series:

Trust, Ethics and Human Reason, Olli Lagerspetz

BLOOMSBURY ETHICS

Autonomy

ANDREW SNEDDON

B L O O M S B U R Y

LONDON • NEW DELHI • NEW YORK • SYDNEY

Bloomsbury Academic
An imprint of Bloomsbury Publishing Plc

50 Bedford Square
London
WC1B 3DP
UK

175 Fifth Avenue
New York
NY 10010
USA

www.bloomsbury.com

First published 2013

© Andrew Sneddon, 2013

All rights reserved. No part of this publication may be reproduced or transmitted in any form or by any means, electronic or mechanical, including photocopying, recording, or any information storage or retrieval system, without prior permission in writing from the publishers.

Andrew Sneddon has asserted his right under the Copyright, Designs and Patents Act, 1988, to be identified as Author of this work.

No responsibility for loss caused to any individual or organization acting on or refraining from action as a result of the material in this publication can be accepted by Bloomsbury Academic or the author.

British Library Cataloguing-in-Publication Data
A catalogue record for this book is available from the British Library.

ISBN: HB: 978-1-4411-5231-2
PB: 978-1-4411-6501-5
ePub: 978-1-4411-6841-2
ePDF: 978 1-4411-6307-3

Library of Congress Cataloging-in-Publication Data
Sneddon, Andrew, 1971-
Autonomy / Andrew Sneddon.
pages cm. – (Bloomsbury ethics)
Includes bibliographical references and index.
ISBN 978-1-4411-5231-2 – ISBN 978-1-4411-6501-5 (pbk.) – ISBN 978-1-4411-6841-2 (ebook (epub)) – ISBN 978-1-4411-6307-3 (ebook (pdf)) 1. Autonomy (Philosophy) I. Title.
B808.67.S64 2013
128'.4–dc23
2012046562

Typeset by Deanta Global Publishing Services, Chennai, India
Printed and bound in India

For Debbie

CONTENTS

PREFACE

The topic of this book is individual autonomy. The roots of the word 'autonomy' are 'auto', or self, and 'nomos', which means 'law' or, more colloquially, 'rule'. To study individual autonomy is to ask questions about the nature and significance of our capacities to govern ourselves. When we think about our lives, it may seem that we understand and exercise control over certain aspects of our identities and not others. We recognize that some of our choices and actions reflect our identity more deeply than other choices and actions. Some of our desires hardly seem to come from us at all, and instead are experienced as stemming from forces external to us. What is the difference between these sources of motivation? What should we make of all this? Should we care about our own autonomy? What about other people and their control over their lives? These are the questions examined in this book. The first half presents an account of the nature of autonomy. The second half addresses why we should care about individual self-rule in both ourselves and in other people.

This book is meant as a provocative introduction to contemporary philosophical thought about autonomy. Philosophers have long been interested in the nature and significance of personal self-governance. However, at the end of the twentieth century, a particularly nuanced body of thought about autonomy was developed by a cluster of English-speaking philosophers. This book presents the themes characteristic of this body of thought, and to this degree this is an introductory book. It is provocative, I hope, because I do not merely present the various debates that have occurred in recent years. I defend a particular account of the nature of autonomy, and I argue that it matters, both in fairly general terms and with regard to quite specific moral issues. Not all readers will agree with the stands that I take. That's good; philosophical thought about autonomy is still developing. If this book prompts readers to develop particular ideas about the nature and significance of self-governance, then it has done more than introduce them to a body of ideas. It will have included them in an on-going philosophical conversation. Maybe it will have made them more autonomous with regard to this topic than they were before. I count this as a good thing.

I have worked, on and off, on the ideas found in this book for a long time. Early versions of some of the material presented here have been published previously. I thank the publishers for permission to reproduce some of the work found in the following articles:

Sneddon, A. (2001a), 'What's wrong with selling yourself into slavery? Paternalism and deep autonomy', *Criticá*, Vol. 33, No. 98 (Aug.), 97–121.

Sneddon, A. (2001b), 'Advertising and deep autonomy', *Journal of Business Ethics*, Vol. 33, #1 (Sept.), 15–28.

Sneddon, A. (2006), 'Equality, justice, and paternalism: recentering debate about physician-assisted suicide', *Journal of Applied Philosophy*, Vol. 23, No. 4, 387–404

A version of the third paper was presented in 2004 at Carleton University; thanks go to the audience members for their attention and helpful criticism.

More personal thanks are also owed. I taught a graduate seminar on autonomy at the University of Ottawa in 2007. I am grateful to the students in this class for their interest in and enthusiastic discussion of this territory. For a few years around the same time I ran a small reading group on autonomy. The most persistent members were Jim Greenwood, Sophie Rietti and Mark Young. Our meetings were fun blends of beer and thoughtful scrutiny of the work of some of the people discussed in this book. Thank you all for helping to sow the seeds of the present project.

I love autonomy. To some ears that might sound like I am some sort of rugged individualist, conceiving of myself and my life as thoroughly isolated from other people. Once you read this book you will see that this is not the case at all. Interest in and respect for self-rule need not involve suspicion and rejection of the influence of other people. Far from it; deep connections to other people can make us more rather than less autonomous. There is one person with whom I run my life—Debbie, my wife. It's not just my life that would be different if we had not been a couple for the last twenty-five years. I would, quite literally, be a different person. I wrote this book, but it stems from personal, educational and vocational processes made possible and deeply shaped by Debbie. This is for her.

CHAPTER ONE

Introduction

I am a middle-aged man. I have a career, a happy marriage, a healthy dog and good relations with my neighbours and relatives. My bills are paid on time. Crucially, I enjoy the liberty and capacity to choose what to do with much of my time and resources.

There is nothing unique in this brief description of myself. These features are shared by millions of people. But something a bit more notable emerges when we put these characteristics into the more extended context of an average life. At the beginning of my life, before my wife, neighbours and dog came along, I had much less liberty and, arguably, none of the capacities that allow me to run my life now. Perhaps the roots of the psychological abilities required for running a life are present in infancy, but there can be no denying that the processes of maturation bring with them great changes in our capacities for taking care of ourselves. When we are completely unable to address our basic needs, others bear the responsibility of ensuring that we are okay. Without this we perish. Typically, we are also denied the liberty to follow our whims in action. Thank goodness! Without such restrictions we would suffer greatly precisely because we are incapable: we lack both the skills and the knowledge to secure ourselves in dangerous circumstances. Ordinary development yields something quite remarkable by contrast. Normal people run their lives – not perfectly and not without challenges, but with a degree of success far-removed from our early helplessness. Others help us with our lives, but in a much different manner from our early years. Then we were helpless dependents; now we are co-operators in the joint venture of living together as adults.

If I live long enough, I can expect things to change again, and not for the better. The average life span of a Canadian such as me is now longer than ever because many relatively sudden and early-in-life causes of death have been successfully curtailed. This is a good thing, but it has a downside. In contrast with our ancestors, average people in countries such as Canada face an increased likelihood of significant, slow degeneration at the end of our lives. The changes will undoubtedly be physical: our muscles will be weaker and our joints more painful, transforming today's effortless tasks into challenges that might be excruciating, even insurmountable. For many the changes will also be psychological. In ways both subtle and obvious, and trivial and deep, our minds will wither. Perhaps particular competencies will be lost. Perhaps we will no longer be the people that we once were. Either way, we will face obstacles in running our lives that we did not suffer in the prime of our lives.

The topic of this book is the nature and significance of personal self-rule, that is, of the psychological capacities that we develop through normal maturation, lose to the scourge of dementia, and that make us capable of running our lives, at least in part. I trust that the general significance of these capacities is clear from the brief look at infancy, maturity and degeneration presented so far. This is enough to warrant studying the topic. For the last three decades there has been growing interest among philosophers in understanding self-rule. We have gone from a position in the 1980s in which this topic got very little direct attention to a position in the twenty-first century in which there are numerous well-developed, intricately detailed theories of self-rule.

Besides being of general theoretical interest, personal self-rule is important in sub-domains of philosophy. To note just two, both medical ethicists and political philosophers wrestle with the nature and significance of the capacities by which people run their lives. In both these cases the stakes are more than theoretical. Just how we understand self-rule will have implications for how we are handled by the state, on one hand, and by medical institutions on the other. The evidence is clear: this is a topic worth studying for both theoretical and practical reasons.

The term commonly used for 'personal self-rule' is 'autonomy'. The Greek roots of this word are 'auto' for 'self', and 'nomos' for roughly, 'rule, law, or government'. In common parlance 'autonomy' is applied to lots of things. As examples, we speak of autonomous robots and states. The present topic is *personal* autonomy – the capacities that render individual persons capable of self-rule. It is quite possible that what we learn about these capacities will tell us nothing about the crucial features of other autonomous things. Presumably when we use 'autonomous' of a variety of types of things we mean to say that they are, for instance, self-controlling, but just what this consists might well vary from one thing to another.

The Greek roots of the word 'autonomy' allow us to construct a variety of terms for contrasting phenomena. Most importantly, the word used for being ruled by others is 'heteronomy'. 'Hetero' is the Greek term for, roughly, 'other'. Autonomy theorists routinely address heteronomy because the control of one person by another is so important, but there are non-personal sources of control worth noting regardless of their relations to heterononomy. Consider a creature with very rigid capacities for tracking certain features of the world. Imagine a type of frog that is very good at catching flies: every time a fly is seen, the frog's tongue automatically flicks towards it. Because this capacity is automatic, the frog does not control it, so it is not autonomous. But the frog is under the control of no other organism either, so it is not heteronomous. Instead the capacity is coupled with the world such that we can say, without too much distortion, that it is under worldly control. Let's call this 'cosmonomy', for rule by (for persons) non-personal features of the world. Finally, there is the possibility of people who are under no control. They act as circumstances and whim dictate, without having the capacities for tracking particular features of the world. Let's call this 'oudenonomy', from the Greek root 'ouden' for nothing. Very young children without adult supervision might, at least occasionally, be oudenonomous.

When theorizing about a topic with which there is a preliminary, non-theoretical familiarity, there are at least two possible sources of disagreement. Obviously theorists can disagree about the details of particular theories. That's what makes up the literature on such topics. But theorists can also disagree about the initial characterization of the topic in question. Both sorts of disagreement are found in the literature about autonomy. Indeed, the little that I have already said about just what personal self-rule is will have rankled some. This is unavoidable. In the remainder of this chapter I will augment our working characterization of autonomy by differentiating it from some related but distinct phenomena.

I shall start with something that sounds like the present topic but isn't: political autonomy. I bring this up at the start because of my experiences in speaking about autonomy with undergraduate students. Depending on their academic background, some students seem to think first of political autonomy when they hear the word 'autonomy'. Moreover, they think of a particular sense of 'political autonomy', which differs from the way the term operates in discussions of personal autonomy. In the sense in which my students think of it, political autonomy is a property of groups, such as states or nations, rather than of individual persons. A nation is politically autonomous when it governs itself. From a sufficiently abstract perspective there is much in common between personal and political autonomy. Both politically and personally autonomous entities exercise control over what happens to them, in at least some respects and to some degree. But as soon as we attend to details it becomes clear that there are deep differences here. Political autonomy will be realized through the collaborative efforts of legislators and through the explicit codes that define legal institutions, including but not limited to constitutions. Personal autonomy is a property of individuals that involves other people in various ways and to various degrees. It is not necessarily collaborative and it is certainly not typically dependent on explicit legal codes or even on anything analogous to them, whatever that might be.

When autonomy theorists use the term 'political autonomy', they are discussing personal autonomy in political contexts. This is particularly important in liberal political philosophy and, indeed, in discussions of democracy in general. The rough idea here is that political power derives its authority from the autonomous consent of the governed. People are politically autonomous when they are sufficiently capable of participating in political institutions, such as voting, in a way that gives expression to their capacity for self-rule. Clearly this notion of autonomy relies on the prior notion of personal self-rule in general. I shall discuss political autonomy in this sense in Chapter 7.

Closer to the topic but still distinct is moral autonomy. This is a somewhat ambiguous notion (as is autonomy itself, of course). Outside of philosophy 'moral autonomy' tends to be used to refer to people who make choices or perform actions on the basis of moral assessment of their options. Morally autonomous action is action that is deliberately performed out of a sense that it is morally permissible or demanded. Philosophers tend to use 'moral autonomy' to refer to people who determine their own moral standards. This stems at least in part from Immanuel Kant's usage of 'autonomy'. To put it roughly, Kant thought that people are free insofar as they are rational. For us to act in ways that have moral worth, Kant held that we have to act out of respect for moral law. Moral laws bind everyone equally, regardless of their desires. This raises a problem: how can free beings be bound by the authority of morality? Kant's answer is that moral laws must stem from rational human nature itself. Autonomous beings are people who give laws to themselves by virtue of their rationality, and hence who bind themselves. We are thus bound by morality but not by any authority outside of ourselves, and hence our freedom is preserved.

It should be clear that personal autonomy, the present topic, differs from moral autonomy. We are self-ruling, in the sense of being able to run our lives, without necessarily giving ourselves moral principles or acting out of an assessment of the moral permissibility of our options. Nevertheless, the contrast between these two notions should not be overstated. There are connections between moral autonomy and personal autonomy, as we will see in the next two chapters.

The discussion of Kant invokes freedom. This is another notion worth differentiating from autonomy. Again there are various notions of freedom, or liberty, both in everyday speech and in academic discussions. Arguably the most famous attempt to specify varieties of liberty comes from Isaiah Berlin (2002). According to Berlin, 'negative' freedom is the absence of external obstacles to acting as one sees fit. 'Positive' liberty is, by contrast, the power to determine the course of your life. Personal autonomy is clearly distinct from negative freedom, although there might be intimate connections between the two. They are distinct because negative liberty is the *absence* of constraint, whereas self-rule consists in the *presence* of specific capacities. Interestingly, it is reasonable to think that negative liberty is an important part of political autonomy as it applies to groups. For nations to rule themselves they must be free of certain sorts of interference from other bodies. This adds another dimension to the differences between personal autonomy and political autonomy. Instead, autonomy is much more like positive liberty, to the extent that we might as well consider them equivalent. However, the differing connotations of the terms mean that they are not usefully substitutable. As we shall see in the next chapter, it is quite natural to speak of autonomy with regard to psychological features which we would hesitate to describe in terms of freedom. Desires can be autonomous, but it strikes my ear as odd to speak of them as free. I take this to be a deficiency of the term 'positive liberty'; 'autonomy' is a preferable word to use to capture the relevant phenomena.

Freedom and moral autonomy point to another concept worth addressing: moral responsibility. We speak of moral responsibility for particular actions and, what is more important for present purposes, of people who are morally responsible in general. The philosophical literature on moral responsibility is voluminous, but thankfully we do not need to delve into these depths to see that being morally responsible is different from being autonomous. There are two features of morally responsible agency of particular importance. First, it is reasonable to assess such agents by moral standards. Second, moral responsibility is something that we attribute to each other, such that a good case can be made for thinking that morally responsible agents must have sufficient interpersonal skills to be participants in this sort of behaviour. If we put together these two ideas we get a sense of moral responsibility as an institution, in the sense of a code-structured social phenomenon. Although, as a matter of fact, most autonomous agents will be morally responsible as well, I think that these observations give us reason to think that these are not quite the same thing. It is conceivable, to me at least, to think of people who are capable of running their lives but who are, in one way or another, not morally responsible agents. Some psychopaths might be like this. Depending on the psychological details of their psychopathy, they might be sufficiently insensible to moral standards as to be unfit for assessment in those terms. However, to the extent that they are capable of self-rule they will nevertheless count as autonomous. High-functioning autistic people present another possibility. Autism is characterized by psychological obstacles to interpersonal activity. Autistic people with severe interpersonal deficits might be shut out of the institution of holding each other morally responsible for action. Nevertheless, if they are sufficiently capable of self-rule then they will be autonomous.

The final topic to contrast with personal autonomy is authenticity. Generally this connotes true or real existence. More specifically we speak of people as authentic when they live in accordance with their 'true selves', which is contrasted with kinds of living that come from external sources. Clearly authenticity overlaps with autonomy. However, depending on just how much we emphasize the contrast between authentic living and external conditions, we should differentiate between these concepts. As we will see in the next two chapters, we can autonomously choose to live according to external demands. We can even autonomously subjugate ourselves to them. However, on the face of it such subjugation is inconsistent with authenticity. This is avoided if authentic living is consistent with subjugation to others, but now the opposing threat is opened up. Perhaps the true self for some people is one that avoids self-rule and instead embraces heteronomy. If this is the case, then we have a different sort of reason for distinguishing between authenticity and autonomy.

So much for what autonomy is not. Is there anything more in an introductory spirit that can be said about what it is? I think that there is. Human psychology is surprisingly multifaceted. Autonomy derives from a variety of psychological sources, but one is particularly important. As we mature, we develop reflective capacities. Our ability to ask questions about the world shows up remarkably early. People with experience with small children will recognize this. But as we mature, we develop and many of us cultivate the capacity to turn our reflective capacities on ourselves. This has unique effects. Such thought about ourselves is not necessary for our actions to stem from ourselves, as opposed to others or the world, but it is, I submit, necessary, in some form, for the fuller sense of self-control that we call autonomy. The details of this view will be developed in the next two chapters. The significance of these capacities will be addressed in the second half of this book.

This book is a suggestive introduction to contemporary thought about autonomy. It is introductory in the sense of providing a survey of central themes in contemporary discussion of personal self-rule. It is a suggestive introduction in that I go beyond merely providing a map to existing discussions to take a stand on them. It is difficult to perform both these tasks at once, but my hope is that the combination is both fair to the work that others have done and sufficiently interesting, in its own right, to be worth taking seriously, as a small contribution to this field. One reading note: I refrain from fine-grained grappling with the details of the literature where I can. Instead, guides to the existing literature are provided at the ends of the chapters. I have two reasons for doing this. First, it increases the readability of the book, which is fitting given my introductory aims. Second, to wrestle with the details of the existing literature would be redundant: this body of work is already characterized by much attentive surveying. A reader who picks up almost any recent book on this topic will find in the first chapter a detailed presentation of prominent themes. I have chosen to introduce autonomy, albeit suggestively, and then to point the way to the literature where the more baroque argumentative nuances can be found.

Reading guide

Introductions to the contemporary literature are often found as part of the development of full-blown theories of autonomy. Some examples: early chapters in James Stacey Taylor's *Practical Autonomy and Bioethics* (Routledge, 2009), Marina Oshana's *Personal Autonomy in Society* (Ashgate, 2006), and Ben Colburn's *Autonomy and Liberalism* (Routledge, 2010). James Stacey Taylor's edited volume *Personal Autonomy. New Essays on Personal Autonomy and Its Role in Contemporary Moral Philosophy* (Cambridge University Press, 2005) is an excellent work to look for both a survey of the field and intricacies of contemporary debate from many key players.

The association of autonomy with the capacity for thought about one's own thoughts stems from Gerald Dworkin and Harry Frankfurt's work. Frankfurt's view, put in terms of personhood and freedom rather than autonomy, is found in 'Freedom of the will and the concept of a person', *Journal of Philosophy* 68 (1971), pp. 5–20; reprinted in his *The Importance of What We Care About* (Cambridge: Cambridge University Press, 1988). Dworkin's view can be found in *The Theory and Practice of Autonomy* (Cambridge University Press, 1988). We will see other versions of this sort of view in the next two chapters. James Stacey Taylor's introduction to *Personal Autonomy*, listed above, is a good introduction to contemporary discussion which focuses on this sort of view as the centre of the field.

The third chapter of Dworkin's book is a trenchant look at differences between personal autonomy and moral autonomy.

Immanuel Kant's work is famous, vast and difficult. His most well known treatment of autonomy is found in *Grounding for the Metaphysics of Morals*. A short discussion of the intricacies of Kant's view has been offered by Paul Guyer, 'Kant on the theory and practice of autonomy', in *Autonomy*, edited by Ellen Frankel Paul, Fred D. Miller, Jr. and Jeffrey Paul (Cambridge University Press, 2003).

The philosophical literature about moral responsibility is even larger than that about autonomy. For a view that famously ties moral responsibility to interpersonal relations, see P. F. Strawson, 'Freedom and resentment'. Strawson's essay is very widely reprinted, including in the still very useful collection: *Perspectives on Moral Responsibility*, edited by John Martin Fischer and Mark Ravizza (Cornell University Press, 1993). Ravizza and, especially, Fischer are leading theorists of moral responsibility. See their *Responsibility and Control: A Theory of Moral Responsibility* (Cambridge University Press, 1998) and Fischer's *My Way: Essays on Moral Responsibility* (Oxford University Press, 2006) for insightful work on moral responsibility that is broadly Strawsonian. Links between moral responsibility and autonomy are discussed by Michael McKenna, 'The relationship between autonomous and morally responsible agency', and Ishtiyaque Haji, 'Alternative possibilities, personal autonomy, and moral responsibility', both of which can be found in Taylor's *Personal Autonomy*.

The literature on freedom is even bigger. Isaiah Berlin's view is found in the famous 'Two concepts of liberty', widely available and reprinted in his *Liberty*, edited by Henry Hardy (Oxford University Press, 2002). Short discussions of freedom and autonomy are provided by Bernard Berofsky, 'Autonomy without free will', Marina Oshana, 'Autonomy and free agency', and Susan Wolf, 'Freedom within reason', all found in Taylor's *Personal Autonomy*. More extended treatments of liberty and autonomy can be found in Berofsky's *Liberation from Self: A Theory of Personal Autonomy* (Cambridge University Press, 1995) and Alfred Mele's *Autonomous Agents: From Self-Control to Autonomy* (Oxford University Press, 1995). Jean-Paul Sartre can reasonably be read as articulating a radical notion of freedom as the capacity to determine the course of your life in 'Existentialism as a humanism', a famous lecture which he gave in 1946 and which is widely available (Yale University Press published a formal edition in 2007).

James Stacey Taylor differentiates autonomy from authenticity in *Practical Autonomy and Bioethics*.

Political autonomy, in the sense of personal autonomy exercised in the political domain, is a central concern of Colburn in *Autonomy and Liberalism* (listed above). Other important work on political liberalism is offered by Marilyn Friedman in *Autonomy, Gender, Politics* (Oxford University Press, 2003) and, especially, John Christman: see his *The Politics of Persons: Individual Autonomy and Socio-historical Selves* (Cambridge University Press, 2009) and the collection, *Autonomy and the Challenges to Liberalism: New Essays*, edited by Christman and Joel Anderson (Cambridge University Press, 2005).

CHAPTER TWO

Faces of autonomy

The project in this chapter is to begin providing a detailed theory of personal autonomy. Before such a theory can be developed, we need to sharpen our sense of just what the theory is about. To this end, I shall start this chapter by making some observations about autonomy. The point of collecting these observations is to construct a baseline account of important features of personal self-rule. If this baseline account is correct, then the adequacy of particular theories can be assessed in terms of how well they explain these features.

1] Ahmed was born on January 1, 1974. On January 1, 2014 he reflects on his life. When he was a young child he wondered about what he would do for a job when he needed one. It scared him to think of adult responsibilities. Now Ahmed proudly owns a own restaurant. The daily responsibilities that once scared him have long since become so easy that they scarcely warrant a second thought. Ahmed marvels at the changes that life brings, although he is unable to pinpoint exactly when these changes occurred.

Observations Part One: As noted in Chapter 1, we are not born with the capacities for personal self-rule. Since adults such as Ahmed are, generally speaking, autonomous, this means that we acquire these capacities somewhere along the way. This should not be a surprise. It is important to recognize the developmental possibilities here. One possibility is that we automatically develop autonomy. Perhaps the psychology of self-rule is like the cognitive capacities for walking or language comprehension, which develop early and effortlessly under normal conditions. Another possibility is that we develop autonomy through difficult, dedicated study, like the capacity for reading. Between these poles are hybrid possibilities which involve both automatic and non-automatic processes. Such blends will be more likely if autonomy is psychologically heterogeneous. Regardless of the details to be found here, we can say at this point that autonomy is a threshold phenomenon: we go from not having it to having it on the basis of the level of development of certain capacities. This does not mean that there is an identifiable point at which a person becomes capable of self-rule. Consider other skills: there is no distinct point at which someone becomes a competent driver. We go from being unable to drive to being novice drivers to being competent, without clear markers that divide levels of competency.

2] This raises an obvious question: just how much of the relevant capacities does one need in order to count as autonomous? How high is the threshold set? Consider Bob and Chantal. Bob is a simple guy. He does what his job requires of him on Monday through Friday. He regularly buys the same things at the grocery store. He grew up playing hockey and still does so on weekends. Occasionally he buys tickets to watch professional hockey. He is not particularly connected to government at any level, but he is not bothered by this, as he is not interested in such things. Bob does not think about the future much. It is important to Bob to do what seems right to him, but he has spent very little time reflecting on values.

Chantal is a chemistry professor. She has made revolutionary discoveries in her particular field of expertise, making her well-known around the world to other chemists. Besides chemistry, Chantal reflects regularly on what makes life worth living, both individually and collectively. She has become active in grassroots political organizations which call for change to legislation and to government practices at every level. She has written some articles for small magazines about these things and is planning on writing a book. She worries a lot about what the future holds for herself and others but is committed to doing things to increase the chances that what she wants will come about.

Observations Part Two: Chantal is clearly autonomous. I shall argue that Bob is too, although this might be contentious. If I am correct then both Bob and Chantal are above the threshold for autonomy. Whatever capacities are central to personal self-rule are found in sufficiently high amounts in Bob and Chantal. Despite being above the threshold, Bob and Chantal are not equally autonomous.

Chantal rules her life to a different degree than Bob, and maybe in different ways as well. There are various theoretical possibilities here. On one hand, maybe autonomy, for people such as Chantal and Bob, is realized by precisely the same characteristics. On the other hand, maybe Chantal's autonomy is enhanced by capacities that are not strictly necessary for self-rule. This possibility presents challenges to the theorist of autonomy. In this case, noting that Chantal's autonomy draws on some particular cognitive capacity does not imply that this capacity is necessary for self-rule. Bob's autonomy need not be represented as deficient due to the lack of this capacity.

3] Compare Dawson, Emilie and Farrah. All are adults. In the past they had no trouble running their lives, but recently obstacles have arisen. Dawson has contracted dementia. His memory is unreliable. He finds ordinary situations baffling at times, although at other times he has no problems. His doctor predicts that his symptoms will inevitably worsen.

Emilie is in her 80s. For decades she lived with her husband, but he died 10 years ago. This, in combination with changes in the world around her, has shaken Emilie's confidence. She no longer feels comfortable in the world. She second-guesses every decision and avoids making them as long as possible. Sometimes this interferes with her getting access to basic necessities such as food. Emilie senses that her life has changed, but she has no clear idea of the extent of the changes or of what might be done to regain control of her life.

Farrah feels fine. She seems to herself to be as she always has been, clear in her views of what she wants and capable of pursuing her desires. However, unbeknownst to her she underwent a serious change when she recently had surgery. An evil neurosurgeon implanted a chip in her brain which substitutes the neurosurgeon's desires for Farrah's own whenever Farrah wants something that the neurosurgeon does not want for her. If she could occupy an objective vantage point on her life, Farrah would say that she has lost control of it.

Observations Part Three: Just as autonomy can be acquired, so can it be lost. Dawson, Emilie and Farrah have all suffered decreases in autonomy, possibly to the extent of losing it altogether. Dawson and Emilie are becoming oudenonomous, but for different reasons. In Dawson's case it is the condition of his brain that is undermining his capacity for self-control. Depending on the causes of his dementia, this could take at least two forms. First, it might be the case that the neurological underpinnings of self-rule are withering with age, as it were. On the other hand, it could be that there is some sort of interfering presence in his brain. In this case his capacities for autonomy are present but hindered. By contrast Emilie's brain is fine. Her loss of self-rule is due to changes in the world and to other sorts of changes in herself. With regard to herself, we might well say that autonomy can be lost due to lack of practice. This viewpoint emphasizes the similarities between personal self-rule and skills in general. The inclusion of environmental factors serves to underline the general way in which cognition can depend on context. While this might hold for our minds in general, it is a particularly important point for the psychology of autonomy, since self-rule concerns, in part, running our lives in the circumstances in which we find ourselves. To some extent individual effort might compensate for environmental changes, but we cannot assume that this will always be possible, and certainly not that it will be easy.

Farrah is heteronomous. The case of the evil neuroscientist is obviously fanciful, but control by others can take more subtle and familiar forms. Suppose that Farrah had fallen under the influence of a charismatic political or religious leader. This can yield the control of one by another without the technical intervention of brain surgery. The important points are, first, that even the autonomous can become heteronomous. Developing the capacities for self-rule does not insulate one forever from the controlling influence of others, although it probably helps to ward it off. Heteronomy can come about by undermining or even usurping one's autonomy, rather than preventing it from developing in the first place. Second, as with oudenonomy, heteronomy can take a variety of forms. We shall look at some of these as we put together the details of the overall theory.

4] Consider George and Hojin. Both reflect on their lives and act accordingly. Hojin thinks regularly about moral values. She reasons about what is right and wrong to do, and she is concerned about making herself into a person who lives a morally acceptable life. George knows about morality but he does not care about it. His reflection is rarely about the moral character of his life. Sometimes he does what is morally required of him, but this is rarely because it is morally required. It is often just coincidental that he lives up to the demands of morality.

Observations Part Four: Although they are very briefly described, we have reason to think that both Hojin and George are autonomous. They control their lives, but they do so in the light of different sorts of considerations. Put abstractly this should seem natural. People have different concerns, so it should be no wonder that they design their lives around differing ideas. The more interesting feature of this comparison is the role of moral values. We might be tempted to think that autonomy requires a concern for morality. Perhaps the self-ruling person must be concerned with the evaluative character of her own life, such that a reflective person who never thinks about moral values cannot be autonomous. There might be a specific sense in which this is true, as we shall see in the next chapter, but as a general point about autonomy it is false. In the present case, George is an example of an amoralist. In typical philosophical discussion, the amoralist is someone who understands moral values but does not care about them and hence is not motivated by them. Just as we can be indifferent to, for example, hockey despite knowing about it and understanding it, so also the amoralist is indifferent to morality. The present suggestion is that just as autonomy is consistent with indifference to hockey, so it is consistent with indifference to morality.

5] Indira is a powerful woman. Long ago she set herself the goal of acquiring a vast fortune. She has chosen a life of crime to accomplish this. She employs a vast network of criminals who do anything and everything necessary to make money: theft, murder, the undermining of elections – nothing is beyond the pale for Indira. Indira knows that her activities are evil, and because of this she often revisits the question of how she feels about living this sort of life. Every time she reflects on her life she ends up recommitting herself to it. Her evil resolve is only strengthened by her reflection. Indira has no plans to change her ways.

Observations Part Five: This is obviously an extension of the previous point. If autonomous people need not be concerned with morality, then they need not be concerned with being good people. 'Autonomy' is not a synonym for 'virtue'. Literature is filled with characters who fascinate precisely because they are both evil and self-ruling. The super-villain often seems more in control of life than the ordinary people who suffer as a consequence.

These last two sets of observations raise questions about the value of autonomy. If we were able to pick our neighbours, but our choices were limited to heteronomous good people or autonomous amoralists, it seems to me that we should choose to live next to the former, not the latter. Nevertheless, this does not imply that autonomy is not valuable at all. Some aspects of the value of personal self-rule are addressed in the second half of this book.

6] Jan is 45 years old. He owns and runs a small logging company. The company is located in the remote town in which Jan grew up. He has spent his whole life there. Most of the people in this town work in the logging industry. There are very few local opportunities to pursue other sorts of careers. None of this matters to Jan: he always dreamed about having his own logging company, to the extent that other careers have barely ever crossed his mind.

Kari is the same age as Jan. She lives in a big city where she owns and runs a small advertising firm. This is one of the things that Kari has long thought about doing, but she has had other opportunities as well. She was attracted by several fields in university, any one of which would have led to a satisfying career. She was also a successful tennis player at the national level and could have pursued a career as a player or trainer. However, once she decided to open her own business she put thoughts of other careers aside. She is very happy with her life and regrets nothing.

Observations Part Six: This is more of an issue to keep in mind than an observation of a straightforward characteristic of personal self-rule. We have already seen one way in which context matters to autonomy; the vignettes about Jan and Kari present another. Kari and Jan are very similar. They are the same age and, professionally, have very similar jobs. We have good reason to think that they count as autonomous. They differ in their environments. Whereas Kari's context is rich in opportunity, Jan's is not. Has Jan's autonomy been diminished by his relatively impoverished circumstances? On one hand we might think that self-rule is at least enhanced by a wide range of opportunities and, even stronger, that it actually requires a minimally rich range of possibilities. On the other hand, given that Jan runs his life in the way that he wants to, we might well think that the addition of possibilities would make no substantial difference to his autonomy. More subtle questions arise when we turn from the choices that Jan and Kari have made to the formation of their desires. Jan has always wanted a logging company, but given that he had so few options for a career can we be confident that he leads the life he really wants to lead? Perhaps a richer array of options is necessary for the formation of desires in a manner consistent with autonomy. Again, we will return to this question in Chapter 3.

7] Lionel designs robots. His current work involves perfecting a robot capable of doing a wide range of tasks without continual instruction from a human overseer. Nicholas calls this robot 'Mibot', short for 'mostly independent robot'. When speaking with his colleagues Lionel refers to the technical problems he encounters in trying to make Mibot autonomous. It turns out to be easy to give Mibot self-controlling capacities in some ways and very difficult to do so in others. Chatting with someone on the train about his work, he is asked whether Mibot is anything like a person. Lionel scoffs at the idea – Mibot has neither a self nor a sense of self, so he's nothing like a real person.

Observations Part Seven: 'Self' is ambiguous in English, and this ambiguity carries over to the ways in which we speak of autonomy. In one sense of 'self', persons and other entities are self-ruling when they are not controlled by others. This is the sense of 'self' and autonomy that applies to Mibot. In principle, and perhaps in reality, very simple mechanisms can be self-controlling in this sense. Let's call this the 'thin' sense of 'self'. By contrast, Mibot has no thicker self than this, whereas Lionel does. Just what constitutes this thicker self is part of our topic in the next chapter. When philosophers speak of autonomy, they mean primarily self-rule in the thick sense of rule by the complex psychology that Lionel possesses and Mibot lacks. But they mean also the thin sense – control by the human organism and not by other things in the wider world. This ambiguity should be kept in mind when assessing intuitions about whether autonomy, in some particular discourse, requires relatively more or relatively less to be realized or respected.

Both senses of 'self', but perhaps especially the thin sense, invite a particular interpretation. To make Mibot self-controlling, imagine that Lionel builds certain behaviour-producing mechanisms and places them within the box that we would describe as Mibot's head. Generalizing, it is tempting to think that the locus of self-rule, in either sense of 'self', must be located within the physical boundaries of the entity in question for that entity to be autonomous. On this view, the capacities that make Lionel autonomous must be located within his physical 'self', presumably in his brain. It is reasonable to think that this is typically and centrally the case, but I shall argue in Chapter 4 that it is a mistake to think that our capacities for self-rule *must* be located within our bodies. Assuming so undervalues the role of the features of wider world, including other people, in our minds.

8] Nicholas exercises control over his life to a high degree. He reflects on both what he wants and what he should want, regularly trying to bring the former into line with the latter. Nicholas is quite successful at this way of running his life, with regard to all domains of his life: health, personal and professional relations, pastimes, *etc.* One day Nicholas is in the mall, passing the food court. The smell of fresh French fries catches his attention. This is the kind of thing that he never allows himself to eat, but today the temptation is too much. Nicholas purchases and consumes a large order of fries. He enjoys the snack but regrets the decision, vowing not to let it happen again.

Olivia has little taste for exercising control over her life. She generally follows whatever desires she happens to have at a given time. Sometimes this has good results, sometimes quite bad ones, but Olivia does not worry about patterns in her behaviour, nor about trying to avoid the bad and pursue the good. She is typically content to satisfy her immediate wants and to let the longer term chips fall where they may. One day Olivia is in the mall, walking by the food court. The scent of fresh French fries hangs thickly in the air. Olivia is hungry and tempted to have them. However, contrary to her usual habits she asks herself, 'Do I really want these?' Despite being tempted, she answers negatively and leaves the food court without buying anything.

Observations Part Eight: What should we say about Nicholas and Olivia? It's reasonable to think that Nicholas is autonomous whereas Olivia is not, but this obscures important details about their actions in the food court. A more nuanced assessment would be that Nicholas is generally but not perfectly autonomous and Olivia is only occasionally so. However, this still leaves out important details. We can be more specific.

It is common for autonomy theorists to distinguish between 'global' and 'local' senses of 'autonomy'. In its global sense, to speak of someone as autonomous is to make a claim about the person's life as a whole or over an extended portion of it. In its local sense, particular actions or choices are autonomous, not larger stretches of a person's life. This gives us something more fine-grained to say about the present case: Nicholas is globally autonomous but fails to be locally autonomous in his action of eating French fries. This action is locally cosmonomous, perhaps. For Olivia it is the other way around: she is not globally autonomous but she manages to be autonomous in the food court, making her decision about the French fries in a locally self-ruling manner.

It is worth knowing about this terminology, but I shall speak in a different manner. The 'global/local' terminology is unnecessarily opaque, especially when there are preferable terms for these phenomena. Moreover, these terms can be misleading. 'Global' connotes, to my mind, 'everywhere', but, as we shall see, the relevant sense of autonomy is not autonomy that is found all through someone's life but something more specific. 'Local', as a contrast to this sense of 'global', can imply something very specific, such as a single decision. The local sense of autonomy can apply to single events, but it need not always. Instead one can be locally autonomous about, for example, a particular kind of decision, such that whenever one makes it one exercises self-rule. In this case, local autonomy is found everywhere that this kind of decision is found in one's life, but now this sounds like something global.

Here is what I shall use instead of the 'global/local' terminology. Nicholas is an *autonomous person*. Autonomy of persons is the topic of Chapter 3, so the details of what this means will have to wait. However, his choice about French fries is made non-autonomously. That is, besides autonomy of persons it makes sense to speak of *autonomy of choices*. By 'choices' here I mean something quite wide. The topic is autonomy in a practical sense, so 'autonomy of choice' should be taken to include decisions, desires and actions at the very least. Olivia's decision and action with regard to the French fries are autonomous, but Olivia is not an autonomous person.

Autonomy of persons and autonomy of choices are intimately related, but they are nevertheless not identical. This is why someone can be autonomous in one sense but not in the other. It is also why I separate these topics into two chapters: autonomy of persons includes autonomy of choices but also involves other capacities. The rest of this chapter will address autonomy of choices.

Autonomy of choice

Autonomy of choice is, essentially, self-control of one's choices, actions, *etc*. This can take the form of refraining from indulging a desire that one has, as is the case with Olivia, but it need not.

Suppose that Olivia had asked herself, 'Do I really want these French fries?' and had answered it affirmatively. In this case her purchasing and eating of the fries would be autonomous. Despite the fact that she would be doing the same thing as Nicholas, she would be exercising self-rule and he would not be doing so. The crucial thing is not what is chosen or done but the manner in which the choice or action is arrived at.

So, what makes a choice (desire, action) autonomous? In what does autonomy of choice consist? In Chapter 1 I briefly suggested that the capacity to think about our own thoughts is central to autonomy. It is now time to develop this idea. In one form or another, this idea is the core of the central position in contemporary philosophical discussion of personal self-rule. James Stacey Taylor calls this the 'hierarchical position', because it portrays autonomy as consisting in relations between hierarchically ordered thoughts (2005, p. 1). Of course, 'in one form or another' is key here: proponents of the hierarchical theory differ over just how to understand it. Here are some possibilities, all put in terms of autonomy of choice even though some theorists who develop these position have autonomy of persons in mind:

a   Having one desire about another desire (choice, *etc.*) makes the second desire autonomous;

b   Having a specific sort of desire about another desire makes the second desire autonomous. For example, interpretations of Harry Frankfurt's position on persons and freedom of the will in terms of autonomy emphasize what he calls 'volitions', which are desires that a certain desire be one's will, that is, that it be effective in bringing about action (1988, p. 16);

c   Explicit reasoning about a desire and its acceptance or replacement makes the eventual desire autonomous;

d   Absence of rejection of a desire after thinking about it makes the desire autonomous;

e   Having feelings of a certain sort about a desire makes the desire autonomous. For instance, maybe certain feelings of satisfaction with desires make them autonomous;

f   (a) – (e) emphasize taking some sort of actual stance towards one's own thoughts or actually reflecting on them.

Another possibility is that a desire is autonomous if one would take some sort of stance towards it (along the lines of (a) – (e)) if one paid attention to it. On this view, desire is autonomous if it passes this hypothetical test, rather than requiring an actual stance towards it.

We will eventually take a look at some of the pros and cons of some of these positions. In general I am inclined to think that a heterogeneous position is plausible. The central characteristic of autonomy of choice is the thought-about-thought structure emphasized by the hierarchical theory. Choices can become autonomous – that is, can come under control by oneself – in various ways and to varying degrees. To see the appeal of this, consider Poya, Quentin and Roberta. All three want a beer. Poya thinks hard about her desire for a Westvletern 12, lists the pros and cons for herself, and on this basis endorses the desire. As a consequence she drinks a beer. Quentin asks himself, 'Do I really want to have a glass of Trois Pistoles?' He observes his own feelings about the possibility without doing any sort of rational calculation and, finding that he is happy with the prospect, has the beer. Both Poya and Quentin, I submit, choose autonomously (other things being equal, as we shall see), despite having different sorts of thoughts about their desires for beer. Both rational calculation and desires about desires deliver certain kinds of self-rule over one's choices. Now for Roberta: On the basis of her desire, Roberta drinks a bottle of Duvel. Poya asks her afterwards if she *really* wanted it. Roberta thinks for a moment and sincerely answers 'yes'. Was Roberta's choice autonomous? If we require actual thought about our desires for them to count as autonomous, then we must say 'no' here. But we would then also rule out the possibility of someone discovering that one of their prior choices was autonomous. Although this is only a suggestive point, this strikes me as undesirable. Why should we not think that we can discover self-rule in our pasts? If we equate 'self' with conscious thought, then, clearly, self-rule is impossible in the absence of explicit thought about our choices. But, as we shall see in Chapter 3, this is an unduly narrow view of the self. Since the self outstrips what shows up in conscious thought, it is possible to discover a rule by oneself in one's past, as in Roberta's case. Roberta's desire is autonomous in a manner different from both Poya and Quentin. Whether these desires are equally autonomous I will leave to the reader to consider.

Some technical terminology is needed at this point. I shall break the terms into two sets:

1] The first set of technical terms concerns what our desires and other mental states can be about. Many mental states are about ordinary features of the world that have nothing in particular to do with our minds. Take Nicholas' desire for French fries or Roberta's choice to have a beer as examples. It is conventional in philosophy to represent the contents of mental states using propositions following 'that'. Nicholas desires that he eats French fries in the food court; Roberta desires that she drinks a bottle of Duvel. These sorts of mental states are called 'first order'. However, some mental states have other mental states as their content. Mental states that have first-order mental states as their content are 'second order' mental states. Take Olivia's endorsement of her desire for French fries and Poya's rational calculation about her inclination to have a beer as examples. Olivia discovers that she desires that she desires that she eats French fries in the food court. On the basis of explicit reasoning Poya endorses her desire for Westvletern 12: she wants that she wants that she drinks a Westvletern 12. More colloquially we can say that, on the basis of their second-order attitudes, Olivia *really* wants French fries and Poya *really* wants a Westy 12.

I take it that this way of thinking about our own thoughts is familiar from everyday life and not a philosophical fantasy. I, for one, sometimes ask myself whether I really want something. I have a sweet tooth, so the desires that I scrutinize are often about the products of the bakeries in my neighbourhood. Sometimes I endorse my desire for a chocolate peanut butter square, sometimes I don't. That is, sometimes I decide that I really want this treat and sometimes I discover that I do not really want it. That I have the temptation to purchase something sweet is undeniable; what is at issue is the status of this desire. Figuring out whether one really wants something requires assessment of more than the fact that one wants it. It requires assessing the place of this desire in a larger network of thoughts, including other desires but not limited to them. Beliefs, attitudes, plans, choices and chains of reasoning are other psychological phenomena relevant to the question of whether one really wants something. This, of course, is not an exhaustive list.

First-order thoughts are about non-mental things. Second-order thoughts are about first-order thoughts. Using this method of classifying thoughts opens up infinite possibilities: third-order thoughts are about second-order ones, *etc*. More important than such iterations is the more general notion of 'higher order' thought. Higher-order thought is thought about thought. Higher-order desires are desires about mental states, *etc*. There are three reasons to be explicit about including this term in our technical vocabulary. The first is convenience: I shall sometimes speak of higher-order desires (*etc*.) rather than of any specific higher order. This is due to the second reason: there is nothing magical about any particular order with regard to autonomy. I shall argue that what is, generally, crucial for autonomy is the capacity for thought about thought, not specifically, for example, second-order thought. Finally, the notion of higher-order thought brings with it a conceptual possibility that the concepts of specific orders alone do not allow. Second-order thought is about specifically first-order thoughts; third-order thought is about specifically second-order thoughts, *etc*. But we can have thoughts about thought in general, including this order of thought itself. The notion of higher-order thought brings with it the concept of thought that is about all thought.

These conceptual distinctions are useful for refining our view of the present version of the hierarchical theory's account of autonomy of choice. The examples given so far include several cases of explicit, conscious thought about what to do – for example, about buying French fries, drinking beer, or eating dessert made by a local bakery. It is worth emphasizing that such conscious thought is inessential to autonomy of choice, by present standards. These examples are useful for motivating the hierarchical theory, but they risk giving a misleading view of it at the same time. In order to portray a clearer view, let's divide action into three categories:

a   uncontrolled
b   controlled by a specific mechanism
c   controlled by relatively central, upstream cognitive processing.

Cases of explicit, conscious reflection on one's motivations and actions fall into (c). However, we should leave open the possibility that actions in category (c) can be controlled by sub-conscious processes as well. This might go for the majority of the actions in this category. At least some of these actions will count as autonomous by the standards of the present theory. Since, at least on the face of it, autonomy involves some degree of self-control, uncontrolled actions are not candidates for autonomous ones, at least not paradigmatically. This is an issue that I shall revisit in Chapter 3. This leaves the rather wide (b) category. Some of these mechanisms will be altogether unresponsive to more central cognitive processing. Reflexes are a good candidate for this sort of action. However, other actions that are immediately controlled by specific mechanisms will also be amenable to the influence of more centralized capacities. This could be through training only, leaving the online performance of these actions under the control of the specific mechanism. However, the mechanism might allow for online intervention by, for example, explicit thought. The skilled movements of athletes are good examples for these sorts of action. They are the result of lots of training. Some are performed automatically – they must be, given the speed at which one must stop a puck or return a serve. However, athletes are often capable of intervening in the performance of their entrenched habits on the fly. This is at least part of what makes creativity in sport possible. Either way, actions performed under the control of these sorts of mechanisms can be, but need not be, autonomous. The crucial issue is not whether conscious thought is involved, but rather whether a choice (action, *etc.*) is made under the control of oneself. This, the hierarchical theory contends, is a matter of the psychological arrangement of the production of the action.

Not just any combination of higher-order attitude and lower-order thought results in the autonomy of choice. Two broad arrangements are worth emphasizing. First, I choose and act autonomously when my first-order choice to, for instance, buy ice cream is accepted (somehow) by higher-order processes and I then go on to buy ice cream. When a first- order choice is endorsed by a higher order but not made effectual in the production of behaviour then we should not see the choice that is made as autonomous *unless* it too is endorsed by higher-order thought. Second, when a first-order desire is rejected by higher-order thought and one then indeed refrains from acting in accordance with the first-order desire, one has chosen and acted autonomously. We saw this in the example of Olivia and the French fries. If I disavow a first-order desire but, contrary to my higher-order attitude, indulge the attitude anyway, then I have failed to choose autonomously. It seems possible, however, to have a conflicting mind about one's motivations, so perhaps one can *both* reject and endorse a first-order desire. In such a case I act autonomously but not as autonomously as if I acted from a more unified mind. I will return to such internal conflicts in Chapter 3.

So far the examples of higher-order acceptance and rejection of first-order desires concern actual, online higher-order attitudes. We should add to this, hypothetical standards of autonomy as well. If I refrain from acting in a way that, were I to think about it, I would indeed reject, then I act autonomously. The same goes for choices to do things that would be endorsed but are not in fact thought about. However, we should see choices (desires, actions) that meet merely a hypothetical standard as less autonomous than those that involve actual, present higher-order attitudes. The reason is that autonomy of choice is, at its core, choice that is under the control of the self, and *actual* control is control to a higher degree than *hypothetical* control. Desires that are what I would desire if I thought about them are in accordance with my control but not really under my control. For this reason they are less autonomous than desires that really are under my control. At the same time we should not think of them as out of my control, and for this reason we should see them as autonomous.

The earlier reflections about Lionel and Mibot are relevant to the present point. Mibot's actions are, by hypothesis, under the control of particular mechanisms that Mibot possesses. For this reason they are autonomous in a thin sense – they are produced by Mibot, not by others. But they are not autonomous in any thicker sense. The reason is that Mibot does not have the psychological capacities required to have a self in any recognizable sense. Human first-order desires that would be endorsed but are not endorsed deliver at least the thin sense of autonomy that Mibot possesses. Depending on the possibilities for integration with the self in the absence of higher-order endorsement, actions on the basis of these desires might count as more autonomous than Mibot's actions. But humans who have thick selves, such as Lionel, are capable of more full-blown autonomy of choice. This is what happens with actual higher-order acceptance and rejection of lower-order mental states.

This finally brings us to the second set of technical terms:

2] This set is about typical features of theories of autonomy. John Christman and Joel Anderson divide the structure of theories of autonomy into two sets of conditions (2005, p. 3). First there are 'competency' conditions. These are specifications of criteria of competence for the particular abilities that we describe as autonomous or not. To spell out the competency conditions for autonomy of choice would be to provide the details about the 'control' aspect of self-control of choice, action, desire, *etc.* For instance, I have spoken of autonomy of choice. This only makes sense for creatures capable of choosing. The competency conditions for this include whatever capacities are necessary for choosing. They can also include more than this. Suppose that autonomy of choice requires explicit reasoning about one's choices. This expands the list of competency conditions beyond just what is required for choice to include whatever capacities are required for explicit rational assessment. Crucially, the mechanisms of control will include processes for acquiring and using information about the choices (*etc.*),. that one has made and that are still in progress. Such feedback mechanisms should be expected to include both conscious and subconscious processes.

Besides competency conditions there are 'authenticity' conditions. Theories of autonomy are theories of, roughly speaking, self-governance. Whereas competence conditions specify the psychological details of governance, the authenticity conditions apply to the self. To spell out authenticity conditions is to specify just what it is for a desire (choice, action, *etc.*) to be governed by oneself.

I suggested above that we should take a heterogeneous view of autonomy of choice. This means that lots of kinds of mental states are relevant to this sort of personal self-rule. For this reason I shall have little to say about competency conditions. I have no doubt that there are interesting things to be said about the details of competent first-order and higher-order thought, but I shall leave such details to psychologists. The tricky philosophical issue, at this point, falls into the category of authenticity conditions. The hierarchical theory should be seen as, first and foremost, an answer to the question of what makes a particular choice (*etc.*) ruled by oneself rather than somebody else (or nothing, or some non-personal feature of the world). Imagine someone competent in all kinds of thought. In what manner must this person think in order to exercise self-rule over desire and action? By asking the question in this manner we effectively bracket the issue of the details of the competency conditions to isolate the authenticity conditions. This shall be the topic for the rest of the chapter.

Authenticity conditions of autonomy of choice

So, under what conditions is desire (choice, action, *etc.*) self-ruled rather than controlled by others (or the world, or nothing)? Let's focus on first-order thoughts: under what conditions does a first-order thought have the status 'autonomous'? The general answer given by the hierarchical theory is that a first-order thought counts as autonomous when it stands in the appropriate sorts of relations to higher-order thoughts. We have seen some details about more specific versions of this proposal. The present task is to reflect on just what these 'suitable relations' might include. I propose to do this by adapting some of the conceptual tools developed by epistemologists. Epistemology is the philosophical study of knowledge. To know, for example, that there will be a lunar eclipse on 28 September 2015 is to have a belief with this content that meets certain other conditions. Just what these other conditions are has proven to be very difficult to pin down, but the perennial baseline answer is that knowledge is justified true belief. Whether a belief is true or not is a matter of its content and the relations of this content to the world. The conditions under which true belief is also justified is a matter of... well, this is the hard part, which thankfully need not be specified for our purposes. I propose that we use some of the major accounts of epistemic justification to build models for authenticity conditions for autonomy of choice. Autonomy of choice seems not to be a matter of what a choice is about, at least primarily, but of other things. The hierarchical theory suggests that relations to other thoughts of a certain kind are the crucial heart of the answer to the question, 'What makes a first order thought autonomous?' Likewise, most major accounts of epistemic justification put the relations between the target belief and other beliefs at their core. On this basis I suggest that we have sufficiently similar issues to allow us fruitful use of the labours of epistemologists to construct models for accounts of authenticity conditions for autonomy of choice.

Note Well: I shall stick to rough details about complex epistemological positions in order to avoid getting sidetracked by technical complexities that are irrelevant to the present issue. For our purposes it is the general theoretical possibilities that are of first importance, not the nuances. Nor need we pick one epistemological account as the correct one about epistemic justification. This would tie distinct issues unduly closely together. One model might fit epistemic justification and a quite different one might suit autonomy. The present project is just to use epistemic positions as a source of structural possibilities for theories of autonomy.

The first answer to the question 'what constitutes epistemic justification?' offers other beliefs linked together like a chain. Picture the theoretical issue via a rhetorical exchange. Steven claims that he knows that the moon is not made of green cheese. Tessa asks him 'how do you know that?' Steven takes this as a challenge to show that he is justified in making this particular claim and answers 'because I know where green cheese comes from and there's no way to get it to the moon from there.' If we generalize, then we get a very natural first try at explaining epistemic justification: a belief is justified if it is part of a chain with other justified beliefs (which might be offered to explain the epistemic basis of the first belief). In particular, a true belief counts as knowledge when it is supported by other beliefs that count as knowledge. Besides chains, another metaphor often used for this model of justification is a ladder. A particular belief has a place on a particular rung of the ladder. To find the reasons that justify this belief, we move along, step-by-step, the rungs of the ladder to which it belongs. If we apply this to autonomy, then we get this answer: a first-order mental state is authentically one's own and hence autonomous when it is part of a chain/ladder with other autonomous, hierarchically arranged mental states. For both autonomy and knowledge, this sort of model portrays the relevant kind of status as being transferred from one mental state to another.

This model generates problems that are famous for both autonomy and knowledge. Suppose that Tessa repeats her question, this time about the new claim – how does Steven know *that*? Steven offers a third claim, which Tessa again questions, *etc.* This is the 'Infinite Regress Problem': the chain of justification threatens never to end, with the result that the original claim is not really justified after all: instead of being completed, the justificatory job is only moved from place to place on the chain. Likewise for autonomy: if a first-order mental state is autonomous because of the autonomy of a second-order attitude about that state, then a new question has opened up. How does the second-order stance come to be autonomous? If endorsement by a higher-order mental state is required for autonomy, then we need a third-order state to deliver the autonomy of the second-order state, and so on forever with the result that the promise of self-rule is never delivered on.

As so far described, the infinite regress problem is a problem only if one thinks that autonomy is possible. If one thinks that personal self-rule is impossible, then the infinite regress 'problem' is perhaps a diagnosis of one reason that this is the case, and not a problem at all. However, the guiding assumption of this book is that autonomy is possible and, indeed, actual for some people. The examples of autonomy that I have offered are not at all outlandish. Instead they are meant to highlight the rather ordinary faces of self-rule. As we will see in the second half of the book, this assumption is shared by applied ethicists and political philosophers: autonomy is given important roles in discussions of the grounds of obligations we have to each in other in various respects. Finally, I take it that people generally assume that control over themselves and certain parts of their lives is possible. On all of these fronts, then, the possibility of an infinite regress signifies a genuine problem.

The infinite regress problem leads to a second problem. The series of rhetorical iterations with which Tessa confronts Steven indicates that the proffered platform which is supposed to shore up a particular belief's status as 'knowledge' is just another belief. The same goes for the second belief's status as 'knowledge', and so on. So, one might ask, what's so special about these subsequent beliefs? Why should we think that they have any greater epistemic authority than the original belief? The same goes for autonomy: a higher-order mental state is offered as what makes a first-order mental state autonomous. Why should we think that higher-order mental states are special, with regard to self-rule, in a way that first-order mental states are not? What gives higher-order mental states authority over first-order ones such that they can make inherently non-autonomous states autonomous? This is known as the '*ab initio*' problem.

Epistemologists have devised various alternatives to the model of justification that gives rise to the infinite regress problem. When pressed into service in the design of models of autonomy of choice, they also promise to solve the *ab initio* problem. The problematic model of epistemic justification has two components: (1) a ladder-like model of inferential relations which (2) offers more beliefs as the epistemic foundation of the starting belief's status as 'knowledge'. Accordingly, either part can be modified to address the infinite regress and *ab initio* problems. The first alternative gives up (1), the ladder-like notion of epistemic justification. So-called 'coherentist' accounts of knowledge emphasize the diverse and independent relations a belief can have to other beliefs (and other mental states). Rather than a ladder, think of a web: put the starting belief in the centre, then trace its complex connections to a ring of other beliefs which themselves have complex links to each other and to further rings of beliefs. Roughly speaking, a belief is justified if it has a place in this web of beliefs; it is not justified if it cannot be placed in the web. So, when one is challenged to justify a belief, one need not rely only on single subsequent beliefs to respond. Instead one can invoke more complex relations between beliefs. This means that the step-by-step process that gives rise to the infinite regress problem is not encountered.

Let's apply this to autonomy of choice. The infinite regress problem arises when a single higher-order state is offered as conferring autonomy on a lower-order state. The reason is that one can ask about the self-ruling authority of the higher-order state, and it seems that one is forced to offer another even higher-order state to deliver this, and so on forever. A coherentist account of authenticity conditions allows one to offer more complex relations between mental states to deliver autonomy. Roughly speaking, a first-order mental state is autonomous when it has the appropriate sort of place in a web of other mental states. Just what sort of place? The heterogeneous list of relations between mental states given above on the basis of extant formulations of the hierarchical account of autonomy gives us the answer, or, rather, answers. A first-order mental state can have various sorts of relations, actual and hypothetical, to other mental states. These relations will yield different sorts of control of the first state by the overall network. If we see these relations as constituting a complex web that persists through long periods of time rather than merely giving rise to occurent, short-term relations between mental states, then we can interpret extant formulations of the hierarchical theory as providing the details for a coherentist model of authenticity conditions.

In the case of knowledge, coherentist approaches give rise to a new worry. Suppose that we ask about the justification of belief A, and its complex relations to beliefs B, C, D and others are offered in response. Now, suppose that we ask about the justification of belief B, and its complex relations to A, C, D, *etc.* are offered. Here is the problem: B justifies (in part) A, and A justifies (in part) B, which means that A plays a role in the justification of A. This, however, is circular reasoning, which is infamously problematic.

This is not clearly a problem for the adaptation of coherentist models for autonomy. Two lines of responses are available. I shall start with the weaker one, although I think that they are both worth endorsing. The first answer emphasizes the role of lower and higher orders of thought in hierarchical accounts of autonomy. It is not just any relations between mental states that are relevant to understanding self-rule. Instead it is relations between (to begin with) the first order and second mental states, and (arguably) while the second order states deliver the autonomy of the first order states, the first order states play no role in delivering the autonomy of the second order states. Hence the first order states play no role in delivering their own autonomy – no circle is found here.

The second response locates the point of disanalogy in a slightly different place. In the case of knowledge, the coherentist model offers, ultimately, beliefs as justifying beliefs. The question of justification arises in the same fashion for every node in a web. But things are different for the autonomy of choice. The issue here is self-rule. We should see the coherentist model as offering not just other mental states, which can be scrutinized one-by-one, as the foundation of autonomy. It offers the self as the foundation for autonomy, by construing the self in terms of a complex web of mental states. So, a first-order desire should not be construed as autonomous on the basis of its relation to another autonomous mental state, or even to a web of autonomous mental states. It should be construed as autonomous because of its relation to the self.

One might think that the circular reasoning problem resurfaces here. It is reasonable to think of at least some of our first-order desires as components of ourselves. But if autonomy of choice really is self-controlled choice, then a coherentist model of authenticity gives first-order desires a role in their own control. There are two potential problems with this. One is a conceptual problem: perhaps it is conceptually incoherent to think of a first-order state as standing in this sort of relation to itself. The second potential problem is, essentially, the *ab initio* problem: if the first-order mental state is not autonomous on its own, then it will not become autonomous by thinking of it as standing in some sort of relationship to itself (especially a conceptually dubious relationship). Why should we think that there is anything special about *that*?

Again, the coherentist response should be to broaden the focus from particular mental states to the overall web of relations. While it might be incoherent to think of a first-order mental state as standing alone in some autonomy – conferring relation to itself, it is not incoherent to think of it as part of an overall web of mental states which, altogether, confers autonomy on this particular part. It is a commonplace that complex groups confer properties on their parts that these parts could not have alone. For example, I am a human male. By virtue of my relations to my parents and brother, I am a son and sibling. I am part of the family unit that confers upon me these properties. It would be a different family without me, and I would not have these relations if I had been grown in a petri dish. In the present case, we should think that there is nothing conceptually problematic or, especially, circular about a coherentist model of autonomy. A mental state can in principle be controlled by the overall psychological system of which it is a part.

The coherentist model of knowledge rejected the ladder-like view of inferential relations that, in part, generated the infinite regress problem. Another way of stopping the infinite regress is to turn from the ladders-or-webs issue to the assumption that a belief must be justified by other beliefs. While this is the case for some beliefs, perhaps other beliefs are self-justifying. If this is possible, then a firm place can be found on which to rest the ladder of epistemic justification. Let's call this the 'foundationalist' account of epistemic justification. Just as examples, here are two candidates for self-justifying beliefs. On one hand, whereas, arguably, beliefs about abstract topics need justification in terms of other beliefs, perhaps beliefs about what is before our eyes (or ears, *etc.*) do not. Immediate sensations are, contentiously, self-evident. On another hand, perhaps some beliefs are justified solely on the basis of the meanings of the concepts involved in thinking such thoughts. The belief that a woman cannot be a bachelor is justified solely on the basis of clear understanding of the meanings of 'woman', 'bachelor' and the terms that link them in this very belief.

It is important to note that the introduction of self-evident and hence self-justifying beliefs provides two ways of assuaging infinite regress worries. First, for self-justifying beliefs themselves, the problem never arises. Second, for non-self-justifying beliefs, chains of other beliefs will deliver the status 'justified' if they can be grounded in self-justifying beliefs.

Let's apply this to autonomy. Are there any inherently autonomous mental states? If so, can they confer autonomy on other mental states? I don't think that there are any inherently autonomous first-order thoughts. Why should we think that, for example, a desire for a certain object, event, experience or state of affairs could be automatically, due to nothing but itself, autonomous? We shall see a particular reason to doubt this possibility very soon. Nor are thoughts at any specific higher order inherently autonomous. These do not differ significantly from first-order thoughts. They just have a specific lower order of thought as their content. In both cases the question 'Do I *really* want this?' has force: we can answer it either positively or negatively, meaning that we could discover that any particular thought of a specific order was not autonomous. However, indeterminately higher-order thoughts are different. Consider the thought, 'I want all of my thoughts to be held to the strictest of logical standards.' Since it applies to all of one's thinking this thought applies to itself, meaning that from it we can derive the more specific, 'I want that my thought 'I want all of my thoughts to be held to the strictest of logical standards' is held to the strictest of logical standards.' The desire expressed in the original thought is self-endorsing – one cannot coherently feel the pull of this desire without *really* having it, so the question 'Do I really want to hold my thoughts to the strictest logical standards?' is automatically answered.

If this is correct, then some mental states are inherently autonomous. However, these thoughts offer no threat to the hierarchical theory of autonomy. The reason is clear: the inherently self-ruling status of these thoughts is delivered by the very relationship between thoughts that the hierarchical theory has at its core. The present account of inherently autonomous thought presupposes the hierarchical account of personal self-rule, and hence it cannot be an alternative to it.

Suppose that, contrary to the line of thought so far offered, there were inherently autonomous first-order mental states. We would still have the reasons that we have already seen to endorse the coherentist hierarchical theory as part of an overall account of personal self-rule. The result would be a fairly deep pluralism about authenticity conditions. Moreover, we would have good reason to think that the hierarchical theory captures a particularly important part of what we mean by 'autonomy', maybe even its core. There are at least two reasons for this. One is that the hierarchical theory offers a preferable view of the self compared to a foundationalist theory, and hence of self-control. The coherentist hierarchical theory offers a network of thoughts as constituting the self and delivering self-rule; a foundationalist theory must offer special kinds of thoughts, without incorporating relationships to other thoughts. I find this unappealing: whatever I am, surely it involves lots of thoughts in complex relationships to each other, so a theory of the self that leaves this out seems to have gone wrong right at the start.

To get to the second reason for preferring the coherentist hierarchical theory to a (hypothetical) foundationalist account of autonomy, and indeed to other views about the nature of personal self-rule, let's turn to a topic that has been conspicuously absent from the discussion so far. Besides the infinite regress and *ab initio* problems, a third problem has been important in the contemporary literature about autonomy: the manipulation problem (Taylor 2005, p. 5). The manipulation problem puts pressure on the idea that higher-order endorsement of a lower-order thought suffices for that lower-order thought to be ruled by oneself. In principle one's mind could be subject to manipulation: another person could implant both the lower-order thought and the higher-order attitude towards it. In such a case we would not want to say that, when one chooses in accordance with the lower-order thought, the choice is autonomous. It seems clearly heteronomous, due to its origins in another person rather than the agent who has it. We can modify the case of Farrah to provide examples of this sort of threat to autonomy. Suppose that the evil neuroscientist implanted chips in Farrah's brain to give her not just first-order desires but higher-order thoughts about these desires. Less fancifully, suppose that powerful political or religious figures have been able to implant such ideas in Farrah's mind. If Farrah chooses on the basis of the implanted thoughts, we have good reason to question whether she acts under her own control.

The manipulation problem threatens any theory, such as the ones examined so far, that explains personal self-rule in terms of relations between thoughts. For any thoughts and the putatively autonomy-conferring relations among them, we can imagine a case in which these thoughts were implanted by another agent in the requisite relations, thereby undermining the autonomy of the recipient of the thoughts and showing that the explanation in question fails to identify sufficient conditions for autonomy. The same problem arises in the epistemological case for the same structural reasons.

Take any account of knowledge that construes justification in terms of relations between beliefs. We can imagine a case in which the beliefs and putatively justification-conferring relations come about in a fanciful way that undermines their ability to deliver knowledge. Suppose, for instance, that one argues that the complex belief 'that Stephen Harper is the Prime Minister of Canada' is typically justified by its relations to beliefs X, Y and Z. Now consider Utley, who has these beliefs in the requisite relations not by virtue of learning about A (and X, Y, Z) but because of a brain tumour. Does Utley *really* know who the Prime Minister of Canada is? Surely not. But this means that these relationships between beliefs do not suffice for knowledge after all.

Epistemologists and autonomy-theorists have taken the same strategy for dealing with this problem. The problematic theories are ahistorical: they offer certain relations between thoughts as sufficient for knowledge and autonomy regardless of how these relations come about. The manipulation problems arise when we turn to the processes by which people might come to have these thoughts in these relations. The solution seems to be to include history in one's account of authenticity conditions and epistemic justification. In epistemology this has taken the form of rejection of the idea that epistemic justification must come via inferential relations between beliefs. Instead, perhaps the processes by which at least some beliefs are generated suffice to justify those beliefs. As one possibility, maybe our sensory capacities are reliable generators of information about the world such that we are justified in thinking of their deliverances as knowledge. For instance, when Victoria, who has healthy eyes and a functioning visual system, sees an apple under normal conditions, arguably, she knows that it is red. She knows this not because of the relation of the belief 'that the apple is red' to other beliefs, but because of the nature of the processes – sensory, neural, perhaps others – that generate this belief. This is known as 'reliabilism' in epistemology.

Should we be reliabilists about autonomy of choice? The appeal is not the same in the two domains. In the case of knowledge, part of the appeal of reliabilism comes from the idea that certain processes (mechanisms, strategies, *etc.*) more or less 'track' certain features of the world and are hence reliable in the information that they convey about these features. Perhaps our visual processing systems reliably track truths having to do with the reflection of light by surfaces and perhaps on this basis we should treat the outputs of these systems as, generally, justified. Once we formulate this idea, the mechanics and evolutionary history of the relevant processes can be made the subjects of empirical inquiry. If we apply this to autonomy, self-ruled choices would be ones produced by processes that track features of the self. 'The self' is a much thornier topic than the things which are the objects of knowledge-producing processes in the most appealing epistemological reliabilisms. What might 'tracking features of the self' mean? The philosophical difficulties here undermine the theoretical appeal of drawing a direct analogy between epistemological reliabilism and authenticity conditions for autonomy. Moreover, I doubt that the tracking model has any pre-theoretical appeal with regard to autonomy, whereas it has (to my mind) considerable appeal in the case of some kinds of knowledge. Instead of attempting to describe autonomy-conducive choice-producing processes, theorists of self-rule have emphasized the absence of autonomy-undermining processes. Put in other words, instead of a 'positive' historical theory, which is what epistemologists have offered, autonomy theorists have generally sought a more conservative 'negative' historical component to accounts of the autonomy of choice. This alleviates the need to provide an account of processes that track the self. Some might worry that this risks triviality: 'the absence of X-undermining processes' does not constitute an account of what makes something an X. However, autonomy theorists who conjoin the negative historical component with additional positive (yet ahistorical) theses go at least some way to describing autonomy of choice in detail and have little to worry about with regard to the charge of triviality.

There is no reason to complain about the inclusion of negative historical theses in accounts of the autonomy of choice. The crucial question is about their importance. Should we see the processes by which desires (choices, actions, *etc.*) are produced as central or peripheral to their rule by the self? Should autonomy theorists be more or less reliabilist? I am inclined to think that negative historical theses are a relatively minor part of the theories of autonomy. Much will depend on whether one thinks the manipulation problem is a big or a small issue. I am not impressed by the manipulation problem. Here's why: all of our thoughts have a history. This is easy to underestimate: we should be broad-minded pluralists about the sources of our thoughts. Some of these histories appear to threaten autonomy, but others, of course, can support or even extend our capacities for exercising control over our choices. Interestingly this can even be the case when mental states are somehow implanted by another agent. Let's change the Farrah case: she encounters a benevolent neurosurgeon rather than an evil one. On the basis of close observation, the benevolent neurosurgeon realizes that Farrah has committed herself to a particular project: drinking more tea. She is generally good at this, but she suffers from a behavioural peculiarity: whenever she sees Kenyan Tinderet on the shelf at the local tea boutique, she immediately turns away and tries something else. As a result Farrah has never tried Kenyan Tinderet. The benevolent neuroscientist has good reason to think that Farrah would both like this tea and endorse her taste for it. Consequently the benevolent neuroscientist implants a specific desire for Kenyan Tinderet in Farrah, to counterbalance her subconscious habit. The next time Farrah visits the tea store, she sees, desires, purchases and enjoys Kenyan Tinderet. Has Farrah chosen autonomously? Although we might quibble about the degree of self-rule that Farrah exercises over her choice, the baseline answer seems to be affirmative. The benevolent neurosurgeon helps Farrah do something that she really wants to do. Her autonomy is supported, not undermined, by the implanted mental state. If this is correct, then the fact that a mental state comes from another person does not suffice for heteronomy.

The crucial issue is not the sources of our thoughts but their overall role in our minds. The difference between the evil and benevolent neurosurgeon cases is that, more or less explicitly, the mental states that are implanted by the evil neurosurgeon are not integrated into the rest of Farrah's mental economy. By contrast the desire implanted by the benevolent neurosurgeon coheres with and facilitates the implementation of a plan that Farrah has, to drink more tea. The general lesson is that when a mental state, implanted or otherwise, is integrated with the rest of one's mind, then choice and action on the basis of that mental state is autonomous. When an implanted mental state is not integrated with one's mind, then action on the basis of that mental state is not autonomous. This lesson holds for combinations of mental states as well. When a first-order mental state and a higher-order endorsing state are implanted (or arise by sheer coincidence, as with Utley's brain tumour), then choice and action on the basis of these states is autonomous when they are integrated into the rest of an agent's mind and non-autonomous otherwise. This is perhaps most obvious when we consider the implantation of a vast complex of cohering thoughts. This would amount to the installation of a new self in an agent, so action on the basis of solely this network, without integration with the agent's original self, could not be 'self' ruled by person A, as it would stem from a distinct self, person B. After integration, however, although the agent in question would have a radically different self, it would still be continuous with the agent's prior self, and action produced by it would be, to some degree, autonomous.

'Integration' deserves further attention, as it comes in several varieties with differing implications for self-rule. Consider an agent who has first-order desires only. Suppose that Wilson likes a wide variety of types of coffee: he likes and desires Arusha, Bergendal, *etc.*, all the way up the coffee alphabet to Ugandan Bugishu with the exception of Maragogipe. If a desire for Maragogipe is implanted by a neurosurgeon in Wilson, then there is a sense in which it is integrated into the rest of Wilson's mind: he likes all other sorts of coffee, so it makes sense that he would like and desire Maragogipe. Let's call this 'content integration'. But other than being about coffee, this desire is disconnected from the rest of Wilson's mind. It is 'functionally' non-integrated. Content integration is insufficient for autonomy of choice. Strictly speaking, when Wilson chooses Maragogipe on the basis of the implanted desire, he chooses heteronomously. Of course, since Wilson has first-order desires only, by the standards of the present position he does nothing autonomously: when he chooses, say, Ethiopian Harar, he does not exercise self-rule, but neither is he controlled by someone else. Assuming that when he encounters the smell of Ethiopian Harar he is not 'led by the nose' by it, he acts oudenonomously when he chooses to drink it.

Functional integration is required for autonomy of choice, but what does this mean more specifically? We can distinguish two types of functional integration. First, a choice is self-ruled when it is produced by and is also, in some way and to some degree, under the control of a self. This requires more than similarity of content between mental states; it requires causal connections, so I shall call this the 'causal' variety of functional integration. Since a mental state must enter into causal relations with other mental states in order for it to be causally functionally integrated, this variety of integration is a matter of history. We cannot tell whether an implanted state has been causally integrated into someone's mind by examining the mind at a split second. Instead we need to know something about the recent and, maybe, not-so-recent history of the mental state. This is not the case with the other sort of functional integration. Besides causal integration, a mental state can be integrated into one's mind if one has the appropriate sort of attitude towards it. Let's call this 'attitudinal' functional integration. One need not have the mental state in question to have a place for it in one's mind, and hence for it to be integrated when one acquires it. This is the case with Farrah and Kenyan Tinderet: she endorses drinking more tea in general, so she has a pre-made mental place for the choice to drink Kenyan Tinderet. When she acquires this first-order desire, it fits into her overall plan about tea, and is hence integrated. This is something that, in principle, can be assessed by taking a 'time-slice' view of a person's mind, without any information about the history of one's thoughts. To the extent that there are the appropriate sorts of attitudes about other thoughts, these other thoughts are autonomous. The more attitudinal integration, the more autonomy there is. In principle one could acquire the lower-order thoughts, the endorsing thoughts, thoughts endorsing *those* thoughts, and more, all at the same moment.

There are three things we can say about both sorts of functional integration. First, the sorts of relations that deliver both kinds of functional integration are those that hierarchical autonomy theorists have already suggested and which I have redeployed so far in developing the coherentist version of this theory; in a slogan: coherence equals integration. Second, although I have emphasized functional integration as necessary for autonomy of choice, it is also sufficient. There is nothing else that needs to be added to an agent for a choice (desire, action) *etc.* to be self-ruled than for it to be functionally integrated with the rest of the agent's mind. Third, although in principle these are separable sorts of integration, in reality they are deeply entwined. An autonomous desire is likely to stand in merely attitudinal relations to some thoughts, in merely causal relations to other thoughts, and in relations of both sorts to still other thoughts. The endorsing thoughts will likewise stand in complex causal and attitudinal relations (and merely content-based relations also) to still other thoughts. 'Coherence' does not entail 'simple'. Nor does it entail 'unified', as we will see in the next chapter.

Attentive readers will note that the list of relations (provided above) that hierarchical theorists have produced includes, as its final item, merely hypothetical endorsement of a lower-order desires (choice, action), and that, on its face, this conflicts with the current emphasis on causal and attitudinal connections between mental states. Let's examine some details. Consider Xavier, who has both first-order and higher-order mental states. A benign neurosurgeon who is not very well informed about Xavier's likes and dislikes implants in Xavier a desire to go to a local vegetarian restaurant. Xavier has no general attitudes that cover this desire, so it does not fit into a pre-existing attitudinal slot that endorses it. What should we say about whether this desire is autonomous for Xavier? It is at least heteronomous, but there are other things we can say about it when we fill in more details. If Xavier would endorse this desire after thinking about it, then it is heteronomous, but it is not autonomy-undermining. Instead, it is autonomy-friendly. Xavier is actually under the control of another, to a small but not insignificant degree, when he acts on this desire, but since it would fit in with his tastes were he to think about it, it is not a threat to his self-rule. By contrast, if Xavier would reject the desire in the event that he scrutinized it, then acting on it is both heteronomous and autonomy-undermining. Xavier's self-rule is diminished by its presence. Finally, there is a third option: Xavier might be indifferent to this desire, neither endorsing nor rejecting it after thinking about it. In this case Xavier's desire to attend the restaurant is heteronomous but autonomy-neutral. It neither complements nor undermines his self-rule.

Heteronomy is not the only possibility here. Consider Yasmine. Whenever she smells freshly baked bread, she seeks out a bakery to buy a loaf. Sometimes the desire is nearly irresistible, other times it is very subtle, but the behavioural pattern is invariable. Yasmine has never noticed this pattern and so she has never thought about her motivations. She is cosmonomous with regard to the smell of fresh bread. If these desires would pass a hypothetical endorsement test, then, as in the case of Xavier, they are autonomy-friendly. If they would fail this test, they are autonomy-undermining. If Yasmine were to decide that she is ambivalent about her scent-induced desire for fresh bread, then her actions are cosmonomous and autonomy-neutral.

What about oudenonomous motivations? These are neither under the control of the agent who has them, nor of another person, nor of a particular feature of the world. Oudenonomous choices that would be rejected or to which the agent would take no particular attitude after thinking about them are respectively autonomy-undermining and autonomy-neutral. Choices that an agent would endorse are different. We should see these choices as actually uncontrolled but, since they are autonomy-friendly and involve no other sources of control, we should regard them as also weakly autonomous. We find here the weakest relation that there can be between a desire (or a choice, an action, *etc.*) and a self, and hence the weakest possible degree of self-rule.

Let's stand back from these cases. The point of the discussion of integration has been to show the appeal of a coherentist version of the hierarchical theory of autonomy of choice. In particular I have been arguing that we should not be, centrally, reliabilists about authenticity conditions for autonomy of choice. Our capacities here do not require a specific sort of history in order to be self-ruling. These reflections also give us another reason for preferring the coherentist approach over foundationalist varieties of the hierarchical theory: foundationalism cannot provide a persuasive answer to the manipulation problem on its own. Inherently autonomous mental states could, in principle, be implanted by another agent, in which case we should see choice and action on the basis of these states as heteronomous: one would be acting under the control of another person. Only when such states are appropriately integrated with an agent's mind do they confer autonomy, but this is to give up foundationalism for a coherentist approach to both autonomy and the manipulation problem. Indeed, the manipulation problem makes clear not the inadequacy of ahistorical accounts of autonomy but instead, the problem with trying to explain autonomy in terms of the endorsement of choices (actions, *etc.*) by single mental states. This cannot thoroughly deliver self-rule because a single mental state does not make a self. A network of mental states does, which paves the way towards appealing to integration to answer the manipulation problem.

Although the hierarchical theory has been central in the contemporary literature, it is not the only game in town when it comes to theories of autonomy. Let's turn to other approaches.

Other theories of autonomy of choice

I shall only briefly discuss other theories of autonomy of choice, for two inter-related reasons. First, the general tendency in recent discussions of autonomy has been to turn away from autonomy of choice to autonomy of persons. Hence I risk distorting extant work if I gerrymander it too much to fit the current focus on choice. A taste of these theories is useful at this point, but to go further is counter-productive. Second, this brevity does not matter: autonomy of persons is the topic of the next chapter, so the themes that quickly pass by here will be duly addressed in their natural home.

One family of theories of autonomy of choice focuses on particular sorts of mental states as the hallmark of self-rule. Broadly Kantian theorists emphasize reason: the self-ruling person is the rational person, roughly speaking. Broadly Humean theories emphasize desires: the self-ruling person is motivated by certain sorts of desires and not by others. Both varieties have pre-theoretical appeal. On the Kantian side, there is much to be said for understanding control in terms of responsiveness to reasons. The clear-headed person is, arguably, a good choice to run a company or country, so perhaps the same goes for running one's own life. On the Humean side, given that motivating states such as desires are at the heart of action, then surely they have a role in our understanding of self-rule with regard to action. The risk of using other sorts of mental states is motivational inadequacy. To capture effective self-rule, desires arguably need a central role.

Within each version of the theories in this family we can in principle distinguish two varieties: those that emphasize taking attitudes of the specified sort towards one's own mental states, and those that do not. Positions of the first sort are more specialized versions of the hierarchical theory, whereas those of the second sort are thoroughly distinct. For example, a particular desire could be autonomous when, for a Kantian, it is rationally scrutinized and guided by reasons, or, for a Humean, when one endorses it with a higher-order desire. I shall put aside these as not really alternatives to the hierarchical position sketched and defended in this chapter. The interesting positions are the non-hierarchical members of this family. I shall return to these shortly.

The other family of theories of autonomy of choice focuses on individuality. Roughly, a choice is self-ruled when it truly comes from oneself. The crucial issue is how to understand what it is to be, truly, oneself, an individual. An important version of this approach construes individuality in terms of values: one chooses autonomously when one chooses in accordance with values that one has chosen for oneself. There is notable appeal to the general idea here: my character can arguably be aptly explained in terms of the things that I value. When I control my commitments to values, then, again arguably, I also control actions and choices taken in the light of those values. Jon Colburn points to Wilhelm von Humboldt as an intellectual forerunner of this sort of theory, so I shall refer to the theories of this family as 'Humboldtian'.

Although very briefly described here, there are three sorts of potential problem that face these theories. The first two are inter related. Let's understand these theories as putative explanations of personal self-rule with regard to choice. To use some technical terminology, we can divide explanations into the 'explanandum', which is the construal of the phenomenon to be explained, and the 'explanans', which is the explanation given of the explanandum. The two families of non-hierarchical theories of autonomy suffer from problems of width with regard to their understandings of either or both the explanandum and the explanans. With regard to the phenomenon to be explained, the first family emphasizes control at the expense of the self, whereas the second family risks unduly emphasizing the self. An adequate theory of autonomy of choice must attend carefully to both: control of one's actions by oneself.

With regard to their explanations of self-rule, the pre-theoretical sources of appeal of these accounts of autonomy are also sources of problems. Both sorts of theory have unduly narrow focal points. The result is that the Humean has an intuitive case against both the Kantian and the Humboldtian, the Kantian has such a case against the other two, *etc.* Call this the 'what's so special' objection. 'What's so special about reason that it accounts for autonomy and desire does not?', the Humean can say to the Kantian. The Kantian can begin to answer, but at the end of the day it looks as if autonomy is delivered by a plurality of mental states, such that the specialized viewpoints of these alternatives to the present version of the hierarchical theory cannot help but leave out important constituents of self-rule.

The third problem arises when we turn to the matter of working out the details of a Humean, Kantian, or Humboldtian theory. For any rational process, desire, or value, one can ask of oneself, 'Do I really think this way?' 'Do I really want this?' 'Do I really value this?' In other words, one can take a higher-order stance towards one's own thought processes. After such reflection one can either acquiesce in the rational process, desire, or value in question, effectively endorsing it, or one can reject it. This higher-order stance might be explicitly rationally reflective, but it need not be. It can, in principle, take a variety of forms, such as merely searching one's mind for the state in question. This phenomenon is, of course, exactly what the hierarchical theory offers as the core of the autonomy of choice. Insofar as control over actions and first-order attitudes is what a theory of autonomy must explain, a place must be made for this sort of higher-order stance. Without being able to think this sort of thought, we lack a crucial source of control over our own minds. In short, the phenomenon emphasized by hierarchical theorists is unavoidable in accounts of autonomy of choice. Non-hierarchical Kantian, Humean and Humboldtian theories will be incomplete. Hierarchical versions of these theories fall into the hierarchical camp rather than offering alternatives to it.

This concludes my look at autonomy of choice, but not at these theories. We shall revisit hierarchical, Humboldtian, Humean and Kantian themes in the next chapter in connection with autonomy of persons.

Reading guide

Marilyn Friedman emphasizes that autonomy is a threshold concept in *Autonomy, Gender, Politics* (Oxford University Press, 2003).

The importance of context and, more specifically, opportunities is at the core of the treatment of autonomy found in Marina Oshana's *Personal Autonomy in Society* (Ashgate, 2006).

The importance of context to the workings of the human mind is the focal point of the debate between 'individualists' and 'externalists' in philosophical psychology. Roughly put, individualists argue that mental states and processes are located within the physical boundaries of organisms such as humans. Externalists deny that these processes must be individualistically located: although they might be, in principle and, arguably, in reality, mental states and processes can extend between individuals and the wider world. A provocative introduction and defence of externalism is found in Andy Clark's *Supersizing the Mind* (Oxford University Press, 2008). A worthy defence of individualism is offered by F. Adams and K. Aizawa in *The Bounds of Cognition* (Wiley-Blackwell, 2010). I develop externalist hypotheses about specific topics in moral psychology in my *Like-Minded: Externalism and Moral Psychology* (MIT, 2011). I return to this topic in Chapter 4 of the present book.

'Global/Local' terminology pervades the recent literature about autonomy. I have used different terminology in three papers: 'shallow' for autonomy of choices and 'deep' for autonomy or persons. I now eschew this way of speaking out of worries that it unduly loads the dice in favour of autonomy of persons and against autonomy of choice when it comes to evaluative questions. For this terminology see 1] Andrew Sneddon, 'Equality, justice, and paternalism: recentering debate about physician-assisted suicide', *Journal of Applied Philosophy*, Vol. 23, No. 4 (2006), 387–404; 2] Andrew Sneddon, 'Advertising and deep autonomy', *Journal of Business Ethics*, Vol. 33, No. 1 (September 2001), 15–28; 3] Andrew Sneddon, 'What's wrong with selling yourself into slavery? Paternalism and deep autonomy', *Criticá*, Vol. 33, No. 98 (August 2001), 97–121.

Specific versions of the hierarchical account of autonomy, none of them identical to the one defended in this chapter, can be found in 1] Harry Frankfurt, 'Freedom of the will and the concept of a person', *Journal of Philosophy*, Vol. 68 (1971), 5–20; reprinted in his *The Importance of What We Care About* (Cambridge University Press, 1988),2] Gerald Dworkin's, *The Theory and Practice of Autonomy* (Cambridge University Press, 1988), 3] Marilyn Friedman, *Autonomy, Gender, Politics* (Oxford University Press, 2003), 4] James Stacey Taylor(ed.), *Personal Autonomy: New Essays on Personal Autonomy and Its Role in Contemporary Moral Philosophy* (Cambridge University Press, 2005) 5] James Stacey Taylor, *Practical Autonomy and Bioethics* (Routledge, 2009). Besides Taylor's edited volume, criticism can be found in 1] Marina Oshana, *Personal Autonomy in Society* (Ashgate, 2006) 2] Ben Colburn, *Autonomy and Liberalism* (Routledge, 2010).

John Christman uses the terminology of competency and authenticity conditions in the introduction to the volume, *Autonomy and the Challenges to Liberalism* (Cambridge University Press, 2005), edited by Christman and Joel Anderson.

The only person of whom I know who has explicitly used epistemological models for theories of autonomy is Laura Waddell Ekstrom. She defends a coherentist version of the hierarchical approach in 1] 'A coherence theory of autonomy', *Philosophy and Phenomenological Research*, Vol. 53, No. 3 (September 1993),

599–616; 2] 'Keystone preferences and autonomy', *Philosophy and Phenomenological Research*, Vol. 59, No. 4 (December 1999), 1057–63; 3] 'Autonomy and personal integration', in *Personal Autonomy: New Essays on Personal Autonomy and Its Role in Contemporary Moral Philosophy* (Cambridge University Press, 2005), edited by James Stacey Taylor. For an introduction to the epistemological models themselves, see, for example, Jonathan Dancy, *Introduction to Contemporary Epistemology* (Wiley-Blackwell, 1991).

James Stacey Taylor presents the infinite regress, *ab initio* and manipulation problems in the introduction to *Personal Autonomy: New Essays on Personal Autonomy and Its Role in Contemporary Moral Philosophy* (Cambridge University Press, 2005).

Whether autonomy should be construed as a time-slice or as a historical phenomenon is at the heart of a debate between John Christman and Alfred Mele:1] John Christman, 'Autonomy and personal history', *Canadian Journal of Philosophy*, Vol. 21, No. 1 (1991), 1–24, 2] Alfred Mele, 'History and personal autonomy', *Canadian Journal of Philosophy*, Vol. 23 (1991), 271–80 3] John Christman, 'Defending historical autonomy: a reply to professor Mele', *Canadian Journal of Philosophy*, Vol. 23 (1993), 281–90. Book length treatments of their respective views can be found in 4] John Christman, *The Politics of Persons* (Cambridge University Press, 2009) and 5] Alfred Mele, *Autonomous Agents* (Oxford University Press, 1995). See also the theory of autonomy offered by Ben Colburn, *Autonomy and Liberalism* (Routledge, 2010).

As noted in Chapter 1, introductions to the contemporary literature are often found as part of the development of full-blown theories of autonomy. These introductions typically include surveys of kinds of theories. My discussion of alternatives to the hierarchical theory draws particularly on the first chapters of the books already cited by Oshana and Colburn. Bernard Berofsky emphasizes rationality and first-order mental states in his *Liberation from Self: A Theory of Personal Autonomy* (Cambridge University Press, 1995).

CHAPTER THREE

Autonomy of persons

In Chapter 2, I introduced the distinction between autonomy of choices and autonomy of persons with the vignette about Nicholas and Olivia. Nicholas, who generally exercises control over his life but who caves into an unwanted desire for French fries, is an autonomous person who makes a non-autonomous choice. Olivia acts autonomously with regard to the French fries in the mall food court but this is a rare occasion, so she is not an autonomous person. Autonomy of choice is a component of autonomy of persons, but the former does not suffice for the latter. What else is needed for self-rule in a wider context than a particular choice? This is the topic of the present chapter.

I shall introduce the answer to this question with a new vignette, but a methodological note is needed first. There is a conceptual tool in analytic philosophy for drawing attention to the importance of history, either immediate or distant, for a given phenomenon: the swamp person. A swamp person is an instantaneously created duplicate of a normal person. Imagine a bolt of lightning striking the ground in the Florida everglades and a newly created person (or other thing) emerging from the muck; only this thing happens, purely by chance, to be molecule-for-molecule identical to another person (or thing). The ordinary person has a normal sort of history: conception, birth, lots of complex interactions with the world and other people. The swamp person lacks a history beyond the moment of creation. The swamp person and the normal person have a lot in common by virtue of their current identical structure. What they do not share is what depends on history. For instance, suppose that I have spent too much time in the sun. Lightning strikes the ground beside me and, completely coincidentally, a perfect duplicate of me emerges from the swamp. I have a sunburn, but my swamp twin does not. Swamp-Andrew – 'Swandrew' – has skin damage that is identical to a sunburn, but in his case it was not caused by the sun, so it is not a sunburn.

With this in mind, consider Viviana. She is hiking through The Great Dismal Swamp. Viviana likes to relax here – besides the exercise she gets, she has a long-term interest in wetland flora and fauna. She has devoted much time and thought to this topic, designing her life to allow her to learn about marshy areas around the world. Viviana sees a plant with which she is not familiar and is tempted to pluck a sample in order to research its identity later. She is not sure whether she should do this – some plants are rare and ought not to be damaged, some plants are dangerous to touch, *etc*. After some consideration, she decides that she really wants to indulge her curiosity, so she picks a sample. Coincidentally, lightning strikes the tree beside her and instantly an exact duplicate of Viviana is created. Swamp-Viviana also takes a sample of the plant.

What should we make of Viviana and her doppelganger? By any standards Viviana is an autonomous person and chooses to pick the plant autonomously. In Chapter 2, I argued that autonomy of choice does not require a history of any particular kind. This means that Swamp-Viviana also picks the plant autonomously. The reason is that she has the right sort of mind at the time of the action: she has a desire which is endorsed by higher-order thought and which is hence integrated with the rest of her mind. She has this because she is a molecule-for-molecule duplicate of Viviana, and Viviana has this sort of psychological arrangement. However, Swamp-Viviana is not an autonomous person. Generally speaking, autonomy of persons consists in the exercise of control over one's life and Swamp-Viviana has not done this sort of thing. She has the capacity for such control but she has not exercised this capacity in the slightest. How could she, since she only just came into existence? More specifically, Swamp-Viviana suffers from two historical deficits that render her a non-autonomous person. First, she has no knowledge about herself. Viviana knows things about herself, so Swamp-Viviana has the same beliefs, but in the case of Swamp-Viviana they are had coincidentally and hence do not count as knowledge. They are like Utley's brain damage-induced beliefs about Stephen Harper. Second,

Swamp-Viviana has not shaped her life in any way. Over time Viviana has reflected on herself, her place in the world and what she finds important, and she has modified herself and her circumstances in the light of this reflection. Swamp-Viviana has not made herself to any degree, and as a result she is not an autonomous person.

Accordingly, here is the general answer to the question asked earlier: besides autonomy of choice, self-knowledge and self-shaping are needed to be an autonomous person. With regard to the latter we may speak of self-'creation', but at the risk of misunderstanding. Talk of creation invites thought about making something out of nothing. Some might think that the autonomous person must make herself completely. This is not the sense of creation that is involved in autonomy of personhood. It had better not be, since it is obviously impossible. Instead, let's take a potter as our model. Imagine a potter who takes a generous blob of clay, drops it on a potter's wheel and forms it into a bowl. The potter has created the bowl by shaping the clay. This is a perfectly natural, and correct, thing to say. But the potter has not created the clay itself. This is the kind of creation that is involved with autonomy of persons: self-ruling persons work with the materials that they happen to have to make themselves into specific types of people. Neither they nor the potter create their products *ex nihilo*. They shape pre-existing materials into new forms. Incidentally, this model of creation also shows why self-knowledge is a vital component of autonomy of persons. If we do not know the nature of what we have to work with, we are at least hampered in our attempts to make both pots and persons of certain kinds.

Let's put aside autonomy of choices and focus on self-knowledge and self-shaping as necessary components of autonomy of persons. These are interrelated topics, so it is a bit distorting to speak of them separately, but I shall do what I can to make the salient points clear first about the one and then about the other. I shall begin with self-knowledge.

Autonomy of persons: Self-knowledge

Self-knowledge is a tricky topic in part because the self is a tricky topic. Although the focus of this section is self-knowledge, discussing this topic will require some attention to the question of just what constitutes a self. This treatment will inevitably be incomplete, given the philosophical difficulties here. Nevertheless, my working assumption is that progress can be made with regard to aspects of the self relevant to autonomy of persons in the absence of a complete account of selfhood.

Very roughly speaking, the more one knows about one's own nature, the more autonomous a person one will be. However, not all sorts of self-knowledge are of equal importance to this aspect of personal self-rule. Since, whatever else it is, autonomy involves somehow exercising control over and hence running one's own life, knowledge of our own motivations is particularly important. Without this our actions will be out of our control. This knowledge can be about particular sources of motivation for particular people. For example, Viviana knows that rare marsh plants will attract her attention and prompt her to act in certain ways. Particularly important among personal sources of motivation are our values. I will attend to this sort of motivation in the next section, in connection with self-shaping. Arguably more importantly we can know about the general kinds of things that motivate us. To acquire this sort of self-knowledge is to learn about the type of thing one is, in contrast to one's individual identity. Knowing about our general sources of motivation gives us powerful tools for, in principle, running our lives. This sort of knowledge provides deep explanations of why we do the things we do and lays the groundwork for both predictions and strategies with regard to our activity in novel circumstances.

So, just what sorts of things motivate us in general? Diana Tietjens Meyers suggests a five-fold conception of the self that serves as a useful classification of sources of human motivation (e.g. Meyers 2005). Here are five vignettes to illustrate Meyer's taxonomy.

A] Yousuf is a young man who loves photography. He likes the idea of a career taking pictures, but, being young, his attention is easily distracted. His parents keep telling him that this sort of career will be very difficult to pursue and that he will need to discipline himself a great deal or he will be disappointed. Through time Yousuf learns that he can devote more time to photography if he develops strategies for directing his attention towards pictures and away from distractions. For instance, when he tires of the darkroom and yearns for the beach, he has discovered that he can recharge his interest by leaving for a few minutes and making a pot of tea. When he is out with his camera and friends invite him for a drink, he has learnt that he can resist by counting to ten and thinking about the strengths of his competing desires for a few moments. Over time Yousuf continues to examine himself and to develop plans for focusing his mind on his passion. He eventually becomes a leading photographer in his nation.

This vignette exemplifies what Meyers calls the 'unified' self. This is arguably the sort of motivation most commonly associated with autonomy: motivation by explicit, conscious, rational reflection. This is where higher-order thought has its most obvious application. Yousuf examines his own tendencies and exercises control by forming thoughts about his own patterns of decision-making. This source of motivation is 'unified' in two senses. First, it stems from the seemingly univocal first-person introspective stance we can take towards ourselves. For most people, apparently, the subjective viewpoint on the world is a unified one, experienced as relatively seamless and as happening to a unitary entity. Our minds are subconsciously much more divided than this, but this is how life typically seems from the inside. Second, efficacious higher-order reflection can impose unity on a more disordered system of motivations. Yousuf is moved by the sun, photography, the beach, friends, *etc.* Higher-order thought marshals these motivations and shuts down some in favour of others. The result, in the present case, is a narrower motivational focus: only some things are allowed to be successful in producing action for Yousuf.

Attending to the unified self can make it seem that autonomy requires a deeply unified mind. This is unduly simplistic. I shall return to this issue after presenting the rest of Meyers' taxonomy, but note: the fact that this classification of human motivations is multi-faceted itself calls into question the assumption that autonomy of persons requires deep and persisting unity of mind.

B] Zeke is a first-generation Canadian living on Cape Breton Island. His parents are Scottish immigrants. Zeke has been brought up in an explicitly Scottish-Gaelic culture. 'There's none more Scots than the Scots abroad', as the song goes, fits Zeke and his family very well. Zeke and his fiancée are planning a wedding. There is not even a second thought about what the groom and his party will wear: kilts will be the official dress of the male members of the wedding party.

This vignette exemplifies what Meyers calls the 'social' self. This sort of motivation stems from one's enculturation. Typically, and perhaps universally, humans are both shaped by the social customs with which they grow up and define themselves with reference to these customs. Such definition can take the form of identification, as with Zeke and traditional Scottish dress, but it need not. One can define oneself through explicit rejection of the features of the cultural milieu in which one develops. This should be seen as part of the social self since we feel no need to explicitly reject features of cultural contexts which are foreign to us. I, like Zeke, am a Canadian of Scottish descent. Turbans play no role whatsoever in this context, and hence I feel no need to define myself by explicitly rejecting or accepting this fashion custom. However, the presence of kilts at my wedding was a different matter: I had to consider them and, consequently, I explicitly rejected them. I do not associate my identity strongly with this practice, although I do weakly associate with it. I recognize, both intellectually and in a more inchoate, visceral manner, that my ancestors wore this sort of garb. I have no such connection to turbans.

C] Alison has a rich family context. Besides her parents she has two sisters and three brothers. She is married with one child. She has rich friendships both with her neighbours and with people with whom she went to school long ago. Alison lives in a city that is growing quickly, which brings with it questions of how to accommodate new residents. Alison is attuned to civic issues and politics. She is wary of both urban sprawl into the countryside and increased population density in existing neighbourhoods. When thinking about which is preferable, she cannot but help thinking about her family and friends, both for now and in the years to come. Despite her own love for the quiet urban neighbourhood in which she owns a home, Alison thinks that increased urban density is preferable to sprawling city boundaries for her family and friends. As a consequence she supports municipal politicians who are in favour of infill developments and opposed to development of rural land for suburbs.

This vignette exemplifies what Meyers calls the 'relational' self. It is similar to the social self in that it concerns our relations with other people. The difference is this: the cultural self is the self conditioned by cultural customs and practices, whereas the relational self is the self that results from particular relations to individual persons such as family members, friends and neighbours. These are obviously related phenomena: family relations are a central conduit for the transmission of cultural customs, after all. Nevertheless these are distinct phenomena. Imagine a person of Scottish descent who lives in a neighbourhood filled with immigrants from India. Social and relational selves come apart here: if this is my situation, then none of my neighbours, to whom I can be very closely attached, share my cultural heritage. I take it that it is a commonplace that personal relations with other people can be an important source of motivation and even identity for people even when the cultural similarities between these people are so slight as to be negligible. This might not be clear to people who live in very culturally homogeneous places. However, for people who live in culturally heterogeneous contexts this will be a familiar phenomenon.

D] Brittany is a university student studying psychology. One day her social psychology class discusses the infamous experiments performed by Stanley Milgram (1963). Milgram solicited participation in learning studies, but this was a set-up. Subjects were given the role of a teacher in these studies, while confederates of the experimenters played the roles of a learner and of a study administrator. The job of the teacher was to ask questions and administer what they thought were electric shocks in response to incorrect answers; no shocks were actually delivered. The 'shocks' supposedly ascended in severity in increments of 15 volts, clearly labelled with very serious warnings for the teacher. When subjects hesitated in administering shocks, the administrator-confederate politely recited a list of instructions to continue. Milgram found that seemingly non-coercive features of experimental situations led ordinary people to administer what they thought were lethal levels of electrical shocks to other ordinary people. More precisely, about two thirds of subjects administered shocks all the way to the final level, and many of the other subjects administered shocks up to very high levels. Brittany's classmates tend to interpret these experiments in terms of external forces subverting one's control of one's actions, but Brittany disagrees. She finds it natural to think of subconscious aspects of herself which might give rise to actions that surprise her conscious self.. She has noticed this sort of surprising motivation in various contexts, and has come to accept it as one of the complexities of the human mind.

This vignette illustrates what Meyers calls the 'divided' self. The division is between conscious and subconscious aspects of one's identity and, consequently, sources of motivation. This is particularly challenging with regard to autonomy. It seems natural to associate 'self' rule with 'conscious' rule, such that subconscious motivation must be out of one's control. This, however, is implausible if we take a moderately broad view of what the self can include. Maybe it is even more generally implausible – I leave it to the readers to decide for themselves just how natural the idea of subconscious aspects of the self seems. If we countenance subconscious aspects of the self, then it is possible that there could be subconscious self-rule. That is, there can, in principle, be subconscious processes on one hand that do not deliver self-rule and there can be others that do, just as there can be with conscious thought processes. I shall return to this shortly.

E] Culver is a highly skilled tennis player. He is very good at all aspects of the game, but he is particularly good when he comes to the net to volley. He has spent hours training his body to volley effectively and creatively. Sometimes Culver forgets to emphasize his skills at the net and gets behind in matches trying to play from the baseline. Today is one of those cases. One of Culver's opponent's shots inadvertently drops short and Culver is drawn into the net to chase the ball. His bodily habits are activated by this occasion and Culver starts to come into the net more often, regaining the lead in the match and eventually winning.

This vignette displays what Meyers calls the 'embodied' self. Generally, recognizing the body, in discussions of autonomy and the self, involves taking account of the ways in which our cognitive capacities depend on our bodily integrity and health. Skilled athletes have extended their control over their lives in a very specific domain by increasing their abilities to deal with their particular sort of athletic challenge. By contrast, illness and disability threaten our capacities for running our lives. At the same time, physical challenges can reveal surprising bodily resources. Meyers relates an anecdote about becoming injured while hiking (2005, pp. 33–4). Her bodily instincts and skills took over and brought her safely off the trail despite her broken bones. Arguably these surprising resources facilitated the maintenance of Meyers' self-rule, given that they brought about not only the completion of the hike but also her continued good health.

This taxonomy of faces of the self could be developed. For instance, sub-categories could undoubtedly be distinguished and put to use to classify our motivations. Perhaps sixth, seventh, *etc.* categories could be added, although this seems more contentious to me. For the present purposes, these rough outlines of sources of human motivation will suffice. When first-order desires arise in one of these categories and are endorsed by higher-order stances, whether introspectively accessible or not, these desires and subsequent choices and actions are autonomous. This is implied by the discussion in Chapter 2. With regard to autonomy of persons, the general point should be clear: the more we know about the nature of our motivations, the better positioned we are to exercise control over them.

This is a multi-faceted and, to some degree, complex view of human motivation. It is, however, important to emphasize our psychological heterogeneity, as it has both practical and theoretical implications. Practically speaking, if the present account is roughly correct, then to think, for instance, that all motivation derives from explicit thought accessible to the unified self is a mistake. Making this mistake undermines our ability to run our lives, both with regard to actions in the present moment and with regard to sorting out what we value and how we should live in general. This mistake is a tempting one, despite our general familiarity with the idea of subconscious motivations of one kind or another. It underlies what I take to be a common assumption that we often know how we are moved on particular occasions. The present view calls this into question. The implication is that it might well take hard work, other people and the principled practices and resources of, for example, psychological inquiry to gain knowledge of the workings of our own minds.

The theoretical implications arise when we consider disavowed motives. Suppose that Doug is a heroin addict. He hates his addiction and wishes that he could be rid of it. He disavows his desires for heroin. Nevertheless sometimes these desires are successful in moving him, so that he takes heroin and maintains his addiction. The crucial question for the present purposes is whether we should think of Doug's disavowed desire as stemming from himself. The correct answer, it seems to me, is that we need more detail to give a determinate answer to this question. Perhaps it is, perhaps it is not – it could go either way, assuming that not all of our motivations should be thought of as part of ourselves. Theories of the self, however, that focus entirely on Meyers' unified self and introspectively accessible thought must locate disavowed desires outside of the self. Doug experiences his desires as an unwanted intrusion, and one way of interpreting this is to deem it a source of motivation outside of the self. If this desire was once part of Doug's self, its current disavowal amounts to a partial disintegration of Doug's self. If he came to endorse this motive, this would automatically be self-expansion. The discovery that this is part of Doug is ruled out as impossible by this sort of theory. 'I didn't know I had it in me!' Doug might say, which sounds like self-discovery. If this is correct, then we need aspects of the self that do not belong to the unified category to account for this possibility.

Delusion is also ruled out by this way of thinking of the self: Doug cannot be wrong about what stems from him and what does not. Moreover, Doug's self is deeply dissociated from his body on this sort of view. Embodied motives must be endorsed by conscious thought to be part of Doug. I take it that these implications are implausible enough to require explicit defence. I prefer a more nuanced view that allows for self-discovery and self-delusion. This is the sort of view delivered by Meyers' taxonomy.

Nevertheless, there is good reason to think that the unified self deserves a special place in accounts of autonomy of persons compared to the other dimensions that Meyers identifies. We can be alienated from the divided, embodied, relational and social aspects of the self in ways that do not fit the unified self. Suppose that I act in ways that I do not like and I chalk this up to a bodily source of motivation, such as a taste for salt. Looking back in time I might well think that I should have taken more control of this aspect of my desires. That is to say, I think that I would have benefited from more higher-order regulation. This is a line of thought that I can, in principle, use to plan for the future. It is unlikely, although not out of the realm of conceptual possibility, that I would wish for other bodily motivations to take over for my taste for salt. I might wish for, for example, relational or social sources of motivation to counteract this embodied one, but given that I am also reflecting on these ways of being moved the unified self is involved in both this motivational reflection and subsequent patterns of motivation. By contrast, when higher-order regulation of motivation goes wrong, recognition of this fact automatically involves the self-regulation of the unified self. Moreover, one of the likely outcomes of this reflection is a desire for more stringent higher-order control although, again, this is not a matter of conceptual necessity. In short, the unified self is at the centre of our powers to take increased control over our lives, whereas the other faces of the self are not.

Increases in self-knowledge serve autonomy of persons in two ways. One is as an aid to self-shaping, which is the topic of the next section. The other is in making possible increased coherence among one's motives. In particular, increased self-knowledge delivers an increased capacity to take account of one's own motivational tendencies in choice and action. This is not to say that either selfhood or autonomy requires perfect psychological coherence. Mental disunity is a familiar fact of life, rendered well by Meyers' account of aspects of the self. There is, obviously, the possibility of disunity between Meyers' categories. Doug, for instance, has embodied motives that differ from and conflict with those of his unified self. I take it that we all do. More subtly, there can be disunity within these categories. Relational and social forces are clearly not subject to forces that produce perfect motivational unity. We can be moved to both endorse and reject simultaneously some options by virtue of cultural inheritance and interpersonal relations. So long as our motivations are in some way endorsed, they will deliver autonomy. Nevertheless, when we discover things about ourselves and achieve increased motivational coherence through reflection, autonomy is increased. Endorsement by the unified self of a motive from some other category *at least* increases autonomy, since the motivation in question is now more integrated with oneself than it was before. It might confer autonomy, if it delivers the first degree of higher-order endorsement of this motive.

Although I have emphasized 'self' knowledge, it should be clear that this involves knowledge of things other than oneself as well. Suppose that I pay attention to my tastes for food and drink, turning myself from an unreflective eater into a gourmand. When I do this I clearly learn about myself, but I also learn about the things that I consume. Foodies know a lot about food, but they get to this point by trying things, seeing what they like and dislike, pursuing ways of developing and extending their tastes, reflecting on both themselves and the ways in which they might experience food, and more. Nevertheless, not all knowledge of other things is relevant to exercising control over one's life. Here is some terminology: 'egocentric' representations of things represent them in relation to oneself. 'Allocentric' representations represent independently of oneself. The knowledge of the world that is relevant to autonomy is egocentric. Allocentric knowledge must be turned into egocentric knowledge for it to be useful for self-rule. In principle one can know a lot about, for example, food – about chemical composition, modes of production – without this knowledge being useful in one's own life. For self-rule this information must be deployed in ways that one can use, meaning that it must be blended with knowledge about oneself.

If we put together the present emphasis on self-knowledge with the line of thought found in Chapter 2, we get this result: false beliefs about oneself are compatible with autonomy of choices but not, strictly speaking, with autonomy of persons. This is important for practical purposes, as we shall see in later chapters. For instance, it is part of the reason that people with religious commitments should be respected as autonomous. Crudely put, religious beliefs are all false. If rendered egocentrically, these beliefs compromise one's ability to rule one's life. But they need not compromise self-control of choices. This has implications for how we understand people who lived a long time ago. In principle, their capacities for self-rule over choices (desires, actions, *etc.*) were no different than ours. But if we assume that we know more about the nature of the world, including ourselves, than they did, and that they had demonstrably false beliefs about themselves that we do not share, then we see that our capacities for being autonomous persons are greater than theirs. I shall amplify this point in the next section, in connection with self-shaping.

The difference between autonomy of choices and autonomy of persons means that, in principle, these can come apart. Indeed, they can interfere with each other. Choices made autonomously can put deep obstacles in the way of our acquiring knowledge about ourselves that would serve our ability to run our lives. Imagine that I choose autonomously to become a slavish follower to an ideology characterized by many false beliefs about humans and the world. This choice interferes with the acquisition of facts about myself, both in general and as an individual, thus interfering with the self-knowledge required for self-rule. I shall return to this point later in the chapter, and it will be of notable importance in the discussion of the significance of autonomy.

A complete view of the importance of self-knowledge to autonomy of persons can be had only in connection with self-shaping, so let's turn to this topic.

Autonomy of persons: Self-shaping

To shape oneself is to exercise control directly over one's identity. I presume that some of our thoughts and actions have no interesting effects on who we are. I am the same person whether I choose orange or tomato juice in the morning. We can divide the choices that do have effects on identity into two groups. First, there are thoughts and actions that have incidental effects on who we are. Suppose that I kill someone and afterwards I experience unexpected changes in the ways that I understand the world and act within it. It would be natural to say that the killing changed me. However, my thought and action at that time (by hypothesis) were not about me – they were about my victim. These are not the sorts of ways of bringing about effects on identity that will concern us in this section. Instead the topic is the second category of identity-shaping thoughts and actions: those that do so directly. It is commonplace to think that we can think about ourselves and thereby make at least some choices about what kinds of people to be and lives to live. This is what is meant by 'self-shaping' as a component of autonomy of persons.

Strictly speaking, self-shaping relies on the two previous topics that have been discussed in connection with autonomy of persons: autonomy of choices and self-knowledge. Consequently self-shaping is at the heart of autonomy of personhood. Here is the point in a nutshell: to shape oneself is to make autonomous choices about a particular topic – oneself. It is not just the topic that makes these choices unique among the myriad of topics about which we can choose autonomously. Instead, these choices have special sorts of effects for autonomy of choice in general. Moreover, given that we are not blank slates, we need some knowledge about ourselves in order for self-shaping to get off the ground. This knowledge concerns us both as individuals and as certain kinds of things – for example, persons, humans or physical objects. Without this knowledge our attempts to make ourselves into certain kinds of being will either be in vain or merely luckily successful. Neither of these captures the idea of exercising control over identity. We exercise control over who we are when we autonomously choose aspects of our identity in the light of information about ourselves.

The relation between autonomy of choice and autonomy of persons can be sharpened by using the distinction between egocentric and allocentric representations. Roughly speaking, autonomy of choice about any topic is, in principle, needed to be an autonomous person. For practical purposes, it is acceptable to think that autonomy of choice is needed for autonomy of personhood. Strictly speaking, however, this is not quite right. It is egocentric choice – choice using representations of things in relation to the self – that is needed for autonomy of persons. Allocentric choice is only indirectly relevant. Suppose that these representational capacities can come apart. This implies that, in principle, some people could have deficits of allocentric representation while being normal with regard to egocentric representation, while others could have egocentric deficits without allocentric ones. Those who are capable of egocentric representations are, strictly speaking, capable of being autonomous persons; those who lack this capacity are not, despite being able to represent things independently of themselves.

Let's get more specific. Just what topics must we reflect upon and choose in order to shape ourselves? A variety of things might be offered here, but two are particularly important. To shape ourselves we must reflect upon and choose with regard to two things:

A   Our lower-order mental states, especially first-order ones, in the light of our values, and

B   Our values themselves.

To do (A) is to assess our thoughts according to some ideal. To do (B) is to choose such an ideal. Doing these two things amounts to shaping oneself if we assume that choosing and living by our values is at the heart of what we mean when we speak, in normal contexts, of identity. If it is our values that define us, then to exercise control over these values and over our lives with these values is to rule ourselves in a very deep way.

In Chapter 2, I defended a version of a hierarchical account of autonomy of choices. Autonomy of choice requires higher-order endorsement of lower-order mental states, but it does not require explicit reasoning as part of the process of endorsing. By contrast shaping oneself requires explicit reasoning. At the core of self-shaping is determining whether lower-order mental states are desirable in the evaluative sense of 'worth desiring'. Doing this is ambiguous, hence the two-fold focus of the account of self-shaping. Part of the exercise of self-rule with regard to the desirability of mental states in answering this question involves assessing what our values are and whether our lower-order desires are consistent with these. More objectively, but also perhaps more difficult to perform, figuring this out can involve assessing whether our values themselves are desirable. In both cases, more is involved than the matching of first-order desires with second-order ones, which is the core of the autonomy of choice. It is reasonable to think that one's values consist of a web of various levels of desires, beliefs, interests and needs. It suffices for our purposes merely to note the sorts of mental states that constitute our values; we need not analyze their complex relationships. More specifically, for (A) the exercise of self-shaping involves having a sense of the structure of one's life and assessing desires against the background of this structure. Moreover, it is reasonable to think that having a sense of the structure of one's life is more than a matter of observing the shape of one's life. Rather, it involves projection of an ideal – conscious reflection about one's values is a combination of description and prescription. So, to examine how one's current mental states about the world match one's values is, at least in part, to ask, 'How do my current first order desires fit the way I want my life to be?'. In so doing, it is reasonable to think that sometimes one will give up on first-order desires, and that at other times one will modify one's values. In considering the coherence of the fit of one's current mental states with the desired shape of one's life, a person is exercising substantial control over his/her own identity. Moreover, this control seems largely rational in the sense of being driven by reason.

The exercise of self-shaping with regard to (B) is somewhat different. To ask whether one's own values are themselves desirable, a person still needs a sense of the structure of his/her life. Now, however, this structure is assessed against other possible ways of living. This requires more than knowledge of one's own mental states and values. It requires a sense of other possible ways of living. In the first case, one's current mental states are assessed against the background of the structure of one's life. In the second case, self-shaping requires the assessment of the structure of one's life against the background of other actual and possible ways of living.

Readers should recall Jan and Kari from Chapter 2, in connection with this point. They both run their own businesses, but Jan lives in a context in which there are very few personal and professional options, whereas Kari has a wealth of options, and knowledge about them, from which to choose. There is some reason to think that, although both choose their careers autonomously, they are not equal with regard to self-shaping. Jan is in an impoverished position with regard to the meaningful consideration of ways of life other than the one that he actually has. Kari, by contrast, has lots of information about different ways of living. At the very least, if we assume that they have both thought about what kind of person to be, we should think that Kari is a more autonomous person than Jan because of the extent of her (B) type self-shaping.

Still, we should not think that self-shaping, as well as autonomy of personhood, has no implications for autonomy of choice. There is an indirect sense in which Kari's choice is more autonomous than Jan's because of the difference in their wealth of options. Autonomy of choice is, essentially, choice by a self, and a relatively wide range of options is not necessary for the existence of a self. However, insofar as a wealth of options increases the determination of a self by making one's self more under one's own control, it also increases autonomy of choice. The reason is that choices made in the face of consideration of a wide range of options stem from a more self-made self than choices made in conditions in which options are relatively more constrained. We might say that the choices in these cases exhibit different 'depths' of integration with the self: the more options one has and the more one has considered them, the deeper a choice is self-ruled.

Both (A) and (B), but especially (B), are characterized by what Charles Taylor calls strong evaluation. I shall rely on Taylor to shed light on some important details about self-shaping. Taylor locates strong evaluation in a family of ideas including others such as authenticity and self-interpretation. Although strong evaluation is of most importance for present purposes, these ideas are best explicated together.

In 'Self-Interpreting Animals' (1985a), Taylor presents strong evaluation in terms we have seen before. Taylor ties his notion explicitly to the work of Harry Frankfurt (Taylor 1985a, p. 66; see also 1985b, p. 15). In this vein, Taylor casts strong evaluation in terms of the evaluation of desires: 'I want to speak of strong evaluation where we 'evaluate', that is, consider good/bad, desirable/despicable, our desires themselves' (Taylor 1985a, p. 65). Elsewhere he says that strong evaluation attends to the quality or worth of our motivation (Taylor 1985b, p. 16). This accords with (A) type self-shaping. However, in *Sources of the Self* (1989), Taylor describes strong evaluation more broadly. Here it is characterized so as not to be limited to the evaluation of first-order desires: strong evaluation involves '. . . discriminations of right or wrong, better or worse, higher or lower, which are not rendered valid by our own desires, inclinations or choices, but rather stand independent of these and offer standards by which they can be judged' (Taylor 1989, p. 4). Whereas strong evaluation in the sense of (A) type self-shaping consists primarily in the assessment of whether first-order desires are consistent with our higher-order preferences, the broader type of strong evaluation addresses the possibility of the evaluation of these higher-order preferences themselves. As such, it matches what I have described as (B) type self-shaping.

Taylor presents two reasons that, together, establish the importance of strong evaluation. First, he tells us that it is unavoidable (1989, p. 42). The reason for this is that strong evaluation, in both the wide and narrow senses, is part of the establishment of one's conception of the good life. The good life is taken here as a broad moral ideal, not necessarily hedonistically, as our vernacular often suggests. We cannot help but live under some conception of how we ought to live, or, in less-demanding terms, of what sort of life is worth living. Figuring this out involves, at the very least, assessing whether we really want the things we seem to want. This is the narrow form of strong evaluation. However, it also involves some form of evaluation of possible ways of living. Here is a fairly trivial example: one may want ice cream, and by performing narrow strong evaluation, one may determine that one wants to want ice cream. In performing a wider strong evaluation, one might compare a life involving the satisfaction of such gustatory desires and bodily appetites with one that shuns such pleasures, or assigns to them a vastly inferior role. The result of this sort of strong evaluation could be that, despite one's first- and second-order desires involving an ice cream, one decides that such items and activities have no or little place in a properly good life.

Second, Taylor argues that, in articulating a notion of the good life and assessing how one's own preferences match that ideal, a person sketches a 'moral map' of him/herself (1985a, p. 67). 'It involves, one might say, attributing to different motivations their place in the life of the subject' (1985a, p. 67). So, strong evaluation is unavoidable inasmuch as it is tied up in the unavoidable activity of operating under some sense of what the good life involves. Figuring out the characteristics of the good life itself necessarily includes a conception of the structure of one's life. Further, as suggested before, the latter activity is not merely descriptive; it is also creative. In articulating the related notions of the good life and the moral map of oneself, one defines oneself. In Taylor's own relaxed terms, 'It involves defining what it is we really are about. . .' (1989, p. 68; see also 1985b, pp. 35–8).

Since strong evaluation is an activity, it can be done well or poorly. What do we need in place to have a chance at performing strong evaluation well? Here it is useful to incorporate Taylor's discussions of other concepts. First, with the idea that strong evaluation involves self-definition, the concept of identity is brought in. In 'Atomism' (Taylor 1985c), Taylor argues that the characteristics of full, rational human existence can only be developed within a social context. In other words, we get our identities from the social context(s) in which we develop. Correlatively, inasmuch as we are properly (and unavoidably) concerned with who we are, we ought to be concerned with the moral character of the social context(s) in which we exist (1985c, pp. 206–7). In terms of Meyers' taxonomy, Taylor emphasizes the social and relational components of selfhood.

Second, with the notion that strong evaluation is central to articulating, defining, and acting out of a conception of what we are really about, the concept of authenticity is brought into the discussion. In *The Ethics of Authenticity* (1991), Taylor portrays authenticity as one of the legitimately central moral ideals of modernity. It is characterized by a call to live one's life in one's own way (1991, pp. 28–9). Obviously, to do this one has to figure out what this way is. Moreover, being true to one's own originality (1991, p. 29) is something one has to figure out and accomplish for oneself. To live up to the moral tenor of our age, one has to undergo or pursue strong evaluation.

The idea of the importance of being true to oneself and the necessity of pursuing this by oneself has led to certain sorts of individualism and relativism; Taylor is concerned about diagnosing and combating with the errors in these views. Two things in particular go overlooked in the modern version of the ideal of authenticity. Both are related to the previous idea that one's identity is determined within a context. First, one must retain, '. . .

Openness to horizons of significance' (1991, p. 66). These horizons correspond to, among other things, the ideas of possible ways of living necessary for the wide sort of strong evaluation. If being true to oneself is absolutely divorced from some assessment of what is really important, then one's attempt to live up to the moral spirit of our age runs the risk of degrading itself to mere narcissism or irrelevance. '. . . one of the things we can't do, if we are to define ourselves significantly, is suppress or deny the horizons against which things take on significance for us' (1991, p. 37). This forces the question of how we come to conceive of these horizons of value upon us; its answer brings the second point out. The source of our horizons of significance is the other people with whom we live. The conversation and interaction which characterize both our adult behaviour and our on-going moral education give us both the roots of and the opportunity to develop our notions of value further. In short, our horizons of significance are rooted in our social context(s). We have also seen that this context is central to the formation of our identities. In Taylor's terms, our conceptions both of value and of ourselves are formed through dialogue (1991, p. 66).

Two things are worth noting about the role of horizons of significance in the exercise of strong evaluation. First, it should be clear that Taylor's idea does not entail that we must sacrifice our reflective authenticity to accord with the context within which we find ourselves. On the contrary, remaining open to such horizons will require searching out information about ways of living that go beyond those we are most familiar with, and that are perhaps even incommensurable with them. Strong evaluation does not require commitment to any particular one of the ways of living we find. Instead, we might find ourselves choosing pieces from any number of ways of living. Second, and relatedly, Taylor stresses remaining open to horizons of significance. This means that strong evaluation is an on-going process. This is another way of putting the earlier point that it is unavoidable.

It should be clear that there is no a priori guarantee that any of the ways of living to which one is exposed will be rationally grounded. Yet exactly these horizons are the source of information used in strong evaluation. Potential problems here with uncertainty as to the rational adequacy of the results of one's strong evaluation can only be dealt with through further testing. One must continue such evaluation. Imagination, time, and work are the only tools one has to safeguard oneself against in making bad choices in the course of strong evaluation.

Three things are worth clarifying about this discussion of self-shaping and strong evaluation. I shall start with the most minor point. I introduced self-shaping in part by saying that this process has unique sorts of effects for autonomy of choice. It should now be clear what the nature of these effects is. When I make autonomous choices about most things, this has no particular effects for the way in which I make further such choices. It might have incidental effects, but nothing more significant. By contrast, self-shaping has direct effects on the autonomy of choice. Mostly this occurs for those choices made deliberately through explicit reasoning. Self-shaping creates the standards by which we judge the adequacy of our options and actions. This is a central part of the point of going through this process. After all, to settle on our values is to set the standards by which we shall try to live. One of the subtle implications of the effects that self-shaping has for autonomy of choice is that it helps to explain why this is an on-going process. Shaping oneself both deploys and affects our capacities for autonomous choices. The effects of today's choices mean that we might want to revisit these very choices and test them against our newly shaped values. If we change things via this round of autonomous choosing, then we are again faced with the option of revisiting these choices with the third set of values, *etc.* On one hand perhaps this sounds exhausting and both intellectually and practically unsatisfying. Must we really go through life absorbed with self-scrutiny? No, but we will be less autonomous for foregoing it. On the other hand perhaps this sounds familiar. As time goes by many see themselves in new ways and commit themselves to new directions in living fairly automatically. The assumption that identity is completely defined once and for all at a given time is a mistake. We both learn new things about and create new features for ourselves all through our life. Autonomous people exercise relatively more control over this process.

Second, and still in a minor vein, in Chapter 2, I suggested that the phenomenon identified by hierarchical theorists – higher-order thought, to put it bluntly – might be unavoidable. The present discussion gives us a new reason to take this seriously. The primary focus of self-shaping is one's values. Our values will be about lots of things including, importantly, our own motives. Recall Nicholas and Olivia. Olivia seems not to have values, but Nicholas does, and some of these are about what motivates him to eat. To the extent that it is unavoidable to value some sorts of motivation over others, we find the pattern of thought characteristic of hierarchical theories of autonomy. Note well that this line of thought is merely suggestive of inevitability of this phenomenon. It is not demonstratively rock solid. Still, it is worth adding to the considerations that we have already seen on this topic.

Let's turn to the third and most significant point. There is debate among autonomy theorists about the scope of ways of living a person can choose among and still be autonomous. Some theorists argue that there is no limit: autonomous people can choose anything and still be autonomous. Others argue that some ways of living are inconsistent with autonomy. The first group of theorists offers 'content-neutral' theories of autonomy. The second group offers 'substantive' accounts of personal self-rule. The kinds of things that substantive theorists point to are ways of life involving domination of one person by another. Good examples are slavery, military service, immersion in a religious context and servant-like devotion of one person to another. Can one, for instance, autonomously sell oneself into slavery and still be autonomous, or is this a choice that necessarily undermines autonomy? Substantive theorists typically argue that slavery is necessarily inconsistent with autonomy. Content-neutral theorists disagree.

One might think that the present account is a substantive account. I have used Charles Taylor's work on strong evaluation and Taylor emphasizes the moral dimension of this sort of thought. Through strong evaluation one projects an ideal for oneself. The resources for performing this sort of projection are social: in large measure we get our ideas of desirable ways of life from the examples and conceptual resources offered by other people. One might be tempted to think that, on this line of thought, autonomous people must choose morally respectable ways of living; kinds of life that fail by moral standards are inconsistent with autonomy. This kind of interpretation of the present view, however, is not required by the sorts of considerations that we have already seen and it is, I think, mistaken. The present view of autonomy of persons is content-neutral despite the value-laden language used by Taylor in connection with self-interpretation and strong evaluation.

We need to be more careful with our technical concepts if we are to see how the present view is content-neutral. The substantive/content-neutral distinction is too coarse-grained to capture all of the relevant phenomena. Consider Erik who is reflecting on what sort of person to be. He uses examples and concepts provided by what he sees around him. However, like all of us Erik is not a perfect replicator of the ideas he encounters, so distortions creep in. I say 'distortions', but some of these might be improvements. Moreover Erik contributes to his stock of ideas from his own imagination. The results of the cognitive processes mediating Erik's context and Erik's thoughts about his context are complex, but one is especially important for the present purposes. We can distinguish between an idea that is represented as morally important by people other than Erik and, on the other hand, by an idea that is represented as morally important by Erik. Let's call the first possibility 'contextual representation' and the second 'individual representation'. Contextual and individual representations can be the same, but they can clearly come apart. Erik can represent something as important, yet the people around him might not share this way of thinking about the topic. Erik can also fail to see the evaluative import of certain ways of being that are valued by his friends and neighbours.

Here is how these distinctions work in the present account of autonomy of persons. The person going through self-shaping reflects upon and even creates for him/herself ideals about how to live. These projected ideals are individually represented as important, but they need not be contextually represented as important. The present account of autonomy of persons is individually substantive: the agent represents some sorts of life as worth living and this probably puts other sorts of life out of reach as inconsistent with the life the agent has shaped so far. But this account of autonomy of persons is contextually content-neutral: in principle agents can give any sort of life to themselves through the process of self-shaping. There will be practical limits imposed upon us by our nature, both biological and individual, but there are no necessary limits on the basis of the nature of autonomy. It is contextual content-neutrality that matters in the contemporary debate about the nature of autonomy. By this measure the present account falls into the content-neutral camp despite the evaluative ways in which agents will experience the possibilities which they consider when shaping themselves.

The crucial thing to address in connection with this issue is this: in order to be autonomous, must a person value autonomy? Can one autonomously choose subservience? Consider Frederick and Gillian. Both are slaves. Frederick was born into slavery. He has never had control of his own life. Gillian is much different. She used to be a free person. She considered her options in life and decided that a life of slavery was attractive to her. She knew that this was a serious decision to make so she spent a lot of time reflecting on what was important to her before selling herself as a slave. She made the decision confidently and has not come to regret it. When she revisits the question of what sorts of life are desirable, she is comfortable with her decision to become a slave.

Although there is something tempting about the idea that subservience is inconsistent with autonomy, there is good reason to think that this is not the case. Frederick and Gillian are both slaves, yet they do not stand in the same relationship to their subservient status. Frederick has never been able to make an autonomous choice about what sort of life to live, nor do we have reason to think that he is an autonomous person. Crucially his slavery is not autonomous. By contrast Gillian is an autonomous slave. Her subservience is an expression of her deeply considered and chosen values. She is an autonomous person with regard to her slavery.

The fact that we can surrender control over our lives autonomously raises problems for one way that some theorists address autonomy. Recent years have seen the use of ideas about narratives to shed light on various aspects of human psychology, including autonomy. There is something appealing about the idea that the autonomous person writes her own narrative. This line of thought suggests that we should think of the autonomous person's stance towards her life and values as an authorial one. While it might be the case that this sort of stance suffices for autonomy, it is not necessary for it. As a model for autonomy it breaks down for cases of autonomous relinquishing of control. The autonomous slave does not write her own story. This goes also for portions of a life. As we shall see in later chapters, we can autonomously surrender control over particular kinds of decisions. The image of an author captures this poorly.

The case of Gillian exemplifies something interesting about the relations between autonomy of choice and autonomy of persons. Should Gillian come to renounce her interest in slavery, she will be stuck in it: she lacks the sort of control over her life needed to get her out of slavery. At this point she will become unable to make autonomous choices that line up with her values, and the reason will be her prior self-shaping and autonomous choice. Even though autonomy of choice is part of the capacity for shaping oneself, the ways of living that we autonomously decide upon can interfere with subsequent choices. Gillian's is an extreme case, as the choice of a kind of life takes a great range of options out of her control. More realistic possibilities involve narrower ranges of possible choices. The kind of life one chooses can pose obstacles to:

1 Making particular choices autonomously, and
2 Making certain kinds of choice autonomously.

With regard to [1], here is an example to which we will return later in the book. Henry is an autonomous person. One of the things that he has thought about and come to value is the limits of his knowledge. Henry is convinced that lots of people know more about important things than he does, and consequently he has chosen a policy of deferring to them on these topics. Medicine is one of these topics. Henry visits his doctor. The doctor explains a few things about an illness Henry has developed and Henry interrupts: 'You take care of it, doc. You know more about this than I do. I don't need to know anything else.' The doctor proceeds to make decisions about Henry's medical care. Because of the kind of person Henry has made himself – that is, a person who values intellectual humility – he does not just put obstacles in the way of making autonomous decisions about his medical care, he gives up on these decisions altogether. Yet since this resignation is an expression of the values he has chosen, Henry is acting autonomously in doing this. This might go well in a case such as Henry's, but it need not: the obstacles that autonomy of persons can pose to autonomy of choices can be undesirable.

Here is a vignette to illustrate [2]: Ike has committed himself to a life of religious devotion. He made this decision after much reflection on what was important to him. He lives in a very secluded religious community with very few connections to the wider world, such as newspapers and electronic media. What Ike knows about the world comes to him via the leaders of this community. Ike is trying to quit smoking. Like many people who try this he is having great difficulty. He is focusing on ridding himself of the desire to smoke, but this seems not to be working. Ike is frustrated about this. As it happens, unbeknownst to Ike there are easily accessible practical aids and sources of technical information that would help him give up smoking by supplementing his strategy. However, Ike has put himself out of reach of these sources of help through the kind of life to which he committed himself. He is failing to give up smoking autonomously in large part because of the kind of person into which he has made himself.

Conclusion

The last two chapters offer a theory of autonomy, in two parts. Chapter 2 contains a version of the hierarchical theory of the autonomy of choice. The present chapter gives an account of the autonomy of persons. This includes autonomy of choice, but it has two other components: self-knowledge and self-shaping. Self-shaping is the capacity for autonomous choice reflectively deployed towards one's own identity. This has unique effects for the standards by which some future choices will be made. This must be complemented by knowledge of oneself, both as a particular individual and in more generic regards. Without this information we are unable to exercise control over ourselves – our attempts at self-shaping will be either merely luckily successful or fruitless. Without self-knowledge, self-shaping is blind and in vain. By contrast autonomous choice in general has no special epistemic component. All that is needed is the knowledge that acting in general requires, whether autonomous or not. The present account of autonomy of persons is contextually content-neutral but individually substantive. The bottom line is that there is no autonomy-based limit to the kinds of life that we can autonomously give ourselves.

Let's finish by recalling the Kantian, Humean and Humboldtian themes raised at the end of Chapter 2. All three show up in the present account. Humean themes are evident mostly in the discussion of self-knowledge. The knowledge relevant to figuring out what sort of person to be centrally includes information about our desires. We can learn about both our particular desires and the motivations we have by virtue of our shared nature as, for example, humans.

Kantian and Humboldtian themes emerge in connection with self-shaping. To shape ourselves directly we must reflect on who we are, who we want to be and what sorts of persons are worth emulating or at least learning from. Otherwise we shape ourselves only indirectly, which does not warrant the name 'self-rule'. Humboldtian theories emphasize individuality, especially as defined by one's values. This is exactly what is formed through self-shaping.

I charged the Kantian, Humean and Humboldtian theories with three objections. None of these apply to the hybrid defended in this chapter, despite the presence of these themes. The third objection charged these theories with neglecting the kind of control that higher-order thought delivers. This clearly does not apply in the present case. As for the others, both 'self' and 'control' are addressed by the two accounts of autonomy of choice and autonomy of persons, so the focal point of the present view is not unduly narrow. Nor is a particular kind of mental state simplistically emphasized over other aspects of our minds. The work of Meyers is particularly useful in answering the 'what's so special?' objection. We have good reason to think that the present two-pronged theory of autonomy is a defensible account of the nature of personal self-rule.

Reading guide

The swamp person device for raising questions about the importance of history for certain phenomena was devised by Donald Davidson in 'Knowing one's own mind', *Subjective, Intersubjective, Objective* (Oxford University Press, 2001).

Diana Tietjen Meyers has written a fair bit about autonomy and aspects of the self. See, for example, *Self, Society, and Personal Choice* (Columbia University Press, 1989) and *Being Yourself: Essays on Identity, Action, and Social Life* (Rowman and Littlefield Publishers, 2004). A brief piece particularly relevant to the discussion in this chapter is 'Decentralizing autonomy: five faces of selfhood' in *Autonomy and the Challenges to Liberalism* (Cambridge University Press, 2005), edited by John Christman and Joel Anderson.

Charles Taylor has a voluminous body of work about many topics which often stand in complex relationships with each other. I have drawn on these for this chapter: 1] 'Self-interpreting animals', in *Human Agency and Language: Philosophical Papers 1* (Cambridge University Press, 1985). 2] 'What is human agency?', in *Human Agency and Language: Philosophical Papers 1* (Cambridge University Press, 1985). 3] 'Atomism', in *Philosophy and the Human*

Sciences: Philosophical Papers 2 (Cambridge University Press, 1985). 4] *Sources of the Self: The Making of the Modern Identity* (Harvard University Press, 1989). 5] *The Ethics of Authenticity* (Harvard University Press, 1991).

The debate over substantive and content-neutral theories of autonomy is at the core of the contemporary literature, so virtually every book about autonomy touches on the subject either briefly or at length. The opposing papers by Natalie Stoljar and Paul Benson provide a useful place to see cases for both sides: 1] Natalie Stoljar, 'Autonomy and the feminist intuition' in *Relational Autonomy: Feminist Perspectives on Autonomy, Agency and the Social Self* (Oxford University Press, 2000), edited by Catriona MacKenzie and Natalie Stoljar. 2] Paul Benson, 'Feminist intuitions and the normative substance of autonomy' in *Personal Autonomy: New Essays on Personal Autonomy and Its Role in Contemporary Moral Philosophy* (Cambridge University Press, 2005), edited by James Stacey Taylor. Marilyn Friedman's attention to this issue is worth noting: *Autonomy, Gender, Politics* (Oxford University Press, 2003).

For a discussion of selfhood, autonomy and narrative, see David Velleman's 'The self as narrator' in *Autonomy and the Challenges to Liberalism: New Essays* (Cambridge University Press, 2005), edited by John Christman and Joel Anderson.

CHAPTER FOUR

Psychological challenges to autonomy

In Chapters 2 and 3, I have sketched a portrait of individual self-rule. It is a multi-faceted view, but at its core is the assumption that we can exercise a certain degree of control over ourselves and our choices. I have introduced both the general contours of this account and some of its details with vignettes that I hope are uncontroversial in what they portray. Consequently, I take it that the idea that we can exercise this kind of significant control over our lives is familiar, attractive, and even commonplace.

It is worth questioning whether this assumption is warranted. The aim of this chapter is to shore up our sense of the control we can exercise – or fail to exercise – over our choices and identities. Here is my strategy: I take it that the vignettes deployed in previous chapters sufficiently illuminate the familiar and common assumption that this sort of control is psychologically possible. Doubts about this have to be prompted, either by argument or by troubling examples of failures of control. So, in this chapter I will confront some classic and contemporary challenges to the psychological possibility of autonomy.

Determinism

The first obstacle to our view of ourselves as capable of ruling our choices and lives stems not from psychology but from longstanding worries about causal determinism. Very roughly, this is the worry that, somehow, the past rigidly determines the future, and hence our present. What we do and think now is not up to us, and hence is not under our control, but rather has been determined by past occurrences. If this is correct, then it seems to threaten our view of ourselves as capable of ruling our lives, which is just what autonomy is.

Determinism is a topic of perennial philosophical discussion. Even if it turns out not to be true – although my guess is with it, not against it – it is instructive for the purposes of understanding the processes that give rise to autonomy to examine the problem it might be thought to pose to our abilities to control our lives. Crucially, autonomy does not require that the doctrine of determinism be false.

Here is a more precise way of formulating determinism. Imagine the world at a particular point in time long ago. Freeze that point of time in your mind. Using common philosophical terminology, we will call the way the world was at that moment the complete physical state P of world w at time t. According to determinism, everything that happens now is necessitated by preceding states of the world such as this. One important way of understanding this is in terms of *laws*: deterministic laws constrain what can happen in w. Consider the law of gravity as an example. At the surface of the earth, objects fall at a rate of acceleration of 9.8 meters per second per second – that is, 9.8 m/sec^2. Objects don't have a choice about this. They – including the physical objects that are human – just fall in this way under appropriate circumstances. So, if a vase is knocked off a window sill, its condition at the moment of collision plus the law of gravity yields its subsequent and all-too-familiar activity. This falling activity, we might say, is determined by the laws and prior state of the world.

Here is the implication of all this put a little more abstractly. Given P and the deterministic laws of w, the states of w at times $t + 1, t + 2 \ldots t + n$ are fixed. There is only one possible future for w. If we had complete knowledge of P and the laws of w, then, in principle we could accurately predict and hence know what the states of w would be at $t + 1 \ldots t + n$. Crucially, if there are any people in w, then they are covered by its deterministic laws. Imagine a person, Leyton, at $t + 1$. Leyton's conduct was fixed by P and the laws of w. There is only one possible future for Leyton, meaning that when he does something, he could not have done otherwise.

This seems to mean that Leyton cannot exercise control over his life. The worry is that determinism makes autonomy impossible.

Readers familiar with the contemporary literatures on freedom and moral responsibility will have perked up at the words 'could not have done otherwise'. For several decades the question of the significance of the ability to do other than what one actually does has been a focal point for philosophical discussion of these topics, but it is relevant to autonomy as well. As with the hierarchical theory of autonomy, the roots of this discussion lie in work by Harry Frankfurt. Frankfurt argued, to put it roughly, that freedom and responsibility are not threatened by an inability to act in ways other than the way in which one actually acts. Here is a Frankfurt-style case modified in terms of autonomous choice. Milos is tempted to assassinate the mayor of the town in which he lives. He thinks about this for a while – assassination attempts are worth careful reflection, after all – and decides that he really does want to kill the mayor. This desire is appropriately incorporated into his overall system of thought; it satisfies the account of autonomy sketched in Chapter 2. Milos forms a plan to kill the mayor, which we should also see as autonomous. Nonetheless, he is sensitive both to thoughts that he really should not do this and to fears about what might happen to him if he carries out his plan. His commitment to doing so accordingly wavers. This worries Brad, a neuroscientist who knows about Milos' desire. Brad wants Milos to kill the mayor, but he is concerned that his fears will overcome him at the crucial moment. To ensure that the mayor is killed, Brad intervenes. He implants a chip in Milos' brain and erases all of Milos' memories of this procedure. The chip does two things: first, it monitors Milos' degree of resolve to kill the mayor; second, in the event that Milos decides to abandon his plan, the chip will activate and interfere with Milos' choosing and action-production capacities, making him choose to kill the mayor. After this implantation, the day to carry out the plan arrives. Milos hems and haws about the assassination, but eventually kills the mayor as he had planned. The chip monitors all of this, but because Milos carries out his original plan the chip remains dormant.

The crucial question is whether Milos' choice to kill the mayor was autonomous. We have good reason to think that it was. It was generated by a combination of desiring, reflecting and planning, so we should see it as cohering with Milos' overall thought. The only thing that raises any questions about the degree of autonomy of the choice is the presence of the chip in Milos' brain. The chip makes it such that Milos cannot choose but to kill the mayor. He cannot choose or act other than the way in which he actually chooses and acts. Since Milos sticks to his own plan, the chip does not make him choose in the way that he does. He could not do otherwise, but he is nonetheless autonomous.

The lesson of the so-called Frankfurt-style cases is that what matters for freedom, responsibility and, for our purposes, autonomy is not whether one can do otherwise, but the nature of the actual processes by which desire, choice, action, *etc.* are produced. Milos' action is under his control. If the chip had been activated, there is an important sense in which Milos would not have been in control of what he did. But since the chip remained dormant, Milos was in the driver's seat of his choice and conduct.

Let's return to Leyton and determinism. Part of the issue was whether Leyton's autonomy was threatened by the fact that, if determinism is true, Leyton cannot do other than what he actually does. We now have reason to think that this is not a problem. The lesson from the case of Milos is that it is the nature of the processes underlying action which matters for thoughts about responsibility, control and autonomy. Contrary to initial appearances, Leyton can exercise control over his life even if our world is deterministic.

We can see this more clearly if we change our focal point. The appearance of a lack of control in a deterministic world is generated by focusing on the distant past and the way that current and future happenings follow from it. In contrast with this, imagine instead the normal way that we explain people's particular actions: we start with an action and work backwards. Suppose that Leyton announces a decision to retire from his athletic career. We ask him why, and Leyton responds that he has reflected on his life, what he has done and what he would like to do, and he has decided that, although continuing with his career has definite appeal, there are downsides to the continuation of this life and there are benefits to changing direction. Reflect on Leyton's decision, but in reverse. There is the decision. Before this there is a process of reflection that includes sensitivity about Leyton's own desires and his place in the wider world. The considerations about the world include both facts about his career – for example, what it will be like to continue, who his opponents are and will be, sources of funding for continuation

– and facts about alternative ways of spending his time. If we work further backwards in time, the sorts of things we will find will seem less relevant to the explanation of Leyton's decision. Suppose that he deliberated over what to eat for breakfast that morning, and that before that he thought about whether to attend a movie the night before, and before that, etc. The causal and explanatory relevance of these considerations fades, even if they are part of the deterministic world in which Leyton's choice arises.

To see what a difference this focus on proximate rather than distal causes makes in a deterministic setting, contrast Leyton with Petr. On the same day that Leyton makes his decision to retire, Petr independently makes the same decision. When asked why, Petr says that he does not know: he just woke up today and the feeling that he should retire seized him. He has not thought about the decision, nor has he reflected on what he wants, what he will do with his time, or whether he will miss his sport. Whereas Leyton's decision arose from a sensitivity to various sorts of considerations about himself and the wider world in which he operates, Petr's consideration has come out of the blue and is, so far as we can tell, completely disconnected from his other wants and needs. Even if one is unsure about the possibility of control in a deterministic world, it should be clear that there are important differences between Leyton and Petr. The causal roots of Leyton's decision are the causal vectors constituted by his sensitivity to information about himself and the world, along with his capacities to think about this information. The causal roots of Petr's decision are much less integrated. Whereas there is a clear sense in which Leyton's decision arises from himself, there is an equally clear sense in which Petr's decision has arisen out of a mood that has fallen upon him. So far as we have information about the respective processes, we should think that Leyton's decision is autonomous and Petr's is not, all within a deterministic setting.

The brain

In thinking about such things as the general consistency of autonomy and determinism, or the more specific topic of the relation of particular thought processes to our brains, there is a common mistake which we should shine some light on and dispel. The mistake is to assume that, somehow, tying our thought processes to causal processes undermines the sense in which the thought processes are our own, performed by us. This is an assumption born of an outmoded dualism about psychological and physical processes. We know enough about the world to know that, however thought works, it is realized by the sort of information-sensitive processes that the brain performs. When you think about autonomy, something is going on in your brain that makes this happen. When you think about a unicorn, something else is happening in your brain. When you decide to make up and tell a bedtime story about a plucky unicorn to your child, something else again is happening in your brain. The thoughts, creativity, choice and love are all yours, but your brain is hard at work making them happen.

Although worries about determinism and control are about as old as philosophy, the lessons learnt here have application to more recent topics of conversation. The late twentieth century saw the birth of powerful methods to study our brains, and there can be no doubt that the twenty-first century will reveal much about the mechanisms of thought. Some important findings can seem to threaten the idea that we have control over ourselves. Because of this they seem to threaten the possibility of autonomy. Consider the famous studies of Benjamin Libet et al. (1983). These researchers used means of measuring 'readiness-potential' – roughly put, electrical activity in the brain, specifically in the motor cortex, associated with voluntary movements and measured non-invasively with sensors placed on the scalp – to compare brain activity with the agents' reports about when they experienced, consciously, a decision to move their hand. To do this, the subjects watched a circle of light moving and reported its position when they had the volitional experience. The findings were striking: brain activity correlated with this sort of decision and movement was consistently detectable several hundred milliseconds before the time at which the subjects reported having the conscious experience of wanting to move their hands. This bears repeating: neural activity is consistently detectable before the point at which subjects report deciding or wanting to move their hands.

It is tempting to think that this sort of finding rules out control over our actions, and with it autonomy, but this is a mistake. Part of the error, arguably, is what we have already discussed: the relation of thought to the brain. Of course there will be brain activity when we decide to do something; thought is realized by the brain, and to think otherwise is to make a mistake about how we work. But this is not the whole story. One can accept this and still be concerned about these findings not because of the role of neural activity but because of its timing: it precedes the reports of the conscious experience of wanting to move. The worry, then, would be that because subconscious neural processes are detectable *before* the conscious experience, control and autonomy are impossible.

This line of thought makes at least one of at least three possible mistakes. Seeing these mistakes requires that we recall some of the discussion from Chapters 2 and 3. Autonomy is, basically, self-rule, and the present chapter concerns challenges to the general idea that self-rule involves the capacity to exercise some degree of control over our actions and selves. The mistakes in question concern the respective parts of the previous sentence: autonomy, the self, and control. I shall start with the error most similar to the issue so far examined in this section: the relations between thought and neural processes. The new(ish) mistake concerns relations between subconscious processes and the self. For Libet's findings to threaten autonomy via the notion of the self, it would have to be the case that the thought processes that constitute the self do not include any subconscious processes (which may occur before, after, or at the same time as conscious ones). But this is deeply implausible, as we saw in the last chapter. Generally speaking, to think this way rules out the very realistic possibility that we can discover things about ourselves by learning about the subconscious aspects of our minds. Such a view excludes from the self everything that Meyers includes as components of the 'embodied' and 'divided' self. Maybe Meyers (and I) are incorrect to include the subconscious as part of the self, but this does not go without saying: without argument to the contrary, we should be willing to include subconscious processes as part of the self.

A second error concerns autonomy itself. In Chapter 2, I argued, as have many autonomy theorists in one way or another, that, for a choice (desire, action, *etc.*) to be autonomous, it must be, in some way, integrated into an agent's mind. Such integration can include both conscious and subconscious processes. Moreover, this general view of the psychology of autonomy makes no claims about which kind must precede the other. It is consistent with subconscious ones coming first. So, for Libet's findings to pose a problem directly to the idea of autonomy, it must be the case that subconscious processes either cannot be part of the integrated web of thoughts that delivers autonomy or cannot, at particular moments, be active before conscious ones with which they are nevertheless integrated. Both of these ideas are gratuitous. We should reject them unless they can be directly argued for, and Libet's findings themselves do not provide this extra support.

Finally, one might think that Libet's findings undermine the psychological possibility of control. The idea would be something like this: for someone to exercise control over their thoughts, and thereby over both their actions and their very selves, it must be the case that conscious thought processes exercise control over both other conscious processes and subconscious ones. Moreover, this cannot happen if subconscious processes precede conscious ones. This line of thought is dubious at a couple of points at least. Most importantly, we should question why control cannot involve, on the controlling side, subconscious processes. Thought and selfhood in general can involve the subconscious; hence to exclude the subconscious from the psychology of control requires direct argument. Perhaps the psychology of control requires conscious processes – I will not examine this idea one way or the other – but this does not imply that it requires *only* conscious processes. Libet's findings arguably reveal mere temporal sequencing; they do not provide extra support in favour of excluding the subconscious from the psychology of control.

The second problem is this: the fact that one thing comes before another does not imply that the first thing is altogether out of control of the second. This is clearer when we distinguish between something happening and the effects that that thing brings about. As I write this, the Conservative Party of Canada constitutes a majority government in the Canadian Parliament. Moreover, this party is widely believed to be quite firmly under the control of their leader and the country's Prime Minister, Stephen Harper. Suppose that a Conservative Party committee comes to a particular policy decision. Stephen Harper has not been part of the committee's deliberations, so we can say quite naturally that the decision occurs before he ever hears about it or thinks about it. The committee communicates their decision to Harper and he disagrees. He communicates a contrary view on the matter to his overall party, to Parliament, and to the Canadian people. It should be clear here that both the topic that the committee considered and the effects of their decision are under the control of Stephen Harper despite their deliberations and decision preceding his. The same can be true of the relations between subconscious and conscious thought processes. The mere finding that subconscious ones precede conscious ones does not imply that either the content of the subconscious processes or their effects are out of the control of the conscious processes. Extra evidence is needed in order to warrant this conclusion.

More recent research provides new empirical details, but the general lessons remain intact. Soon et al. (2008) note that the readiness potential stems from relatively late stages of motor processing. To gain access to earlier stages, these researchers used functional magnetic resonance imaging (fMRI). Subjects watched a stream of letters on a screen. When they felt like it, they were to press a button using either the left or right index finger – the subjects were free to choose which finger to use. They were also asked to recall which letter was present when they made the decision to move the finger. Soon et al. claim that predictive information about the choice of finger to move was detectable using fMRI a full seven to ten *seconds* – not *milli*seconds, which is the scale of measurement used by Libet et al. – before the subjects' reported time of awareness. This is dramatic evidence, in the realm of brain research, but it affects none of the points made so far. It shows nothing about autonomy or control or integration of the conscious with the subconscious. Hence no sceptical conclusions about autonomy can be drawn directly from this research.

The wider world

Apparent challenges to our control over our choices, our actions, and our selves arise not only from research into the brain, but also from studies of the sensitivity of our thought and behaviour to the situations in which we find ourselves. The extent and nature of the contextual sensitivity of human action is fairly well known, the contextual sensitivity of our thought less so. I will present some details – the research is striking and worth knowing about regardless of one's interest in autonomy – and then I will show why autonomy is still possible regardless of these findings.

Let's start with action. This is the subject of the so-called 'person-situation' debate. This debate was initiated by Walter Mischel's 1968 review of the literature on personality and action production.

After this, social psychologists, sometimes called 'situationists', and personality psychologists carried out a vigorous and very interesting discussion of the relative contributions of personality structures and the environment to the production of behaviour. Very roughly, personality psychologists argue that variation in behaviour between individuals is due to variation in certain sorts of psychological traits possessed by those individuals. Exactly what sorts of psychological traits is part of the debate. So, for example, if you are interested in explaining why Katelin does well at school but has few friends, and why Adam does relatively more poorly at school but has lots of successful personal relationships, the broad approach offered by personality psychology directs you to find out about certain character traits that produce this behaviour. As a specific example, the Five-Factor Model of personality associated with, among others, the work of Lewis Goldberg (1993), Robert McCrae and Paul Costa (1996), presents personality as composed of five traits, sometimes given these names:

1 Extraversion
2 Agreeableness
3 Conscientiousness
4 Emotional Stability
5 Openness to Experience

The general idea is that differences in these five factors account for differences in personality and hence for differences in behaviour. Five-Factor theorists would attempt to explain the differences between Katelin and Adam in terms of these traits. Correlatively, if you were interested in predicting how Frank and Kim would perform in a particular institutional setting, personality psychology would advise you to find out about their personality traits, either according to the Five-Factor model or some other model.

By contrast, and again very roughly, situationist social psychology argues that variation in behaviour is due much more to differences in situations than we are inclined to think. Importantly, there is considerable evidence that offers support for situationism. At the beginning of the twentieth century situationist tradition stands *Studies in Deceit* by Hugh Hartshorne and Mark May (1928). Hartshorne and May performed a long term study of deceit involving thousands of children in classroom settings. They used a variety of tests to assess their subjects for deception and honesty in various forms, such as cheating on tests or lying to teachers. What they found is that the correlation between different sorts of honest behaviour or deceptive behaviour was remarkably low, leading them to infer that the variation in behaviour was better explained by variation in properties of the immediate context than by some sort of personality trait.

Subsequent studies provided evidence in support of this idea. In Chapter 3, I mentioned Stanley Milgram's infamous studies on obedience (1963). To repeat: Milgram solicited participation in learning studies, but this was merely an experimental ruse. Subjects were given the role of 'teachers', while confederates of the experimenters played the roles of 'students' and 'study administrator'. The job of the teacher was to ask questions and administer electric shocks in response to incorrect answers. No shocks were actually administered, but the subjects were under the impression that they were delivering real punishment to the 'students'. The supposed shocks ascended in severity in 15 volt increments. Some were clearly labelled with very serious warnings. When 'teachers' hesitated in administering shocks, the administrator-confederate had a list of instructions about continuing, which they read to the subjects. Milgram found that seemingly non-coercive features of experimental situations led ordinary people to administer what they thought were lethal levels of electrical shocks to other ordinary people. More precisely, about two thirds of subjects administered shocks all the way to the final level, and many of the other subjects administered shocks up to very high levels.

Other studies assessed helping behaviours rather than harming ones. For instance, Alice Isen and Paula Levin (1972) found a very high correlation between the performance of helping behaviour and seemingly insignificant good fortune, such as finding a dime in the change slot of a pay phone. In their experiments, subjects (unsuspecting ones, not solicited ones) were people who went into a payphone. Some found a coin in the change slot, others did not. When they left the phone booth, an experimental confederate posing as a passer-by dropped a pile of papers, apparently accidentally, outside the phone booth. Of the 16 people who found coins in the phone, 14 helped and 2 did not. Of the 25 people who did not find coins, only one person helped with the dropped papers. John Doris (who makes much of the dime study) reports that overall, more than 1,000 studies have produced results like these about helping behaviour alone (2002, p. 34).

Overall, the situationist suggestion is that the variation in behaviour exhibited by an individual should be accounted for in a way that gives a substantial role to variation in context. Just what sort of role, and just what sort of contribution is made by individual psychology, is again part of the debate. To explain the differences between Katelin and Adam, situationist social psychology would look at least in part to the contexts in which they perform. For the purposes of predicting how Frank and Kim will behave within a given institutional setting, situationist social psychology *might* direct us to find out about the details of this context, but it would more likely advise us to find out about how people generally behave in this sort of setting.

In presenting these findings in the context of the person-situation 'debate', I mean to convey the sense that there is still work to be done here to explain what is going on in these findings. The apparent challenge to autonomy arises to the extent that the situationist case is vindicated. So, for the purposes of argument, let's assume that the situationists are correct. Does the significant sensitivity of human behaviour to our contexts undermine the possibility of autonomy by undermining our control over our actions and ourselves? Here are four reasons to think that it does not.

First, the situationist case is not that context accounts 100 per cent for our behaviour. My students often make this point when we discuss this literature in class. There is clearly a role for a significant individual contribution to the production and control of behaviour even if situationism is true. It is worth noting that most personality theorists also think that agents' contexts make a considerable contribution to behaviour, despite these theorists' emphasis on the personality traits being putatively responsible for action. The real issue is not whether the roots of action are rooted within agents or outside of them, but how to understand the person-context dynamics that give rise to behaviour. This way of framing the issue has plenty of room for familiar senses of control.

The second and third points stem from the fact, implied by what has just been discussed and, really, contested by no one, that the situational effects of situations vary. Some situations, or features of situations, seem particularly potent, whereas others are not. The Milgram studies, for instance, have been rerun in many variations.

When features of the experimental context are changed, the degree of obedience elicited from subjects also changes. This opens up two lines of thought about how we can exercise control in the fact of situational contributions to behaviour. One way is by doing exactly what we are doing now: learning about the results that situationist experimenters have achieved and the phenomena that they have observed. It is one thing to find oneself in Milgram's setting completely unaware of the power of this sort of situation. It is quite another to be in there and to be somewhat aware of how seemingly insignificant features of situations can play a role in our conduct. Knowledge is power, as the old saying goes.

However, it might be unwise to rely on our knowledge to arm us against the situations in which we find ourselves. It is arguably better to use our knowledge less directly. Instead of trying to stand up against the pressures to, for example, shock an innocent neighbour to death – which have, let's recall, been demonstrated to be surprisingly powerful – we should be wary of such situations and avoid getting into them in the first place. Forewarned is forearmed, in more ways than one.

So far, the responses to situationism have been in the spirit of defending autonomy in spite of these putative facts about how our minds work. The fourth point to be made against the thought that situationist psychology undermines the possibility of autonomy takes a more conciliatory tone. It is a mistake to think that self-rule must be independent of significant contributions from the environment. The reason is the very idea at the core of the present account of autonomy and the one we have seen already in this chapter: psychological integration. For action to be autonomous, it must be produced by oneself, and I have argued that this requires that it be produced by processes that are sufficiently integrated as to constitute a self. These processes need not be located solely within our skin; 'self' rule is not necessarily the same as 'internal' rule. To the extent that there are psychological processes responsible for action which are environmentally dependent yet integrated into our overall minds, they are conducive to autonomy. To the extent that such processes are not integrated, they are autonomy-undermining. These are the same possibilities that exist for psychological processes that are isolated from such notable environmental dependence.

For some decades there has been a debate about this general issue within philosophical psychology. The topic has come to be known as the Extended Mind Hypothesis. Defenders of this hypothesis are typically known as 'externalists'; those who deny it are 'individualists'. In very general terms, the debate between individualists and externalists is about how to understand the role of an agent's context in the agent's psychological functioning. Externalists argue that context plays important roles of various kinds, whereas individualists restrict context to the psychological background, capable only of providing input to an agent's psychology and of receiving output from it. At the risk of oversimplifying, let me suggest that situationism and externalism fit together nicely. To the extent that our psychological processes involve the wider world beyond our brains and bodies, environmental dependence *per se* poses no threat to autonomy.

The details of debate over externalism would take us too far afield, so I will not review them here. However, here is an imagination exercise to suggest why we should take externalism seriously. First, the primary topic in the situationist literature is action, so imagine a part of your brain particularly important to the production of behaviour: the motor cortex. Suppose that the neurons that constitute your motor cortex are degrading. You face the prospect of losing the ability to act voluntarily. However, Susan, a neuroscientist, tells you that she can build an artificial replacement for your motor cortex. It will be made out of silicon chips rather than carbon-based neurons, but it will do the same job. Instead of losing your ability to act voluntarily, Susan will remove your meat-motor cortex and instal a silicon-motor-cortex in its place, thereby saving you from your biological predicament. The day of your operation comes, Susan does her job, and you leave the hospital with a hybrid silicon-carbon brain.

However, imagine that you start to have problems with your new part. Susan runs some tests and discovers that she needs to add more chips to your silicon-motor-cortex. This in itself is a not a big problem, but doing so will make the new part too big to fit into the space where your meat-motor-cortex once was. You and Susan talk things over and decide that you really have no choice but to go ahead with the change. Where will your silicon-motor-cortex be located? You have a variety of choices: it can sit on top of your head, as near as possible to its old location without actually being within your skull. Or, Susan can use longer connections and you can carry it in your breast pocket. Longer wires still will allow it to be kept in a bag that you hang from your shoulder.

Suppose that the enlarged silicon-motor-cortex is constructed. You experiment with location, and you don't like any of the options. It looks too odd on top of your head. You don't always have a breast pocket, and you don't want to carry a bag around everywhere. Susan thinks for a little while and comes up with a solution: instead of hard-wired connections between you and your silicon-motor-cortex, she can devise a wireless set-up. This will allow you to leave the silicon part at home. A transmitter, located in the neural cavity where your meat-motor-cortex once was, will communicate with your silicon part, thereby allowing you to perform voluntary actions in relative comfort.

The point of this series of imaginary developments is to convey the sense that the location of the components that give rise to thought, either within our physical bounds or outside of them, does not really matter. In this made-up tale, you perform voluntary actions from beginning to end. At the beginning the physical basis of your capacity is located entirely within the physical confines of your body. At the end it is not: a crucial part is physically outside of you, but psychologically part of you. What matters is what these components do, and if there are ways for psychological processes to happen between agents and their environments rather than within agents, so be it. Brains are wonderful, but they are not magic, and in principle the things that they do can be performed by other sorts of things, either by themselves or in combination with brains, as in this imaginary case. Since we do not have magical antennae that connect us to the environment, these processes will happen via our familiar senses. If the situationists are correct, then these senses open us up to surprisingly powerful psychological forces.

So far I have been addressing contextual sensitivity of the psychology of action, and the apparent challenge this poses to autonomy. Action is the primary topic of the person-situation debate, and particularly important to considerations of autonomy. However, it should be clear that the externalist/individualist debate is about all aspects of our thought. My imaginative exercise can be modified to apply to the neural basis of any kind of thought whatsoever. As it happens, psychologists have revealed considerable environmental sensitivity for lots of kinds of thought. This is often spoken of in terms of 'situated' cognition. The general idea is that we should think of these psychological processes as happening between agents and features of their physical, social and cultural contexts. Although the details are interesting, I will not rehearse them here, as they involve no new lessons about autonomy. Mere external influence does not necessarily undermine self-rule. For one thing, the extent of external psychological forces can be mitigated through reflection and preparation. For another, such psychological resources can be integrated into our minds and hence they can be part of the psychology of autonomy rather than threats to it.

Conclusion

It is easy to assume that we are identical with the small window of conscious awareness via which we experience the world. If we do this, then the myriad happenings both within our own bodies and in the wider world that we do not experience seem to take place outside of our selves. This would mean that they can pose threats to our capacities to control our choices, actions, and identities. From this perspective, it seems that self-rule requires that determinism and situationism be false, and that thought occur in substantial independence from the causal workings of our brains. But such a bifurcation between ourselves and the wider world is too harsh. Once we reflect on the details of our involvement with our pasts, our brains, and the situations in which we find ourselves, we discover that both our own natures and our opportunities for control are more complex and nuanced than we might have thought. What seems like a threat need not be one; the details matter. Although much depends on argumentative and empirical details that are still to be worked out, I trust that this chapter suffices to set aside some challenges to the psychological possibility of autonomy.

Reading guide

Determinism is a venerable topic. It is often addressed in connection with free will, naturally enough, about which there are many books and articles both introductory and advanced. For an introduction to determinism itself, see the entry in the online *Stanford Encyclopedia of Philosophy*: http://plato.stanford.edu/entries/determinism-causal/.

Harry Frankfurt's famous contribution to thought about freedom, responsibility and the relevance of our ability to do otherwise than we actually do is found in his 'Alternate possibilities and moral responsibility', *Journal of Philosophy* (1969), 829–39, reprinted in his *The Importance of What We Care About* (Cambridge University Press, 1988). An important response comes from Peter van Inwagen: 'Ability and responsibility', *The Philosophical Review*, Vol. 87, No. 2 (April 1978), 201–24.

Libet's most famous work, written with colleagues Curtis A. Gleason, Elwood W. Wright, and Dennis K. Pearl, is 'Time of conscious intention to act in relation to onset of cerebral activity (readiness-potential)', *Brain*, Vol. 106 (1983), 623–42. There have been lots of responses to this work, from both psychologists and philosophers. Notable philosophical treatments come from 1] Daniel Dennett: (a) *Consciousness Explained* (Penguin Books, 1992), and (b) *Freedom Evolves* (Penguin Books, 2003), and 2] Alfred Mele: (a) *Free Will and Luck* (Oxford University Press, 2006) and (b) *Effective Intentions: The Power of Conscious Will* (Oxford University Press, 2009). For a provocative review of the territory written by a psychologist, see Daniel Wegner's *The Illusion of Conscious Will* (MIT Press, 2002). The collection of empirical details continues just as much as the overall discussion. As an example, see Chun Siong Soon, Marcel Brass, Hans-Jochen Heinze, and John-Dylan Haynes, 'Unconscious determinants of free decisions in the human brain', *Nature Neuroscience*, Vol. 11, No. 5 (May 2008), 543–5. For a relatively recent and influential discussion of possible implications of brain science for thought about legal responsibility for action, see Joshua Greene and Jonathan Cohen, 'For the law, neuroscience changes nothing and everything', *Phil. Trans. R. Soc. Lond.* B, Vol. 359 (2004), 1775–85.

For partisan accounts of the person-situation debate, see: 1] John Doris, *Lack of Character* (Cambridge University Press, 2002). 2] D. C. Funder, *Personality Judgment* (Academic Press, 1999). 3] L. Ross and R. E. Nisbett, *The Person and the Situation: Perspectives of Social Psychology* (Temple University Press, 1991). The roots of this debate can be found in H. Hartshorne and M. A. May, *Studies in the Nature of Character I: Studies in Deceit* (MacMillan, 1928). The 'debate', although not the empirical work itself, was sparked by Walter Mischel, *Personality and Assessment* (John Wiley and Sons, 1968). Stanley Milgram's landmark study was reported in

'Behavioral study of obedience', *Journal of Abnormal and Social Psychology*, Vol. 67 (1963), 371–8. The curious dime studies are reported in A. M. Isen and P. F. Levin, 'Effect of feeling good on helping: cookies and kindness', *Journal of Personality and Social Psychology*, Vol. 21 (1972), 384–8. Here are two important papers in defence of 'personological' approaches: 1] L. R. Goldberg, 'The structure of phenotypic personality traits', *American Psychologist*, Vol. 48 (1993), 26–34, and 2] R. R. McCrae and P. T Costa, Jr., 'Toward a new generation of personality theories: theoretical contexts for the five-factor model', in *The Five-Factor Model of Personality: Theoretical Perspectives*, edited by J. S. Wiggins (Guilford, 1996).

Book length treatments of cases for and against externalism can be found in 1] Andy Clark, *Supersizing the Mind: Embodiment, Action, and Cognitive Extension* (Oxford University Press, 2008) and 2] Frederick Adams and Kenneth Aizaw, *The Bounds of Cognition* (Blackwell Publishing, 2008). I defend both externalism and situationism, especially with regard to the production of action, in *Like-Minded: Externalism and Moral Psychology* (MIT Press, 2011). For an influential and short introduction to the territory, and one which uses both imaginary and real scenarios with which to supplement the silicon-motor-cortex example, see Andy Clark and David Chalmers, 'The extended mind', *Analysis*, Vol. 58 (1998), 10–23 (reprinted in Clark's *Supersizing the Mind*).

Situated cognition is a label for a pretty vast territory. Perhaps the best starting place is a similarly big book: *The Cambridge Handbook of Situated Cognition*, edited by Philip Robbins and Murat Aydede (Cambridge University Press, 2008). For a review of some findings particularly relevant to autonomy, see Susan Hurley, 'The public ecology of responsibility', in *Responsibility and Distributive Justice*, edited by Carl Knight and Zofia Stemplowska (Oxford University Press, 2011).

The debate over the extended mind hypothesis has occurred in parallel with a debate over social relations and autonomy. Feminists in particular have pursued these issues, in much the same spirit as the present chapter: some see social influence as raising problems for autonomy, others have instead sought to develop accounts of relational autonomy. I am inclined to think that the psychological issues raised when we attend to social (and other) relations are better treated by the extended mind literature, but the relational autonomy literature is nevertheless worth a look. Here are a couple of good places to start: 1] C. MacKenzie and N. Stoljar (eds) (2000), *Relational Autonomy: Feminist Perspectives on Autonomy, Agency and the Social Self* (Oxford University Press), and 2] Chapters 4 (especially) and 5 of Marilyn Friedman's *Autonomy, Gender, Politics* (Oxford University Press, 2003).

CHAPTER FIVE

The significance of autonomy

The last three chapters offer an account of the nature and possibility of self-rule. 'So what?' one might ask. Fair enough. This chapter marks a change in the topic of this book. Instead of the nature of autonomy, the remainder of the book will address the significance of personal self-rule. In this chapter, I address the following questions: Does autonomy matter? If so, why? How? Subsequent chapters will address evaluative questions about autonomy in more particular contexts.

Philosophers have addressed these questions quite generally, as will I in this chapter, but it is worth noting one methodological point at the outset. Practical and evaluative issues about self-rule have been particularly important in medical ethics over the last half century. It is not an undue simplification to claim that medical ethics after World War II has been marked by an increased focus on patient autonomy, such that it is now as central a value in this field as patient well-being. Upon reflection, this is no surprise: when ordinary people (i.e., people who are not medical experts) go to the doctor, they enter a complex joint decision-making situation. The patient has the medical issue and stands to gain or, more likely, lose due to it, but doctors and other medical experts have all of the knowledge and access to medical resources with which to address the issue. One way of safeguarding the patient in such a complex situation is to emphasize, both formally and informally, his or her capacity and right to control what happens, at least to his or her body. That is, an emphasis on autonomy is a natural part of reflection on the complexities of modern medicine. A consequence is that medical ethicists have been particularly attentive to the evaluative and practical significance of self-rule. This means that, for this chapter, much (but not all) of what I discuss will be drawn from medical ethics. Readers who are interested in other domains are urged to be patient and to wait for the next couple of chapters. The lessons sketched here will turn out to apply, one way or another, to non-medical contexts.

Implicit in these remarks is something that might seem curious: the particular account of autonomy that has been developed in Chapters 2 and 3 has not so far been mentioned. Indeed, it should be clear that we can have ideas about the value of autonomy independently of having a theory of autonomy. Not just any old ideas either: medical ethicists have well-developed ideas about the value of autonomy without, in many cases, having anything like an explicit theory of self-rule. The possession of such ideas (whether preliminary or well worked out) might be just what leads someone to read a book such as this one. So far, so good: we can value autonomy without thinking much about its nature, and our ideas about its value need not be deficient as a consequence. At the same time, it is also reasonable to think that a theory of autonomy should contribute substantially to our understanding of the value of personal self-rule. A good theory can be expected to sharpen and even to modify our initial sense of the value of autonomy. Both of these points have implications for this chapter (and for subsequent ones). Some of the ideas marshalled about the significance of autonomy will be theory-neutral. These should be worth scrutiny even if the present theory of autonomy is incorrect. However, other ideas will depend on the theory presented in Chapters 2 and 3. I shall start with theory-neutral considerations.

Does autonomy matter?

Does autonomy matter? When the question is put so coarsely, I can offer only a suggestive answer to it. The conceptual refinements to come should sharpen our sense of the nature and extent of the significance of personal self-rule. Here is the suggestive general answer: yes, autonomy matters, in more ways than one.

Marilyn Friedman offers a very direct argument in favour of the value of autonomy: self-rule is valuable because the alternatives are so much worse (2003, p. 57). The alternatives are heteronomy and lack of control altogether, as Friedman sees them. Here are two reasons why autonomy might seem better than the alternatives. The first, which Friedman does not really consider, is taste. But as soon as we get this potential reason out in the open, we can see how weak it is as a foundation for the value of autonomy. Certainly, it will be distasteful to many to relinquish a significant degree of control over their lives. However, to an important number of people this will not be counter to their desires. These people will be content with turning control over to others, for instance, and maybe even quite happy with it. So, it does not seem that our tastes can be relied upon to deliver the strong conclusion that Friedman envisions.

Instead of taste, Friedman appeals to having a sense of self. Friedman thinks that heteronomy and oudenonomy come at the price of the loss of our sense of ourselves (2003, p. 57). The reason is that having a sense of self will involve having a sense of how one wants to live or ought to live. The worry is that giving up control, either altogether or to others, undermines our living in the ways in which we think we want to or ought to. But this is too quick. The reason is that some people will value precisely being controlled by others, or being subject to no personal control whatsoever. These people will lose nothing about themselves if they are not autonomous. Consequently, I think that Friedman overstates her case.

At the same time, I think that Friedman is looking in the right place for the roots of the value of autonomy. Here is a tentative argument in favour of the idea that we value autonomy more than we might actually think. This line of thought draws from part of the same territory as Friedman – relations between autonomy and heteronomy – but in a more defensible fashion. Consider Jenny, a competent adult who thinks that she does not have the moral right to control her own life. She has the capacity for personal self-rule, with regard to both herself and her choices, but she does not think that she is entitled to exercise such rule. She thinks that other people should run her life for her. On the face of it she values heteronomy but not autonomy. She does so not out of any concern for other values but just because of self-rule and other-rule themselves. Her attitudes are about the value of both autonomy and heteronomy and of nothing else. Given that the present topic is the value of personal self-rule, it is tempting to ask whether Jenny is making an error by not valuing autonomy. However, I think a more fundamental question must be addressed: is the case of Jenny described in a coherent way? Is it actually possible for someone to value heteronomy but not autonomy? Only if this is possible can we meaningfully ask whether Jenny is making a mistake in thinking this way. If it is not possible, then the case must have been 'misdescribed', and we must describe it accurately before assessing whether mistakes are made.

So, can we, as Jenny seems to, value heteronomy without valuing autonomy? Answering this definitively would take us too far afield, but here is a reason to think that we cannot. To value heteronomy as Jenny does is to think that it is appropriate for one person to determine the course of the life of another competent person. Why might this be appropriate? We can put aside all arguments that rely on religion, culture or law as either mistaken or, more importantly, as addressing the wrong kind of value. The question is about the moral value of autonomy and heteronomy, and hence the moral appropriateness of one person exercising control over another. All laws, religious codes and cultural practices can legitimately be assessed in terms of whether they meet the demands of morality or not. So we can just put these concerns aside and focus directly on morality. Under what conditions would it be morally appropriate for one person to dictate the course of another person's life, to the extent of shaping the kind of person the controlled person is and of making the controlled person's decisions for her? A full answer to this question will be very complicated, I suspect, but we need not get into all of the details, for the very first step of the case will be a requirement that the controlling person be capable of controlling a life. Without such a capacity, it will be morally inappropriate for this person to attempt to control the life of another. To have the capacity to determine the character and choices of another person is to have the capacity to do so for oneself, barring special psychological deficits that prevent one from having at least the sort of access to one's own thoughts that one has with regard to other people. So, to be capable of heteronomy is to be capable of autonomy. Correlatively, to value the capacities that make heteronomy possible is, at the same time, to value the capacities that make autonomy possible. One cannot value heteronomy without valuing another's autonomy in virtue of the psychology that makes both possible. But this, on the face of it, is just to value autonomy, albeit for another person and by another name. Jenny is making a mistake, but it's not the mistake of undervaluing autonomy. It's the mistake of thinking that she can value the control of one person's life by another person without thereby also valuing autonomy. She is also being inconsistent in her thought: she is psychologically competent and, let's say, so is the person she thinks is authorized to control her life. She values the other's control in virtue of that person's psychological capacities, but she fails to see that she has the same capacities and hence should be due to the same value regarding her right to control lives.

Note: the force of the present argument is that insofar as we value personal control, we cannot help but value autonomy. The argument does not apply to people who value non-personal control or lack of control, but who do not value personal control. Cosmonomy and oudenonomy can be valued without thereby committing oneself to the value of autonomy. So be it: it is conceptually possible not to value autonomy, because it is conceptually possible not to value personal control. For practical purposes, however, this will not apply to many cases. So far as I can tell, people tend to value personal control in one form or another. That is, they explicitly value heteronomy or autonomy, or both. Very few real people value only non-personal forms of control or lack of control altogether. The upshot is that, for practical purposes, we can assume that people value autonomy explicitly or are committed to its value by their valuing of heteronomy.

Let's get more specific by attending to some conceptual distinctions. Here is a case to introduce the first distinction. Novak has a respiratory problem. It comes and goes in severity. Sometimes it is so bad that it ruins his day, making it difficult to do such normal things as sleep. On other days it is much better, but Novak has serious athletic interests and even on good days his breathing problems interfere with these. Novak does not know what the cause is. He goes to the doctor in the hopes of having his problem solved. However, Novak is shy, so all that he tells his physician is that he is having a breathing problem. He does not tell her about other aspects of his life, such as his sporting activities. His doctor is content to try out conventional treatment options on Novak. These have two consequences. One is that, although they alleviate his breathing issues to some extent, they do not do so enough for his particular interests. He can now sleep much better, but his athletic pursuits are still hindered by his respiratory problem. The second is that the conventional treatments introduce new problems. The medication that his doctor has prescribed interferes with Novak's ability to concentrate, which makes his athletic activities difficult in a new way. After trying his physician's recommendations and reflecting both on the outcomes and on what he wants, Novak decides to exercise more control over his medical treatment. On his next visit to the doctor, Novak initiates a more active but still joint approach to his problem. He explains to his doctor the important details about his life and about the outcomes he desires with regard to his breathing. His doctor takes in this information and changes her recommendations for Novak in multiple ways. Over time they tinker with Novak's treatment and eventually find a satisfactory combination of chemical, dietary and behavioural measures that get him the desired results.

The case of Novak is designed to show the 'instrumental' value of self-rule. Things (actions, persons, whatever) have instrumental value when they are valuable as tools. Tools are valuable not (primarily) in and of themselves, but as ways of getting what we really want or value. So, to have instrumental value is be valuable because of a relation to something else that is valuable or valued. In Novak's case, self-rule is instrumentally valuable in several ways. It serves as a way of accomplishing his goals. It turns out to be valuable because of its relation to his health as well. This is one of the main reasons that patient autonomy is emphasized in medical ethics: recognizing and giving patients an active role in their own health care is a useful way of solving their medical problems. The more that medical problems are problematic because of their relations to particular details about patient's lives – such as Novak's breathing is related to his athletic pursuits – then the more that medical expertise itself is ill-suited to revealing these problems. Information about patient's lives is needed to uncover the details of the problem, and the most direct way of getting at this information is to make medical decision-making properly joint, between medical expert and patient. That is, giving patients an active role in their medical care is a valuable means of serving their well-being.

Instrumental value is not the only sort of value there is. It had better not be: if it were, then nothing would be valuable at all. Things (acts, persons, whatever) that have merely instrumental value derive all of their value from other things (acts, persons, *etc.*). If those other things have merely instrumental value, then their value also stems from other things. If *these* other things have merely instrumental value, then the chain continues, and it will continue forever if everything has merely instrumental value. If this is the case, then instrumental value amounts to no value at all: the evaluative buck is always passed, never made good on. It seems that something must have value in and of itself, not just in relation to other things, for anything to have value of any kind. This kind of value is typically called 'intrinsic' or 'inherent' value. I will call it 'intrinsic'. To be instrumentally valuable is to be valuable because of relations to other things. To be intrinsically valuable is to have value in and of oneself, regardless of relations to other things. Some things are instrumentally valuable, some things are intrinsically valuable, and some are both: there is no reason to think that one kind of value rules out the other.

Is autonomy intrinsically valuable as well as instrumentally valuable? It is difficult to establish that something is intrinsically valuable. In support of this idea I shall offer a range of cases in which autonomy is valued apparently for itself and not because of its relations to other things which we value. Such a case must be incomplete. The reason is that we can, by normal standards, mistakenly value things that are not really valuable. More specifically, we can value things intrinsically when they are not really intrinsically valuable. For instance, many people seem to make this mistake with regard to money. Money is valuable only because of what we can do with it. That is, it is valuable only in relation to things other than money: it is merely instrumentally valuable. However, many people seem to treat it as worth pursuing in and of itself. This is a mistake: just ask a financial planner, and you are likely to receive an explanation of why this attitude towards money is mistaken. All of this granted, when we try to determine whether something has intrinsic value, our judgements and actions involving that thing, whether considered or not, are the best evidence that we have. My argument for the intrinsic value of personal self-rule will consist in the enumeration of some of these judgements and actions. At the same time, I acknowledge the incompleteness of this argument.

Ok: on to cases that provide some support for thinking that autonomy is intrinsically valuable. First, consider little children. As I noted in the first two chapters, normal human development consists in part in changing from being non-autonomous to being capable of various sorts of self-rule. My impression of little children is that two things are worth noting of them, for present purposes, as they develop. First, they increasingly want to do things. Crudely put, normal human development is marked by movement from relative inactivity to relative activity and by increased desires to be active. Second, and relatedly, they increasingly want to accomplish things by themselves. From a sufficiently rough vantage point, human development seems to be characterized by a growth of natural interest in greater personal self-rule in itself.

Before moving on to other cases, let's reflect on the epistemic status of both the present point and similar sorts of activity. Chapters 2 and 3 provided an account of autonomy in terms of, primarily, psychological states, but this observation of young children emphasizes their behaviour and only secondarily the psychological roots of such behaviour. This should prompt questions about just what inferences we can draw about our minds from observations of behaviour. Here are two possibilities. First, behaviour can be evidence of certain sorts of thought. This makes the behavioural observations epistemically defeasible: while they provide *prima facie* support for claims about the mind, they are not definitive and hence the psychological inferences that we draw can turn out to be incorrect, on the basis of other evidence and, perhaps, other sorts of considerations. Second, behaviour can be criterial of certain sorts of thought. This relation makes the behavioural observations epistemically definitive, other things being equal: the accurate observation of certain sorts of behaviour requires (perhaps conceptually) that certain sorts of thought have happened. If behaviour were criterial of thought, then we could draw very firm inferences about minds from such observations as the one I have just made about little children. But I am suspicious of such a stance, and hence I am inclined to treat our behaviour as merely defeasible evidence of certain sorts of thought. This weakens the strength of the inferences that we are entitled to draw from behavioural observations, but I regard this as a strength rather than a weakness. It guards us against hasty inferences by encouraging us to seek multiple sources of support – of evidence – for conclusions about psychological processes. It is in this spirit that I offer the present array of cases for the intrinsic value of autonomy. Here is how this works in the present case: the publicly observable interest of children in both activity and accomplishment of things by themselves is taken as defeasible evidence of both their burgeoning capacities for autonomy of choice and autonomy of personhood and their embrace of these capacities. Development, on the face of it, is marked by an increase in our valuing our control over our own activity for its own sake.

Mature adults offer an array of phenomena with which to supplement this general developmental point. Some of these are dramatic, world-changing series of events. Consider the centuries-long and occasionally fitful move humans have gone through from general acceptance of human slavery to its widespread rejection. Without doubt there are multiple values at work here. In many of its forms slavery is brutal and a clear threat to the well-being of the enslaved, for instance. But arguably the defining feature of slavery, if there is one, is the denial to slaves of control over their lives. The extent to which such control is curtailed varies among the culturally and historically specific forms that the institution of slavery takes, and doubtless there are also differences in the degree to which individual slave-owners interfere with the lives of their slaves. Still, to be a slave is to lack, because of others, a significant degree of power to exercise self-rule. Correlatively, much of what seems wrong with slavery is this interference with autonomy. This can be turned into a thought experiment, or even a psychological tool for assessing attitudes: ask yourself and others to see if people would consent to become slaves if they would be benevolently treated. My guess is that many would say 'no', and that the degree of well-being required to turn these answers into 'yes' would often be very high. Such attitudes about slavery, both actual and hypothetical, point to our intrinsic valuing of personal self-rule.

Another world-shaping manifestation of our esteem for autonomy is found in the spread of democracy throughout the world. As with slavery there are, of course, multiple values at work in such grand social developments. Sometimes people revolt and seek democracy because their prior mode of government had turned out to be such a threat to well-being that it is no longer acceptable, nor even worth suffering anymore. But also, as with slavery, in such changes a central value is the importance of individual self-rule in and of itself. Put aside instrumental reasons for which citizens value participating in the means of governing their countries. Arguably citizens deserve an active role in civic government precisely because they are capable of, and hence deserving of, controlling their own lives. After all, civic governance is governance of citizens, and hence can be thought to fall into the class of things to which personal-self rule applies. As we shall see in the Chapter 7, there is another sort of reason to link democracy with individual autonomy. A theoretical underpinning of liberal democracies concerns the legitimacy of the coercive powers of the state. Government authority is not legitimate under just any conditions – we can all think of cases in which it clearly is not. With regard to creatures capable of ruling their lives, governmental power is legitimate only when it is suitably related to the autonomy of citizens. The legitimacy of state power has its roots in the value of personal self-rule. Democracy is the form of government best suited to respecting this constraint on state power. The spread of democracy can legitimately be seen, if only in part, as evidence of increased recognition of and insistence on the intrinsic value of personal autonomy.

As with slavery, we can deploy ideas about democracy in thought experiments and interpersonal surveys to assess the ways in which we value personal self-rule. Ask yourself or others about which is preferable, in the sense of which you would vote for: a social arrangement in which your well-being is assured but in which your right to run your life will be strictly curtailed, or a social arrangement in which your well-being is just as assured as in the first case but in which you will be treated as autonomous, having wide freedom to determine the course of your life. If autonomy is of value only as a tool for securing our well-being, then there should be no difference in our voting preferences. The cases are equal with regard to well-being, so the second case should seem just as good as the first. To the extent that second case is the one we would vote for, autonomy has value independent of well-being. If there is no other value from which personal-self rule derives value, then it must be its intrinsic value that makes the difference.

There are famous thought experiments, designed by Robert Nozick, which can arguably be used as evidence for the intrinsic value of autonomy. Nozick was arguing against the idea, at the core of the moral theory called 'utilitarianism', that the only things that have intrinsic value are experiences of pleasure and pain. Nozick asks us to imagine a machine which will give us any experiences we desire. For instance, suppose you want to do a space-walk around the international space station. You could plug into this machine and get exactly this experience. You would not actually go on a space-walk, but, from the inside, the machine-generated experience would be indistinguishable from the real thing. Nozick argues that most people would not choose the machine experiences over real life. With regard to the suggestions that we want to be certain sorts of people and that we want to bring about effects in the world, Nozick asks us to imagine other machines that would do these things for us. For instance, suppose I want to be a brave and honest person and that I currently am not: I could plug myself into the character-machine and make myself brave and honest. Suppose that I wanted to write a book: I could plug myself into the result-machine and it would produce a book, brand new in content, with my name on it. Nozick argues that many people would still not use these machines, even though they may have more concern for things other than experiences. He suggests that the reason is that we value being really connected to the world and that these machines sever this connection. More to the present point, he claims that these thought experiments illuminate the fact that we value actively living our lives, not having the significant parts of our lives brought about without much in the way of active contributions from ourselves (other than programming the machines in the right way). In the terms of the present book, the machine thought experiments can arguably be seen as pointing to the intrinsic value of personal self-rule. When we live our lives via these machines, we abdicate control over our experiences, character and worldly contributions to them. The character-machine, for instance, clearly takes self-shaping out of our hands, and hence at least compromises our autonomy of personhood. To the extent that we value autonomy intrinsically we will be hesitant about these machines, and to the extent that autonomy really is intrinsically valuable our reticence will be justified.

Let's return to the real world. Along much the same lines as our ruminations about slavery and democracy, consider the equality movements that have marked the last couple of centuries of western civilization. Many values have been at the root of attempts to bring about formal and informal gender and racial equality, but there can be no doubt that respect for the capacity and exercise of personal self-rule is a central one. These movements stand with anti-slavery and pro-democracy developments as evidence of the valuing of individual autonomy partly for its own sake.

Even more specifically, there is the ascendance of patient autonomy as a central value in both medicine and medical ethics. Greatly simplifying, decision-making in medicine, both in practice and in reflective theoretical assessments, used to be assigned only to physicians. Patients were understood to have the role of following doctor's orders. The guiding value of this arrangement was patient welfare. The assumption was that medical expertise was required to secure this goal, and that patients who lacked such expertise could appropriately be relegated to the sidelines of medical decision-making. Social and intellectual changes have led to widespread rejection, both in practice and in thought about medical ethics, of this doctor-orders model of patient-physician interaction. Instead, patients are now recognized to have a legitimate place in medical decision-making. I have already discussed the instrumental reason for doing this. But this is not all there is to this issue. Besides health outcomes, it is respectful of patients to give them this role. The reason is the capacity and hence, arguably, the right that patients have to run their lives. This is a way of saying that patient autonomy matters in and of itself, not just because of the ways in which it serves patients' health.

I shall finish by presenting without endorsing a version of an argument from Marina Oshana (2006, pp. 131–3). I say 'a version' because I am rephrasing it in terms of intrinsic value; if this distorts the original argument, the responsibility is mine. The present version of this argument locates, at least in part, the intrinsic value of autonomy in its relation to choice. It should be clear that choices are significant due to their content – that is, to what is chosen. The person who chooses to pursue the pleasure of others rather than their pain makes, on the face of it, a good choice because of the nature of pleasure and pain. Oshana points out, however, that there is another way in which choices can have significance. It seems to matter to us that at least some of our choices are *really* ours, in contrast to other choices which we merely make and to still other choices which we technically make but disavow, for example because they were made under duress. The thing that makes the difference is autonomy: autonomous choices are ours in the significant sense whereas non-autonomous ones are not. So, as Oshana puts it, autonomy lends significance to choice.

So far, so good; I see the appeal of this classification of choices and their relation to autonomy. However, I am not sure that it stands up to scrutiny. Compare two people who pursue the pleasure of others rather than their suffering. Steffi chooses to do so autonomously: she thinks about her options and desires, and eventually chooses, in a way which she endorses, to give a large amount of money to a charity. The charity goes on to use that money to benefit one hundred suffering people far away. Pete gives the same amount of money to the same charity and brings about the same results, but he does so non-autonomously. The feeling just comes upon him, as if out of nowhere, and he acts on it without giving it a second thought, completely out of character. Is Steffi's choice really better because it is autonomous? I am not convinced that it is. Perhaps we should prefer people like Steffi because they are more likely than people such as Pete to benefit us and others, but this is a separate issue. The present point is the significance of the choice, and I cannot see that being autonomous or non-autonomous makes a difference. The same goes, I think, if we imagine people who choose others' pain instead of pleasure. Such a choice is neither better nor worse for being produced autonomously, and indeed we might prefer to be around non-autonomous pain producers rather than autonomous ones: they arguably pose less of a risk to us.

I have already noted that I have modified this argument to put it in terms of intrinsic value. Oshana claims instead that the present point shows the 'symbolic' or 'demonstrative' (2006, pp. 132–3) value of autonomy. Maybe this is different from intrinsic value, but Oshana makes clear that it is also meant to be different from instrumental value (p. 132). Autonomous choice symbolizes or demonstrates that a person is in control of herself and her actions, and perhaps that the person is a unique self, whereas non-autonomous choices show none of this. This is an interesting line of thought, but it is incomplete because of our poor understanding of the nature and significance of symbolic value. Is Steffi's choice better than Pete's because of being symbolic of herself and her ability to control what she does? We do not know. This needs attention before we can answer this question, and hence before we can assess the importance of Oshana's argument, suggestive as it is.

More can be said, I'm sure, but the overall point should be clear: there are lots of aspects of human life that provide some sort of reason to think that we value personal self-rule in and of itself, not just as a tool for achieving other things that we value. To the extent that such a multi-faceted case is ultimately defensible, we have good reason to think that autonomy is both instrumentally and intrinsically valuable. I will let matters rest with the merely suggestive case for the intrinsic value of self-rule.

Besides the inherent interest of the question of whether autonomy is valuable in these two ways, this is a matter with practical implications. Consider decision-makers who must wrestle with the value of individual autonomy for practical purposes. For instance, consider politicians, lawyers, hospital administrators and other people responsible for designing policies that will apply to patients under the care of medical institutions in a particular jurisdiction. Suppose that these policy-makers meet and have a lengthy discussion about how to respect patient autonomy. If autonomy is intrinsically valuable, then these policy-makers are discussing a legitimate value, and probably one that really is central to the institutions and activities that they regulate. Therefore there should be no question that they are focusing on something genuinely important. But if autonomy is only instrumentally valuable, then there is much more room to question whether these policy-makers are spending time on a secondary concern. If autonomy is only instrumentally valuable, then the evaluative work is really being done by other values, and the policy-makers run a risk of missing something of proper importance by discussing autonomy so much. Autonomy might be a genuinely important tool for accomplishing the things that the policy-makers need to accomplish, so their attention on it might be vindicated, but nevertheless its instrumental status as a value would open them up to a risk of missing the things that are really important. So, to address the question of the kind of value that autonomy is should clarify one parameter that structures practical discussions of the significance of self-rule.

For the rest of this chapter we can relegate the intrinsic/instrumental distinction to the backburner (but please keep it in the back of your mind). For the rest of the book I shall assume that autonomy has intrinsic value and is hence worth attending to directly.

How does autonomy matter?

Let's turn to our next major conceptual distinction. Generally speaking, we can value autonomy either, on the one hand, as a 'constraint' or 'limit' on our choices and actions, or, on the other hand, as a 'goal' or 'ideal'. I shall refer to this as the 'goal/constraint' distinction. First I shall explain what this means generally, then I shall explain it in terms of a particular debate from medical ethics.

To value autonomy as a goal or ideal is to see it as a value towards which the appropriate stance is one of promotion. We should take 'promotion' to have a wide meaning. On one hand by 'promotion' I mean attempts to increase the amount of something. On the other hand I mean to include protection of something against loss. For example, imagine that you hire a financial advisor with the aim of promoting your wealth. This person has two jobs, by the standards of the present understanding of 'promotion': she is to try to make you richer and, failing that, she is to protect you from losing money.

So, if we understand autonomy as a value of this kind but then arrange our behaviour, either in general or in particular contexts, such that we do not promote autonomy, then we fail to live up to the proper value of personal self-rule.

By contrast, to value autonomy as a constraint or limit on our behaviour is to recognize it as a legitimate parameter that structures the appropriate ways in which we can behave without insisting on its promotion. If we understand autonomy as a value of this kind but then arrange our behaviour, either in general or in particular contexts, such that we do not promote autonomy, then we do not necessarily fail to live up to the proper value of personal self-rule. There will be things, however, that we cannot do without thereby failing to live up to the demands of autonomy.

This is all rather abstract, so let's turn to specific examples in order to make this distinction more concrete. First I shall present a trivial example, solely about the goal/constraint distinction and then I shall examine a more serious example about this conceptual issue and autonomy.

Here is a relatively trivial case to the illuminate the goal/constraint distinction. There is a landscaping company that operates in my neighbourhood. I would not have noticed them except for a sticker on their trucks which raises my philosophical hackles. It reads, 'Safety is our goal.' Strictly speaking, if you are in the market to hire someone to do anything other than make you safer and you encounter this sort of claim, you should hire someone else. Clearly, safety is not the goal of this landscaping company, in the sense of something they aim at and wish to promote. Their goals are making money and making yards look good by cutting grass, trimming trees, *etc.* No one who wanted to promote safety would be out mowing lawns – they would be doing other things that actually promoted safety. Rather than being their goal, I am willing to believe that safety is a constraint on the activities of this landscaping company. They will take care of your property, but not in ways that put you or their employees at risk. Safety sets parameters within which they operate, doing the things that make them money. This makes it a limit on their behaviour, not a goal like their real aims.

So much for the trivial example; let's turn to the more serious case. I have already remarked that medical ethics since World War II has been marked by increased emphasis on patient autonomy. This did not happen all at once, either theoretically or in clinical settings.

As the sense that patient autonomy should be given more value grew, there were discussions over just how to understand patient autonomy, on the one hand, and on the other over how to change medical practice in order to incorporate the demands of the value of personal self-rule. The most important place now to look to find the stages of this conversation is in the literature about patient-physician relations, especially from the 1970s and 1980s. A particular mode of thinking about patient-physician relations emerged during this discussion. It focused on models or metaphors for understanding patient-physician relations. The point of the images used as models or metaphors was to illuminate certain features of patient-physician relations and the relevant values that accompany these features and, at the same time, to relegate other features of medical interaction to the background. The doctor's orders model of the Hippocratic tradition, which was to be overcome because it cast medical experts as the proper decision-makers and gave patients no official active role in medical decision-making, was represented in 'priestly' and 'parental' models. Parents legitimately make important decisions for their children, and priests have moral authority over at least the spiritual matters of parishioners, if not their entire lives. The question, in medical ethics, was what alternative metaphors better captured the importance of patient autonomy.

Robert Veatch (1972) and others argued for a 'contractual' model of patient-physician relations as an alternative to the parental/priestly model. Contracts come in a variety of forms, but they all derive their legitimacy from the coming together of competent parties who agree explicitly to the terms of some sort of arrangement. For instance, when one person buys a house from another person, they typically go back and forth in a discussion of price, time of exchange, inclusions and exclusions, practical and financial responsibilities for repairs, *etc*. The agreement that is reached about these things is morally valid due to the competency and attention of the two parties. In principle, medical interaction between patient and physician could be just as explicit and formal. However, it need not be, as the significance of some contracts is more symbolic than the one in the house-buying example. For example, Veatch held up marriage contracts as a more apt model for patient-physician relations than purchasing or employment contracts. Regardless of the heterogeneity of the class of contracts, the crucial aspect of the model is the moment of explicit agreement between parties which thereby legitimately binds them to perform certain activities or to exchange certain defined things. Without this explicit moment of agreement, no contract has been entered and the parties are not bound by the corresponding terms. Applied to medicine, the idea is that legitimate medical care cannot take place, under normal conditions, unless doctor and patient enter into some sort of explicit agreement about what is going to happen. In terms of autonomy, legitimate medical care requires the exercise of the patient's autonomy about treatment at one point, at least. By emphasizing that patient autonomy must be exercised over treatment options in order for ethical medical decision-making to happen, the contractual model of patient-physician relations represents patient autonomy as an ideal. Doctors (and other medical professionals) must insist on the exercise of patient autonomy in order to live up to the ethical demands of their profession. This might involve taking steps to bolster the patient's capacities for autonomy. All of this is just to say that the contractual model represents the appropriate stance of medical professionals towards patient autonomy as one of promotion.

Some medical ethicists and doctors thought that, while the contractual model might be an improvement over the priestly/parental model, it was also problematic with regard to the way it portrayed patient autonomy within doctor-patient relations. Patients come in many forms, even under fairly normal conditions. Some have the taste and ability for participating actively in their healthcare, but others do not. To think that doctors ought to prod hesitant patients into an active role in their own healthcare struck some as undesirable. Moreover, it seems to run counter to the spirit of respecting patient autonomy. Why should we think that competent patients cannot choose to let others make decisions about their healthcare? James Childress and Mark Siegler (1984) offered a 'negotiation' model of patient-physician relations as preferable to the contractual model with regard to patient autonomy. The negotiation model represents patient autonomy as a constraint on the choices and activities of medical professionals, not as a goal. Here is how. Negotiation is a process of discussion. In principle lots of aspects of medical care can be subject to negotiation. The negotiation model applies to all of them, but for present purposes let's focus on patient autonomy and patient participation in medical decision-making as particular potential topics of discussion between patient and medical professional. Competent patients could, on one hand, decide to be active participants in decision-making about their medical care. On the other hand, they could decide to let others do all of the decision-making. By Childress and Siegler's standards, this could be legitimate by the standards of patient autonomy. There is no need to force patients to take an active role in their healthcare in order to respect their autonomy. Under certain conditions, patient autonomy could be respected while competent patients opted not to participate in medical decision-making.

'Under certain conditions' is crucial here: it is certainly not the case that anything goes for medical experts once patients opt to let others make medical decisions for them. If this were the case then there would no sense in which patient autonomy constrained the decisions and actions of medical professionals. Patient autonomy puts two broad limits on the activities of medical experts by the standards of the negotiation model. First, the process of discussion must always be, in principle, open to continuation. This means that patients must always have the chance to revisit the terms of their interaction with their medical experts. In cases where patients have relinquished control of their medical care to their doctors, they must always have the chance to take this control back into their own hands. To keep this option open for them is to respect them as autonomous and hence, in principle, as deserving a say about what happens to their bodies. To deny them this option is to infringe against their autonomy-based authority to control their bodies. Second, medical professionals must not unilaterally do things to patients that undermine their capacity to control their medical care and hence their physical persons. Suppose a patient has relinquished control over general medical care to his physician. It is one thing for this physician to decide on behalf of the patient to remove the patient's gallbladder. The gallbladder has no constitutive role in the physical processes that realize the psychological capacities that constitute the patient as an autonomous agent. It is quite another thing for the doctor to decide unilaterally to perform a frontal lobotomy on the patient. This sort of brain surgery compromises the patient's decision-making capacities, and these are constitutive of the psychological basis of the patient's autonomy. To respect the patient's autonomy as a limit on the doctor's activities, the latter sort of procedure cannot be legitimately chosen without the patient's explicit agreement, whereas the former sort can be.

As applied to the value of autonomy, the goal/constraint distinction lines up with another distinction from which it is technically distinct. Indeed, our talk of autonomy is shot through with ambiguity due to lack of attention to this latter distinction. When we speak of autonomy, and especially when we speak of autonomous people, we can mean one of two things. We can have in mind people who have made themselves autonomous – that is, people who have exercised their capacities for self-rule. On the other hand, we might mean people who have the capacity for self-rule whether or not they have exercised this capacity.

The 'mere capacity/exercised capacity' distinction, for lack of a better name, is not specific to autonomy and shows up in connection with other topics. For instance, imagine speaking of someone as musical. You might mean that the person pursues musical interests, such as playing an instrument, being part of a band, *etc.* On the other hand, you might mean that the person has musical aptitude even though they do not take part in musical activities. The latter sense refers to the mere capacity; the former refers to the exercise of the capacity.

This distinction can also be found in discourse about values. Consider, as an example, speaking of the value of free speech and of practical measures to live up to the demands of this value. Just what practical steps are appropriate will depend on just what we mean when we speak of the value of free speech. We might mean the exercise of free speech: what should be promoted and protected is the public sharing of opinions, at least on topics of importance by some (other, probably) metric. Suppose instead that we mean the capacity for free speech, regardless of whether it is exercised. The same practical measures as in the first case might still be relevant, but it seems to me that they will be less central now. Instead, it will be more important to focus on education, to ensure that people have the capacities to form opinions and to defend them, should they wish to do so.

Let's return to autonomy and the goal/constraint distinction. To value autonomy as a goal is to value the exercise of autonomy. To value autonomy as a constraint is to value it primarily as a capacity. This should be clear from the discussion of models of patient-physician relations. The contract model insists on the exercise of patient autonomy about treatment in order for ethical medical interaction to happen. The negotiation model does not insist on such exercise of autonomy: patients need not exercise their autonomy about treatment in order to receive ethically appropriate medical treatment. However, the patient's capacity for autonomy serves as a limit that constrains the domain of things medical experts can legitimately do to the patient. This capacity is not adequately respected if the patient is refused a chance to exercise control over medical treatment or if the medical experts take this capacity away from the patient through medical means without giving the patient a chance to say whether this is acceptable.

Attentive readers will have noticed that there has been hardly any discussion in this chapter of the most important distinction in this book: the distinction between autonomy of choice and autonomy of persons. You are correct: it is important to bring this distinction back into the discussion, and not just out of interest in details and completeness. When we turn to practical issues, the choice/person distinction will matter just as much as the goal/constraint distinction. However, first things first: both autonomy of choice and autonomy of persons can be valued either as a goal or as a limit. This is just to say that both can be valued either as mere capacities or as actually implemented. In cases in which autonomy seems to matter, it will be important to sort out just what is meant: autonomy of persons, autonomy of choices, or both? How are these valued: as a goal, or as a constraint, or, in principle, as both?

We have already seen examples of autonomy of choice and autonomy of persons which can be usefully put in terms of goals and constraints. Recall Nicholas and Olivia in the food court with French fries, from Chapter 2. I shall start with autonomy of choice. Although Nicholas is an autonomous person, he fails to choose the fries autonomously. However, he is generally capable of doing so; it's just that in this moment he failed to exercise his capacity for autonomous choice. Olivia normally chooses non-autonomously, but she refrains autonomously from eating in the food court. Her exercise of her capacity for autonomous choice demonstrates that she too has the capacity and is generally capable of choosing autonomously, despite her habits.

As for autonomy of persons, recall Viviana and Swamp-Viviana from Chapter 3. Viviana is an autonomous person, which means that she has exercised self-rule over her own identity. Strictly speaking, to be an autonomous person one must exercise the relevant capacities – that is, the abilities for autonomous choosing, for acquiring self-knowledge, and for using these two things together with regard to one's identity. However, we can speak loosely of autonomy of personhood and mean the mere capacity. Swamp-Viviana has the capacity to be an autonomous person, but she is not one. She can't be one at this particular moment: she has just come into existence, but autonomy of personhood requires a history of acquisition of self-knowledge and use of this knowledge to choose (autonomously), roughly, the kind of person to be. Swamp-Viviana has no history, so she obviously does not have the right kind of history to be an autonomous person. She has the capacity for this however, because she is a physical duplicate of Viviana, and Viviana has the capacity to be an autonomous person – after all, she is one.

Here is a simple graph of the conceptual possibilities (not including the distinction between instrumental and intrinsic value; this graph is to be understood in terms of intrinsic value):

Valued as Goal	Valued as Constraint
Autonomy of Choice	
Autonomy of Persons	

FIGURE 5.1

There is a feature of this graph that is worth emphasizing, for both theoretical and practical reasons. To value, for example, autonomy of persons as a goal, one does not necessarily value autonomy of persons as a constraint. Moreover, although there is a sense in which this requires valuing autonomy of choice as a goal, they are not the same thing. So, for practical purposes, it is worth thinking of the conceptual possibilities located in these four quadrants as distinct. This means that designing the appropriate means by which to live up to the value of autonomy in practice will require getting straight about which sense(s) of autonomy and which sense(s) of value are relevant to the particular issue. We shall see some examples of this in the remainder of the book.

Before moving on the evaluative and practical implications of these distinctions, it is worth reminding ourselves of something. Since my topic is the nature and significance of autonomy, other values have not really entered the picture. However, it is rare for autonomy to be the only value relevant to a practical issue. As we have seen in the discussion of patient-physician interaction, well-being is of equally central relevance here. So, perhaps, are other values, such as equality. So, the arguments that are found in the rest of the book should be understood as 'autonomy-based' arguments, and hence as potentially incomplete with regard to the practical issues that they concern. In some cases, if not all, it will be important to balance autonomy-based considerations against other sorts of value in order to act ethically. Doing this, however, goes beyond the bounds of the present discussion. Occasionally, I shall remark on the relevance, or irrelevance, of other values, but hopefully readers will keep in mind the autonomy-based nature of these discussions. The discussions in this book are not intended to preclude the possibility that, although an account of a particular issue shows that a particular choice or way of life is consistent with autonomy, it fails by the standards of other moral values that are sufficiently important to warrant rejecting it altogether. Put the other way around, some ways of behaving might be unjustified from a perspective that focuses just on autonomy, but justified on the basis of other values and justified overall. In some cases, these actions will be justified overall. In Chapter 8, I will raise some questions about the implicit view of the relation between autonomy and other values that I am using here, thereby complicating things even further. First things first, however: it is time to show the present view of the significance of autonomy at work.

Reading guide

Many authors address the question of the value of autonomy, one way or another. A well-known account of the value of autonomy, including an attempt to explain why autonomy is intrinsically valuable, is offered by Tom Hurka in 'Why value autonomy?', *Social Theory and Practice*, Vol. 13, No.°3 (1987), 361–82. Marilyn Friedman's argument can be found in Chapter 3 of her *Autonomy, Gender, Politics* (Oxford University Press, 2003). Friedman argues for the intrinsic value for autonomy. Marina Oshana argues for the intrinsic value of autonomy in Chapter 6 of *Personal Autonomy in Society* (Ashgate, 2006); she also draws attention to connections between autonomy and democracy. Ben Colburn argues for the intrinsic value of autonomy in Chapter 3 of *Autonomy and Liberalism* (Routledge, 2010). James Stacey Taylor argues against the intrinsic value of autonomy, and for its instrumental value only, in Chapter 10 of *Practical Autonomy and Bioethics* (Routledge, 2009). Robert Nozick's machine thought experiments can be found on pp. 42–5 of his *Anarchy, State, and Utopia* (Basic Books, 1974). Taylor criticizes both Hurka and Nozick.

The line of thought that instrumental value cannot be the only sort of value is derived from the first chapter of Aristotle's *Nicomachean Ethics*, which is widely available in many editions from many publishers.

Accounts of the long-term shift from Hippocratic paternalistic attitudes about patient-physician interaction to an emphasis on patient autonomy are common in introductions to medical ethics. Two examples: Chapter 2 of Robert Veatch's *The Basics of Bioethics, 3rd Edition* (Pearson Education, Inc., 2012) and Chapters 1 and 2 of *Biomedical Ethics* (Oxford University Press, 2005) by Walter Glannon. Robert Veatch's work on the contract model of patient-physician relations is best found in his 'Models for ethical medicine in a revolutionary age', *Hastings Center Report*, Vol. 2 (June 1972), 5–7. James F. Childress and Mark Siegler offer the negotiation model in 'Metaphors and models of doctor-patient relationships: their implications for autonomy', *Theoretical Medicine and Bioethics*, Vol. 5 (1984), 17–30. Childress and Siegler attribute the goal/constraint distinction to Chapter 3 of Childress' book *Who Should Decide? Paternalism in Health Care* (Oxford University Press, 1983). Childress attributes the distinction to Nozick: *Anarchy, State, and Utopia* (Basic Books, 1974), pp. 28–30.

CHAPTER SIX

Autonomy and paternalism

'Paternalism' is the name of one of the most fundamental evaluative and practical issues one must face when addressing the significance of autonomy. Arguably it is the most fundamental, given how generally applicable this issue is. Very generally put, to act paternalistically is to do something for the good of another person but without, or even against, that person's will. The word 'paternalism' connotes the kind of decision-making parents – etymologically, fathers, but we can safely generalize here – justifiably perform for very young children. I say 'very young' here, because as a child's autonomy develops and increases with normal development, it becomes increasingly inappropriate for parents to make decisions for the child without or despite her will. Autonomy is at the root of the moral problem of paternalism. The question to be asked in this chapter is under what conditions, if any, is paternalistic interference with autonomy justifiable. To answer this I will deploy the more general ideas about the significance of autonomy that were presented in Chapter 5.

We are all familiar with paternalistic practices because we all face them. Examples of state paternalism—that is, of interference by the government in the lives of individuals for the good of those individuals whether they want it or not—include laws requiring competent adults who ride motorcycles or bicycles to wear helmets, stop signs, laws requiring the wearing of seatbelts, and the legally mandated addition of fluoride to drinking water, just to name a few. Very few of us have explicitly consented to these practices; as time goes by, this number will decrease because new people will be born into a context in which these measures are already in place and those of us who were around when these practices were introduced will die. So, to put it bluntly: these laws are in place without our explicit consent. For those of us who mind these practices, they are in place despite our desires. But the good that these policies aim at is independent of such desires. Clearly, these policies aim at our well-being whether we like it or not.

It is more difficult to find shared cases of individual paternalism – that is, of one person interfering in the life of another for the second person's good but without or even against the second person's consent. Presumably we are all accustomed to family members or friends, or neighbours or even strangers, who intervene in our lives for our good but despite or against our will. I will let you think of such cases from your own life. Medical contexts provide territory ripe for this kind of paternalism. When a medical authority takes steps to pursue a patient's health either without or against that patient's consent, that medical authority is acting paternalistically.

It should be clear that paternalism can appear anywhere. To think about the moral justification of paternalism – about whether such interference in the lives of autonomous people can be justified, and, if so, on what grounds – is to scrutinize an autonomy-based moral problem of wide, perhaps even unbounded, relevance.

Here is another point that might appear to be clear, on the basis of these examples, but which is actually mistaken. The examples are put in terms of a conflict between a person's autonomy and her well-being. Take Freeman: he lives in a Canadian province which has laws which require him to wear a seatbelt when he travels in a car. He resents these laws. A family member died in a car accident while wearing a seatbelt and Freeman believes that the belt might have made this person's injuries worse rather than keeping the person safe. Despite his recalcitrant resentment of his provincial motor vehicle laws, there is plenty of evidence that seatbelts save lives and prevent injuries, even if Freeman is correct that they contribute to injuries in some cases. Freeman is safer because of his province's laws, not worse off. Given all of this, it might seem that the issue of the justification of paternalism should be put in terms of, on one hand, the improvement to a person's well-being at which the paternalistic measures aim, and, on the other hand, the interference with people's ability to control their lives.

This way of framing the issue, while legitimate in part, is not necessary, and to insist on it is, I think, a mistake. To seek a justification of paternalism in terms of the improvement to well-being to be achieved by a particular paternalistic measure is to pursue a justificatory strategy that cannot help but be unsatisfactory. The reason is that the best result that this strategy can yield is an uncomfortable face-off between different sorts of values. Worse results all amount to unjust infringement of autonomy in the name of meagre competing values. Think about it: we have a rough sense of what sorts of interference with people's control over their lives are justifiable and of what sorts are not, but we have nothing approaching a specific sense. Speed limits on roads are, in part, a paternalistic measure: they are in place to benefit those whose self-control they limit. 'Speed kills', so it is said; this points to an obvious practical measure: people's lives will be saved if we require drivers to proceed as slowly as possible. Suppose that a state imposed a maximum speed of 15 kilometres per hour on every public roadway. This would reduce the number of injuries and fatalities due to accidents on these roads, so the measure would clearly serve the well-being of the affected drivers. But it would be greatly resented by these same drivers. If you doubt this, ask some people about how they would feel about this measure. Not only would it be resented, but many would think that such a law 'goes too far', as we might say: the benefits to be had do not justify the degree of interference with people's lives. But very few people object to the very common 50 kilometre-per-hour limits on public roadways. This degree of interference is, on the face of it, acceptable. Supposing that this is correct, we are faced with the problem of being precise about just what sorts of benefits justify just what sorts of interference with people's authority over their lives. I doubt that such precision is possible. The implication is that attempts at justifying paternalism in terms of benefits are bound to be rough at best and, just as likely, to be unsatisfying tug-of-wars between different sorts of value. I shall call this the 'Tug of War' problem.

At the same time, there is something correct about this tempting thought. Paternalistic measures appear to wear their justification on their sleeve: they are aimed at the good of the people with whom they simultaneously interfere. Surely it is the good in question that justifies these measures, if anything does; this is what points us in the direction of well-being as the potential foundation of the justification of paternalism. With this general point in mind, here is a suggestion: rather than construing a person's good in terms of well-being and thereby trying to justify paternalism, a more promising strategy is to attempt to justify paternalism in terms of autonomy itself. That is, the good at which justified paternalistic measures aim must be construed in terms of the autonomy of the agents affected by the measures. The reason this should be done is that the problem with paternalism is generated by interference with autonomy. If an autonomy-based justification can be provided, it could, in principle, be decisive. The reason is that the same value that generates the problem also generates the solution, and we need not make do with an uneasy juxtaposition of different sorts of values. I say 'in principle' because the details, perhaps in general but at least in particular cases, might be sufficiently complex to prohibit the specification of a wholly satisfactory solution. Such complexity, of course, is faced by any strategy to justify paternalism. So, at the outset we have good reason to think that the prospects of framing a satisfactory justification are better if we pursue an autonomy-based route than one based on well-being.

If by 'autonomy' we meant just one thing, the prospects for finding an autonomy-based justification of paternalism would not be very good. The reason is that paternalistic measures, by any standard, interfere with our autonomy by, at the very least, limiting our powers of choice over some topic. A new stop sign means that we can no longer legally choose to drive straight through a particular intersection; forced medical treatment takes the possibility of choosing to avoid that treatment completely out of the realm of possibility. For any attempt to justify such interference in personal self-rule by reference to autonomy itself, a quick rejoinder is always available: autonomy is more straight-forwardly respected by not performing the paternalistic measure in the first place. Let's call this the 'Shortest Route' objection. Perhaps there are ways of responding to this challenge, but it should be clear that the person who defends paternalistic interference with autonomy in this manner faces an uphill battle.

However, I have argued at length that by autonomy we should not mean just one thing. I have defended a distinction between autonomy of choice on one hand and autonomy of persons on the other. This distinction gives us the possibility of a different sort of autonomy-based justification of paternalism. As should be clear from the discussion so far, insofar as paternalistic measures interfere with our autonomy, it is autonomy of choice that is compromised. The Shortest Route objection can be mounted to any attempt to justify such measures in terms of autonomy of choice, but it is not available to justifications in terms of autonomy of persons. So, here is a general suggestion about justified paternalism: interference with the autonomy of choice of another person for that person's good is justified when the measure sufficiently serves that person's autonomy of personhood. Let's be clear: the word 'sufficiently' hides a lot of difficult issues. In order to get at some of these issues, more details are needed.

Before getting to the details of this position, there is a general issue to address. If we are going to justify interference with autonomy of choice on the basis of the value of autonomy of persons, then we seem to be assuming that autonomy of personhood is more valuable than autonomy of choice. This does not go without saying, and hence one might resist paternalistic interference with autonomy of choice on the basis of one's autonomy of personhood by putting one's foot down and insisting on the superior importance of choice. What can be said to support the idea that autonomy of persons is more important than autonomy of choice? There will be fuel for this issue later in the chapter, but here is an important line of thought. Our choices can be made, in principle, about anything. This holds whether the choices are made autonomously or not. Some of our choices will be about serious things, while others will concern trivial matters. Recall, once again, Nicholas and Olivia. They both make choices about French fries; Olivia's is autonomous, but Nicholas' is not. French fries, in and of themselves, are a pretty trivial matter. However, autonomy of personhood concerns something that is not trivial: our very selves. Things that are, in and of themselves, trivial gain a non-trivial status when they are incorporated into the processes of self-shaping. The argument is not that valuing things makes them valuable. It is the following more complex inference:

1 Premise one: Human selves have value.

2 Premise two: Such selves stand in complex relations, including constitutive ones, to, in principle, anything.

3 Conclusion: Anything, when standing in the appropriate relation to human selves, acquires value derivative from that of these selves.

Overall, insofar as we value human selves, we have some reason to think that autonomy of persons is more important than autonomy of choice.

Okay, let's turn to the details of this way of justifying paternalism. First, it is desirable to sharpen our understanding of the forms paternalism can take. People who write about paternalism make many distinctions, not all of which are relevant to the present purposes. I provide a brief list of some of these at the end of the chapter. Here is a distinction to add to these that is useful for present purposes. We should distinguish between what I shall call 'positive' and 'negative' paternalism. Positive paternalism occurs when one's freedom of choice is limited by an action or policy that introduces something into one's life for one's own good, but without one's consent and perhaps despite one's wishes to the contrary. Actions/ policies that introduce something into one's life without restricting the range of choices one faces are not paternalistic. An example of positive paternalism is the addition of fluoride to public water supplies. Such a policy does something for the good of the people who use the public water supply, but in a way that restricts their freedom of choice. Specifically, before this step was taken, people had the following two options: drink from the public water supply and not consume fluoride, or drink from the public water supply and consume fluoride (from some other source). After fluoride is added to the public water supply, the first option is no longer open to people.

Negative paternalism is merely the restriction of one's behaviour for one's own good by some action or policy, but without one's consent and perhaps despite one's wishes to the contrary. An example is the law that prohibits selling oneself into slavery. This restricts one's freedom of choice for one's own good, but the restriction is direct; nothing is added to one's life that indirectly limits one's choices, as in the case of the addition of fluoride to drinking water.

At base, negative paternalism is merely the restriction of one's freedom of choice for one's own good. This implies that all positive paternalism is simultaneously negative, in that it restricts choice. By contrast, not all negative paternalism is also positive: there can be purely negative paternalism, such as the law prohibiting selling oneself into slavery. Such complications do not matter for the present purposes. Arguably it is negative paternalism that captures the defining core of paternalism in general: the restriction of freedom of choice. Consequently, let me suggest that we focus on justifications for negative paternalism. If the negatively paternalistic aspect of some example of positive paternalism is justified by the standards of a legitimate test of justified negative paternalism, then it is justified *qua* paternalism *tout court*. The extra aspects that make it a case of positive paternalism will require justification on other grounds, but these will have nothing in particular to do with paternalism. For instance, consider the introduction of fluoride into sources of public drinking water as an example. To justify the negatively paternalistic aspect of this is to justify its limitation of choice. That which makes it positive – the addition of fluoride into people's bodies via drinking water – will require justification in terms of health benefits, which are not intrinsically linked to paternalism.

Another distinction is needed before we address the question of how paternalism might be justified. Negative paternalism takes what I shall call 'weak' and 'strong' forms. Weak negative paternalism occurs when some policy or action puts an obstacle in the way of one's free choice without absolutely prohibiting one from doing otherwise. An example is the erection of a stop sign at a junction where one was free to pass through before. This restricts one's range of choice: one is obliged, by law, to stop at this place or to face legal consequences. Strictly speaking however, one is not absolutely constrained to reckon with this stop sign. One is free to take other routes, to walk instead of driving, *etc.* Such paternalism can be more or less restrictive; the less restrictive it is, the less justification it needs.

By contrast, strong negative paternalism limits one's freedom of choice by absolutely prohibiting one from doing otherwise than what the policy or action indicates. Under strong negative paternalism, it is in some sense impossible to do otherwise. I say 'in some sense impossible' because there are different ways in which things are possible or, vitally, impossible. Here are examples of two of these ways. First, some forms of strong negative paternalism are *physical*, and hence they make it *physically impossible* to do otherwise. An example would be forced medical treatment (which is simultaneously a case of positive paternalism). If one is forced to take some medicine or to undergo an operation against one's will, then it is literally physically impossible to do otherwise. Once the injection is given, there is no going back. Second, other forms of strong negative paternalism make it *legally* impossible to do otherwise. A law against selling oneself into slavery is strongly paternalistic in this sense: it makes it legally impossible to sell oneself into slavery in, for instance, Canada.

Since the restriction of one's freedom of choice under strong negative paternalism is stricter than that under weak negative paternalism, my intuition is that the former must pass a stiffer test that the latter for it to be justified. Nevertheless, both justifications are framed in terms of autonomy of persons. The two tests that I shall propose for assessing weak and strong negative paternalism respectively are differentiated in terms of the distinction between valuing something as a goal and valuing it as a limit. Very roughly put: weak negative paternalism is justified when it lives up to the demands of autonomy of persons as a goal, whereas strong negative paternalism is justified when it lives up to the demands of autonomy of persons as a limit. Alternatively, we can say that weak negative paternalism is justified when it promotes and protects the exercise of autonomy of personhood, whereas strong negative paternalism is to be justified in reference to the mere capacity for autonomy of personhood.

Let's start with weak negative paternalism. Generally speaking, to value autonomy of persons as a goal is to adopt a stance of promotion towards it. Recall that, for practical purposes, 'promotion' involves either trying to increase the amount of something or trying to prevent the loss of something. So, for weak negative paternalism to be justified, my suggestion is that the measure in question must serve autonomy of persons, either by promoting it or, which is more likely, by preserving it. Stop signs at intersections pass this test. They do this by reducing accidents and thereby increasing our health. Besides the fact that healthy people face more options than unhealthy ones – that is, they have a greater range for autonomy of choice – avoiding accidents also preserves their ability to consider what sorts of things are worth having, what sorts of lives are worth leading, and related questions. These issues are at the core of self-shaping, which is one of the pillars of the autonomy of personhood. The erection of stop signs at intersections protects this aspect of autonomy of persons very directly, by reducing the number of head injuries.

Although this test is put in terms of autonomy, it is strictly a consequentialist test for paternalism. Here, autonomy of persons is treated as a good that ought to be promoted or protected from diminution. This satisfies the search for an autonomy-based rationale for weak negative paternalism; it also happens to preserve some of the appeal of the sort of value that gives rise to considerations of paternalism in the first place. At first glance, it seems that paternalistic policies ought to be justified in terms of the end they serve: that is, in terms of the good that is done for the person whose freedom of choice is limited. The test for weak negative paternalism construes autonomy of persons as the relevant good by which particular paternalistic policies are to be measured. This way of framing the value of autonomy invites the rough-and-ready use of balancing considerations (and metaphors): the good to be gained by paternalism, in the sense of the contribution to the exercise of the capacities that make us autonomous persons, is to be weighed against the disvalue that comes from the limitation of freedom of choice. Some paternalistic measures that serve autonomy of persons will not serve it enough to be justified: an example might be the erection of stop signs every 20 feet along a roadway. Here there is great inconvenience in the form of limitation of choices, but the added protection of autonomy of personhood is distinctly minimal.

Strong negative paternalism is different. Here the issue is the justification of *absolute* prohibition of some sort activity for the good of the very same person whose conduct is limited. Weakly negative paternalistic policies put an obstacle in the way of some choice without limiting it absolutely. Whereas construing autonomy of persons as a goal provides a promising foundation for the justification of weak negative autonomy, such a strategy is much less promising for strong negative paternalism. The reason is that, due to the complexity of the forms which meaningful human living can take, the apparent disvalue that attaches to the direct destruction of the capacities that make us autonomous persons can be part of a life-plan, autonomously considered and chosen. To put up a single stop sign is to take a step that preserves autonomy of persons at that intersection, but it does not absolutely prevent people from deliberately and autonomously structuring their lives in part around activities involving very fast cars and the associated increase in risk of head injury.

It is reasonable to think that the mere avoidance of bad consequences will not suffice to ground the absolute prohibition of some activity. In the face of this sort of risk, caution and safeguards are warranted, not prohibition. Instead, a stronger sort of justification is needed. To my mind, the most convincing reason to absolutely prevent someone from doing something is not that there is a possible bad effect of the action, but that the course of action is *wrong*. *Prima facie*, it is justifiable to prohibit people from doing things that are demonstrably wrong. So far I have put this merely in terms of prohibiting people from doing things, but paternalism is narrower in scope than this. Paternalistic measures interfere with freedom of choice for one's own sake. So, for strong negative paternalism to be justified it must prevent one from doing something that is wrong with regard to oneself; if one is prevented from doing wrong to others, then one's conduct is limited primarily for the sake of those others, not for one's own sake.

For this to be an autonomy-based rationale for strong negative paternalism, the wrong in question must be put in terms of the autonomy of persons. To see how this might work, let's consider the legal prohibition against selling ourselves into slavery. Since this is an absolute prohibition, it is an example of strong negative paternalism. I shall start with slavery in general. Regardless of the bad effects that typically stem from slavery, I'm inclined to think that the fundamental problem with it is that it is unjust. It is unjust because (to follow Aristotle's famous way of framing the issue) it fails to treat people who are equal in important ways as equals. The relevant facts to consider here are those associated with the self-shaping component of autonomy of persons: the ability to reflect on a life-plan and to live in accordance with this reflection. Both slaves and slave-owners, insofar as they are normal, healthy, mature adults, have the brain structures that realize the cognitive capacities by virtue of which we are deeply autonomous. If there is any moral value to autonomy at all, it supervenes upon these structures and capacities. But a state that countenances slavery divides people who are equal in this respect into different moral groups: some deserve respect due to their ability to form and enact a life plan – the slave owners – and others deserve no such respect, despite having the same abilities –the slaves. Put in another way, slave owners are acknowledged as having a right to self-rule, based upon their capacities for it, but no such right is acknowledged for slaves, in spite of the fact that they have the same capacities. Since such a social arrangement treats equals unequally in a relevant respect, it is correspondingly unjust. Since the matter in connection with which equals are treated unequally is an important one, states that countenance slavery are unjust in an important way. Laws against slavery are paternalistic only when the issue of selling oneself into slavery arises. The same pattern of unequal treatment of equals arises with regard to selling oneself into slavery. Such a sale presupposes that one has the right to direct the course of one's life *before* the sale is made. This is the very right that is given up by entering slavery. One has this right by virtue of the capacities and structures that realize the sorts of thoughts characteristic of autonomy of persons. When one becomes a slave, one loses the right (socially speaking) to direct the course of one's life but not the capacities by virtue of which one had this right. A person before entering slavery is *non-morally* equal to his/her future self after entering slavery, but *morally* unequal. A state that countenances such a possibility is one that, through time rather than at a particular moment, treats equals unequally, which is unjust in the way that we have already seen. To try to do this to oneself is to treat one's present and future selves as morally unequal when one's present and future selves are equal with regard to the non-moral facts that ground this moral status. To sell oneself into slavery is to commit an unjust act with regard to oneself. The paternalistic law that prohibits this is justified because it prohibits such injustice. This law limits one's autonomy of choice, but out of respect for the moral value of autonomy of persons – that is, for the value attached to the capacity to frame and pursue a plan for one's life.

One might think that we can acknowledge a right to control our lives, yet insist that nothing unjust is done by selling ourselves into slavery for the following reason: one of the things that we can legitimately do with rights is to waive them. To waive a right is to refrain from enforcing it. The person who sells himself into slavery waives his right to control his own life. Since waiving rights is within the legitimate powers of competent rights-holders – that is, of autonomous people in general – there is nothing necessarily unjust about doing so by selling ourselves into slavery.

The problem with this line of thought is that waiving a right is consistent with still having it. To refrain from exercising a right is not necessarily to give it up altogether. In cases in which we have rights, and perhaps other sorts of moral value, in virtue of our constitution rather than our choices, we will retain the right even while we waive it. For example, suppose, as seems reasonable, that

I have a right to prevent others from violating the physical bounds of my person. I have authority over my body. Suppose that I waive this right and allow medical experiments to be performed using my body. This waiver does not imply that I give up my right to control my body altogether: I retain it, but I allow others to use my body, which is within my rights. In the event that I decide to assert my right and terminate the experiments, the medical researchers have no moral grounds on which to insist that I have given up my right to control what happens to my body. Likewise, exactly this line of thought applies to selling ourselves into slavery: although I can legitimately waive my right to control my life, I retain it since it is delivered by my physical constitution. But the institution of slavery is structured in such a way that slaves are not recognized as having a right to control their lives. They are treated as having given this right up altogether. This is not the case, even if we recognize that the relevant rights can be waived. Consequently, no defence against the charge that selling ourselves into slavery is unjust is found in the idea of waiving a right.

To return to the general case: strongly negative paternalism is justified when it prevents one from doing something wrong with regard to oneself *qua* deeply autonomous. The injustice attached to selling oneself into slavery is an example of such a wrongful act. If such injustice is the only way that one can do the relevant sort of wrong to oneself, then the test for justifiable strong negative paternalism can be modified: it is justified when it prevents one from doing unjust acts towards oneself. This test for justifiable paternalism is deontological in spirit: instead of a goal to be promoted, autonomy of persons is here construed as a limit on behaviour. The kind of wrong that arises in the slavery case is to be prevented even if, for example, somewhat more happiness would result from the performance of such injustice. This is, to my mind, the appropriate sort of value for an absolute prohibition, unlike consequentialist values.

An example: Assisted suicide

Let's see how these tests for the justification of paternalism work when applied to a poignant and live moral issue: assisted suicide. As of the time of writing these words, there is a lively debate about whether helping others to end their lives can ever be morally justifiable. There has been a growing interest in getting such help from medical experts as Western populations have aged and, ironically, grown healthier. The increased health has led to two things: longer lives ended by degenerative diseases. Many people do not want to go through the entire dying process that these diseases involve, and would prefer to die by their own hand at some earlier time. Medical aid in dying is desirable because it is the best means of ensuring that the choice is being made with an accurate view of one's physical condition and treatment options, and that the action taken to end one's life is painless. Laws that prohibit such aid, which are more common than not, are paternalistic: they limit the autonomy of choice of the people who want help in dying, ostensibly for their own good. More specifically, they are negatively paternalistic: choice is limited directly, without the introduction of anything else into one's life. This means that such legal measures can be assessed by the tools developed in this chapter. I shall not decide whether such laws are strong or weak versions of such paternalism; instead, I shall evaluate them using both tests.

A] Suppose that such laws *absolutely* prohibit this sort of conduct. This means that such laws exemplify strong negative paternalism. Since these laws limit freedom of choice, they limit autonomy of choice. Accordingly, an autonomy-based rationale for paternalistic legal prohibition of assisted suicide should be put in terms of autonomy of persons. More specifically, the law should prohibit people from doing something wrong with regard to themselves *qua* autonomous. In general, it seems to me that such laws will fail this test: so far as I can tell, there is nothing *a priori* wrong, in connection with autonomy of persons, with killing oneself. Suicide is certainly not unjust in the way that selling oneself into slavery is. When one sells oneself into slavery, one treats one's present and future selves as having different moral statuses despite non-moral equality. But when one kills oneself, one destroys the non-moral capacities that realize our deep autonomy. Insofar as one's future moral status is implicitly treated as different from one's current moral status, it is accompanied by a more fundamental change in the non-moral properties that ground such moral status. One's present, living, autonomous self and one's future, dead, non-autonomous self are non-morally unequal, so no injustice is done if they are also implicitly treated as morally unequal. Unless a different deep autonomy-based rationale for prohibiting assisted suicide is forthcoming, we have reason to think that this sort of paternalistic policy is not morally justified.

B] Suppose that laws against medical assistance in ending our lives do not absolutely prohibit us from getting such help. I realize that this seems not to be the case – the point of these laws, after all, is exactly to prohibit such assistance absolutely, at least by legal standards. Nevertheless, since it seems, to me, conceptually possible for legal prohibitions to be non-absolute, let's examine the conceptual possibility that such laws are weakly negatively paternalistic. Construed this way, for laws against assisted suicide to be morally justifiable, they must promote or preserve autonomy of personhood. This is what must be demonstrated to justify weak negative paternalism in general, because this test is framed in terms of seeing autonomy of personhood as a goal. Do such laws deliver on this score?

To answer this, let's look at some details from a particular autonomy-based argument against assistance in suicide. Jerome Bickenbach argues for continuing legal prohibition against assistance in suicide on the basis of what he calls 'inequality of autonomy' (1998, p. 126). What this means is that able and disabled persons face the issue of whether to take their own lives in different ways. Bickenbach argues that, unlike able-bodied persons, for the disabled, '. . . it is more likely than not. . . [that] the decision to kill oneself, or to seek assistance to do so, is a coerced, manipulated, or forced decision.' (1998, p. 127) That is, able and disabled do not face the issue of suicide with the same free ability to choose. According to Bickenbach, the value of equality calls for prohibition against assistance in suicide because when the choice is made by disabled people, we have good reason to think that it is not made autonomously, but is in fact coerced. A prohibition against assistance in suicide thus helps the disabled retain control over their persons and lives.

Bickenbach identifies two sorts of coercion that the disabled face. The first is psychological. Psychological coercion stems from pressures experienced by the disabled person as a direct result of their disability. To determine whether a choice has been made under conditions of psychological coercion, case-by-case examination is required. The goal of such examination is to assess whether the will of the decision-maker is unduly over-powered by the contingencies of their condition (1998, p. 127).

The second sort of coercion is moral (1998, p. 128). Bickenbach thinks this is much more important than psychological coercion. Moral coercion occurs when the issue of whether to end one's life arises in a context where one's sort of life is devalued and where one's options for how to continue are limited by the choices of others. Bickenbach argues that both of these are the case for disabled people. The prevailing social attitude is that the lives of people with disabilities are devalued. Bickenbach argues that this attitude *itself* devalues life. It certainly reduces its quality. For example, when this attitude affects policy decisions, it can translate into a 'justification' of limitation on resources available to persons with disabilities (1998, pp. 127–8). Moreover, the choice to die is made against a background of other options. These options are themselves determined by prevailing social attitudes and policy decisions informed by these attitudes. Such attitudes and decisions can, and often do, limit the alternatives available to people dealing with disabilities. These limitations are far different from those imposed by nature – they are neither inevitable nor the effect of our natural allotment of talents, physical conditions, *etc*. Instead they are produced or maintained through human decisions and activities, both of which could be conducted in other ways as a matter of human choice (1998, p. 128).

The implication of these reflections is the following: there is inequality of autonomy with regard to decisions about suicide. In contexts where the lives of people with disabilities are systemically devalued, the choice to die is coerced by the attitudes and decisions of others. The same choice made by the able-bodied is not subject to such coercion. This is unfair. To combat unequal ability to choose for oneself on such a fundamental matter, Bickenbach thinks (continuing) state prohibition against assistance in suicide is warranted.

So much for the argument. Does this position pass the test for weak negative paternalism? Does it serve autonomy of personhood? We have good reason to think that this is not the case. The problems that Bickenbach identifies for disabled persons' abilities for self-rule regarding end-of-life decisions concern, in particular, the attitudes of others that devalue the lives of the disabled, limit resources available to the disabled, and artificially constrain options for the disabled. These are all problems for self-rule, but they call for more direct redress than that provided by prohibition against assistance in suicide. Two more direct responses are obvious:

I   Education is needed to counter the prevailing social
    attitudes about the value of the lives of the disabled.

II Resources are needed, especially to counter the artificial
    limitation of options for how to live which are available to
    the disabled.

If prohibiting people from getting assistance in suicide accomplished
either [I] or [II], then we would have some reason to think that
autonomy of persons was well served by legal prohibitions against
assisted suicide. But this is not the case. In particular, we have no
reason to think that prevailing attitudes would be *changed* by
continuing legal prohibition against assisted suicide. Of course not
– in Canada, for instance, these attitudes exist in a context in which
such assistance is *already* officially prohibited. There is no reason to
think that leaving the law the same would bring about any changes of
attitude at all. The same goes for resources: we have no reason to think
that the disabled would receive more resources than they currently do
on the basis of *continuing* legal prohibition against assisted suicide.
Since the problems faced by the disabled with regard to decisions
about whether to continue living call directly for *new* education and
resources, and since the legal prohibition against assisted suicide
indirectly provides neither of these, we can confidently claim that
the value of autonomy of persons does not justify the curtailing of
autonomy of choice that is the effect of laws against assisted suicide.

Perhaps these results come as no surprise. When we reflect on
suicide and autonomy of personhood directly, it is clear that there
is no *a priori* reason that prevents suicide from having a place
in the considered structure of one's life. As such, it is consistent
with autonomy of persons. If this is the case, then our *prima facie*
assumption should be that assistance with suicide is also generally
consistent with self-rule.

Concluding reflections

There are three things worth emphasizing about this discussion of
paternalism and physician-assisted suicide. First, in order to show
how these tests of the justification of paternalism work, I have
argued that paternalistic measures against assistance in suicide fail
these tests. While it might seem peculiar to show how these tests

work by showing how certain measures fail to be justified by these standards, it is actually quite important. Paternalism is a serious issue, and I do not mean to suggest that a successful argument in favour of the justification of paternalism implies that just any paternalistic measure can now be legitimately performed. On the contrary, I think that the autonomy-based standards for justified paternalism are quite importantly high. To demonstrate *this,* it is vital to show how real world paternalistic measures can be ruled out by these standards. Second, while it is certainly suggestive, the argumentative dialectic grapples with a particular argument – the one from Jerome Bickenbach – and hence should not be taken as exhaustive. The primary point is to exhibit how the present treatment of autonomy and paternalism works, not to provide an exhaustive treatment of the ethics of physician-assisted suicide. This brings up the third point: it is important to reiterate that the challenge of justifying paternalism – or, failing this, of condemning it – does not fall to medical ethics alone. This might get lost given the focus on physician-assisted suicide, but paternalism, in principle, is a moral challenge that can appear anywhere. The other examples that are sprinkled through the discussion should help to remind us of this.

This discussion raises harder issues than these. Most importantly, it should be evident that having a general treatment of the justification of paternalism does not suffice to settle the question of whether particular paternalistic measures are justified. Besides questions about the adequacy of the account of paternalism itself (which are perfectly reasonable, as we shall momentarily see), there is the unavoidable fact that, for application, general accounts must be combined with more particular details. These details, for other issues just as much as for physician-assisted suicide, invariably bring with them poignant complexities which elude the general account. For the present example of the application of these two tests of the justification of paternalism, the difficult issues concern just how particular social and cultural contingencies compromise autonomy, both of choice and of persons, and the realistically available options to deal with these challenges.

That said, there is another way in which particular details matter for consideration of such issues as whether paternalistic prohibition of expert medical assistance in taking one's life is justified. They provide us with an important perspective on the Tug-of-War problem and the Shortest Route objection. Put crudely, the lessons are that the Shortest Route objection is less important than I have presented it whereas the Tug-of-War problem is arguably more important.

Let's start with the Shortest Route objection. This is the general rejoinder to attempts to justify paternalistic interference with autonomy on the basis of autonomy itself that the promotion and protection of autonomy is most directly served by avoiding paternalism, both in general and with regard to the specific measures being considered in a particular place at a particular time. The details of the arguments about paternalism and physician-assisted suicide should make us pause to think about whether things in the real world are really as simple as the Shortest Route objection portrays them. Although I have argued that Bickenbach's considerations do not justify the paternalistic measure of legally prohibiting expert assistance in ending one's life, I have not argued that these considerations are crazy or so misguided as to be disregarded altogether. On the contrary, I think that the kinds of coercion to which Bickenbach draws our attention are very important, and consequently I think that they need reflective attention. While the shortest route to the promotion and protection of the autonomy of the able-bodied might be through non-paternalistic legal settings, I agree with Bickenbach that it needs extra argument to show that this is the case for the disabled. Even if my overall argument against legal prohibition of assistance in suicide is correct, I agree with Bickenbach's implicit point that the best ways of protecting autonomy need not be the ones that appeal to us at the outset. It might take considerable wrestling with details to clarify just what the best ways of living up to the demands of autonomy are.

The Tug-of-War problem is trickier still. I argued that attempts to justify paternalism in terms of well-being are destined to end, at best, in a stalemate between different sorts of values, and that hence we should seek justifications of paternalistic interference with autonomy on the basis of autonomy itself. But once we attend to the distinction between autonomy of choice and autonomy of persons, the Tug-of-War problem risks reappearing. Maybe autonomy of choice and autonomy of persons are sufficiently different as to be incommensurable. If this is the case, then to invoke autonomy of persons to justify interference with autonomy of choices will be very difficult to do convincingly. It might even be doomed to failure, for exactly the same reasons that undermine attempts to justify interfering with autonomy on the basis of well-being.

Here are two lines of thought in defence of the suggestion that the Tug-of-War problem is not as damning for attempts to justify paternalism on the basis of autonomy as it is for attempts based on well-being. Both considerations deploy reflections about relations between autonomy of choice and autonomy of persons. First, consider a possible objection to the conceptual coherence of the attempt to justify interference with autonomy of choice on the basis of autonomy of persons. This objection turns on the idea that since autonomy of personhood requires autonomy of choice as a component (along with the capacities for self-knowledge and self-shaping), infringements of autonomy of choice cannot help but also infringe against autonomy of personhood, and so the value of the latter cannot justify interference with the former. We might respond to this by recalling the distinction between egocentric and allocentric representation. It is not autonomy of choice *per se* that is required for autonomy of persons. It is egocentric autonomy of choice. Interference with autonomy of choice need not interfere with the right kind of autonomy of choice, and hence, in principle, we can still rely on the value of autonomy of persons to justify interference with autonomy of choice. Regardless of what one thinks of this rejoinder to this problem – for instance, one might object that to interfere with autonomy of choice from without is to interfere with autonomy of choice *tout court*, regardless of what different sorts there might be from the inside once we attend to the psychological details – it provides a way of resisting the deployment of the Tug-of-War problem against intra-autonomy justifications of paternalism. The Tug-of-War problem requires that autonomy of choice and autonomy of persons be so different that they are incommensurable as values, but this is implausible. They are intricately interwoven even if they are distinct, and so the issues that arise when trying to assess their comparative value should not be thought to be as difficult as those that accompany the comparison of the importance of well-being with that of autonomy.

Here is a second response. It is a response not only to deployment of the Tug-of-War problem against intra-autonomy justifications of paternalism but also to the worry that autonomy of personhood is not necessarily more important than autonomy of choice. The spirit of the discussion of paternalism presented in this chapter is that autonomy of persons is more important than autonomy of choice. Why might this be the case? A simple answer relies on addition:

autonomy of persons requires, in some respect at least, autonomy of choice. Since autonomy of personhood is composed of autonomy of choice plus the capacities for self-knowledge and self-shaping, it must have more value than autonomy of choice does. The only situation in which this would not be the case would be one in which the combined value of the capacities for self-knowledge and self-shaping was negative, but this is so implausible that I know of no one who has defended it. So, at worst, autonomy of personhood seems to be equivalent in value to autonomy of choice; the more likely situation is that it has greater value. This holds even if we reject the relevance of the egocentric/allocentric distinction for assessments of the relative value of autonomy of choice and autonomy of persons, which means that this response is independent of the previous one. The implications for the Tug-of-War problem are the same as those of the first response, however: given their intricate relations, we should not think of the values of autonomy of choice and autonomy of persons as being just as incommensurable as the values of well-being and autonomy.

It is worth noting that the Shortest Route objection and the Tug-of-War problem pull in opposite directions. The spirit of the Shortest Route objection is that the considerations that are offered to justify paternalism are insufficiently different from autonomy to pull off this justificatory role. Insofar as autonomy is the real issue, the shortest route to living up to its demands is to refrain from paternalism. This pushes us away from autonomy-based justifications of paternalism. The spirit of the Tug-of-War problem is precisely the opposite: justifications of paternalism in terms of things other than autonomy are bound to fail or to result in an uneasy truce between different sorts of values. To avoid this we should seek autonomy-based justifications of paternalism. The spirit (if not the letter) of the present argument, which draws on intra-autonomy distinctions to justify paternalism, is perhaps the best hope for justifying paternalism in the face of this uncomfortable combination of considerations. I take it that the responses to the Tug-of-War problem make the importance of these intra-autonomy relations clear.

In Chapter 5, I presented a general account of the significance of autonomy, drawing particular attention to the distinction between valuing it as a goal and as a constraint. This distinction was deployed in the present chapter to shed some light on the possibility of justifying paternalism. Although particular issues have been discussed, especially physician-assisted suicide, these two chapters have focused on rather abstract aspects of the significance of autonomy. Things are more specific in the next chapter, where the topic is, to put it roughly, the political significance of personal-self-rule. The final chapter is more specific still. Nevertheless, the choice/persons and goal/constraint distinctions will be important to both chapters.

Appendix: Varieties of paternalism

Here are some distinctions that are often drawn in discussions of paternalism. This list closely follows Gerald Dworkin's entry in the *Stanford Encyclopedia of Philosophy*.

1] Hard and Soft Paternalism: This distinction is drawn on the basis of the knowledge of the person whose actions are being interfered with. Soft paternalism is interference with someone's activities when that person either does not know what stakes they face, or the interferer does not know if the interferee knows what they face. For instance, suppose that Maria is about to drink from a glass and that Brad takes it away from her forcibly. The glass is filled with poison; Brad is saving Maria's life. This is clearly paternalistic. If Maria does not know that the glass is filled with poison, or if Brad does not know whether she knows this, then the act is soft paternalism. By contrast, hard paternalism is interference with a person's actions for that person's good even if they know what they face. If Maria still tries to drink the poison once she knows what it is, and if Brad interferes with this, Brad is committing an act of hard paternalism.

2] Broad and Narrow Paternalism: The discussion in this chapter has been broad, in that it addresses paternalism whether it is performed by the state or by individuals. Some think, however, that state paternalism raises somewhat different issues than individual paternalism, and hence focus more narrowly just on state interference with individuals for the good of those individuals.

3] Pure and Impure Paternalism: This distinction is often lost when we focus on interference with individuals because it concerns larger groups of people. In pure paternalism, the people interfered with are exactly the same as those whose good is sought, no more and no less. In impure paternalism, more people are interfered with than are protected. Legal prohibition against selling certain sorts of drugs is impure paternalism: everyone's activity is limited, but for the benefit of would-be drug consumers only. A school rule preventing students from running in hallways for their own good is an example of pure paternalism.

4] We have already seen, implicitly, that we can distinguish varieties of paternalism on the basis of the nature of the good that is offered as a justification. Dworkin divides 'welfare' paternalism, which is what I have described above as paternalism aimed at the well-being of those whose activities are limited, from 'moral' paternalism, which aims at the moral good of the people interfered with. Both categories could be sub-divided if we wished; arguably the present account focusing on autonomy does just this. Another example could be 'aesthetic' paternalism, which would be interference with someone's activity to bring about beauty in that person's life. I shall leave it to readers to decide whether this would fall under the well-being or moral categories, or whether it is a third sort of good at which we might aim.

5] Weak and strong paternalism: This distinction is not the same as my differentiation between weak and strong varieties of negative paternalism, despite the overlapping terminology. The conventional distinction is drawn on the basis of considerations of means versus ends. Weak paternalism is interference with someone's activity because of a mistake that person is making about the means that are necessary to accomplish something. Suppose that John wants to impress Ivan and thinks that becoming an athlete will accomplish this. Chris, who knows that Ivan dislikes athletes, prevents John from enrolling in athletic training so that John does not frustrate his own aims. This is weak paternalism. Strong paternalism is interference with someone's activity for their own good on the basis of a conviction that the person who is interfered with is making a mistake about what is worth seeking or about what sort of life is worth living. If Chris interferes with John because Chris thinks that intimate interpersonal relationships are not worth pursuing and hence that John is making a mistake in trying to impress Ivan, Chris' actions count as strong paternalism.

Reading guide

For a classic discussion of paternalism different from the present one, see Gerald Dworkin, 'Paternalism', *The Monist*, Vol. 56 (1972), 64–84. Dworkin is also the author of the entry on paternalism in the online Stanford Encyclopedia of Philosophy: http://stanford. library.usyd.edu.au/entries/paternalism/. For those who want a slightly more detailed look at relatively recent work on paternalism, David Garren has pair of essays: 'Paternalism, part I', *Philosophical Books*, Vol. 47, No. 4 (October 2006), 334–41, and 'Paternalism, part II', *Philosophical Books*, Vol. 48, No. 1 (January 2007), 50–9.

Jerome Bickenbach makes his anti-physician-assisted suicide argument in 'Disability and life-ending decisions' in M. Battin, R. Rhodes and A Silvers (eds), *Physician-Assisted Suicide: Expanding the Debate* (Routledge, 1998), pp. 123–32. I discuss this at greater length in 'Equality, justice, and paternalism: recentreing debate about physician-assisted suicide', *Journal of Applied Philosophy*, Vol. 23, No. 4 (2006), 387–404.

CHAPTER SEVEN

Autonomy, democracy and liberalism

In Chapter 6, I discussed both state and merely interpersonal versions of paternalism. The matter of individual relations to the state is the topic of the present chapter, broadly put. When speaking of autonomous individuals, as I have been doing for six chapters now, it is easy and, indeed, reasonable to have in mind interpersonal relations of a fairly simple one-on-one sort. But, as the discussion so far has shown, we interact in more complex ways than this. We cooperate and conflict not just on a directly individual basis but also via complex institutions. The most powerful and generally applicable such institution – or set of institutions, if one prefers – is the state. We lead our lives together not just individually but also within the formal and informal confines of certain sorts of political arrangements. What are the relationships between self-rule and state rule over self-ruling individuals?

This is a big question; it is arguably the defining question of political philosophy. I cannot hope to give it a definitive treatment in a brief chapter in a book about personal self-rule rather than political philosophy in general. Consequently, I shall restrict my focus. The parameters of this discussion are provided by philosophical thought about liberalism. There are two reasons for this. One is that liberalism is, arguably, the central ideology in mainstream political philosophy. Consequently, much discussion of relations between individual autonomy and the state is put in terms of liberal ideas, even by those who are not proponents of liberalism. Second, readers who are not attracted by particular ideologies are nevertheless likely to be sympathetic to democracy. However, as we shall see, there is reason to think that there is a close fit between liberalism and democracy. I am inclined to think that much of the discussion in this chapter could be rephrased in terms of 'liberal democracy' rather than 'liberalism' without much loss, except for the connections with the extant literature about liberalism. Hopefully the connections with democracy suffice to make the topic of this chapter interesting to those who are ambivalent about ideology, and even to those who are opposed to liberalism. Regardless, I shall remind readers of the restricted focus and hence of the extent of the omitted considerations which would need to be examined in a thorough treatment of these topics by including qualifying remarks about the force of at least some of the arguments presented in this chapter.

Politics: Equality and autonomy

People have lots of different features and we stand in many sorts of relations to each other. Some people are hairy, some have blue eyes, some are philosophy professors; some people are strangers, others are neighbours, some are siblings, all are children etc, Which features and which relations, if any, are the proper topics on which to focus when thinking about politics? Ronald Dworkin suggests (and Will Kymlicka notably follows him in this) that equality is the fundamental relation between individuals, and hence the fundamental value, for political theories (e.g., Dworkin 1977, pp. 179–83; Kymlicka 2002, p. 3). There is an important sense in which all major contemporary political philosophies, regardless of their differences, are egalitarian. Their differences, however, point to an important theoretical and practical question. Suppose that we are committed to being political egalitarians. People are equal and unequal in myriad ways. My neighbour and I are male, hence equal in this respect. However, we are of different ages: unequal. He has hair on his head, whereas I don't: unequal. Both of us work in the field of education: equal. This listing exercise could go on for a long time, and it would concern just two people. Which are the relevant kinds of equality and inequality for politics? In the event that we can satisfactorily answer this question, we will still be faced with the challenge of designing institutions, laws and policies to do justice to the value of equality.

In a discussion of utilitarianism as a political philosophy, Kymlicka suggests that part of its appeal is its secular focus on humans (2002, pp. 11, 36). This suggests a way of getting at the kind of equality that matters for politics: we are all equally human, so all humans should matter equally from the perspective of the state and for those concerned to delimit the nature and bounds of political power. While the secular nature of this suggestion should be attractive, it is insufficient as it stands. The reason is that 'human' needs specification. This word is used in a variety of ways. Let's suppose that these are all acceptable connotations of 'human'. Not all of them imply that we are equal; hence they fail as interpretations of the egalitarian basis of contemporary political thought. Others deliver equality, but in a way irrelevant to morality and, consequently, to politics. I shall provide one example of each problem, then move on to a different sort of interpretation of equality and politics.

I am a professor of philosophy. It is common to speak of philosophy as a discipline that is part of 'the humanities'. Some universities even use 'humanities' as a formal designation for a certain cluster of topics of study. Philosophy and literature belong to this group, medicine and engineering do not. Does this cluster tell us anything about the politically relevant sense of 'human'? It is hard to see how it does: professors in the humanities study a diverse group of activities, achievements and kinds of thought. Not all politically relevant people contribute to, care about, or even understand the concerns of this group of studies. Not even close. For instance, I am a competent adult, so I am a central example of the sort of person who counts as politically relevant: I am a citizen capable of active participation in government. I am an expert in certain areas of philosophy, but not in most. Most people are not experts in any areas of philosophy. Nor do they necessarily care about them. My experience with people outside of philosophy is that attitudes are more likely to be indifference or hostility or condescension towards philosophy rather than to be interest in or sympathy towards these topics. It should be clear that the concerns and abilities that define this particular corner of the humanities are not equally shared by all adults. As for other sorts of concern that fall into the humanities: I have little expertise or care for many of them; some other people will be much the same, others will be baffled or hostile, and still others will be engaged, impassioned experts. Overall, it is implausible to think that this group of studies denotes something especially 'human' that sheds light on the egalitarian basis of politics. After all, the vast differences in the relations between people and the concerns of the humanities seem to amount to inequalities.

Let's turn away from the humanities and to another facet of human life: our shared biology. Whatever else we are, we humans are all members of the same species, *homo sapiens*. This is typically referred to as the 'human species', so it is reasonable to think that one central use of 'human' is as a name for a species. For what it's worth, I am inclined to think that this is, or should be, the fundamental interpretation of 'human'. Although the issue of just what it is for an individual to be a member of one species rather than another is a matter of on-going study, the generally accepted rough-and-ready idea is that individuals who are, under the appropriate conditions, capable of producing living, reproductively viable offspring are members of the same species while individuals who, under the same conditions, are not capable of this are not members of the same species. Simplifying greatly, since this kind of reproductive capacity depends on the possibility of sharing and recombining genes, we can say that members of the same species share a genome, whereas members of different species do not. From this biological perspective, all humans are equally human. But this notion of equality is morally and politically irrelevant. To think that our genome confers on us some sort of value is to fetishize our genes. This is particularly clear when we think of the deep similarities between the human genome and those of other species. Genetically, we are all composed of the same basic materials; the differences lie in the number and organization of these pieces. More importantly, it is not the genes themselves that really matter, but what they build – that is, the organisms and, crucially, the capacities that they construct. Humans are directly politically relevant and spruce trees are not, but the reason is not, in the first place, differences in our genes. It is differences in the kinds of lives and concerns we can have. Our genes are the more distal causes of these politically relevant differences, but they are not these differences themselves.

This line of thought points us away from our humanity and towards something more specific as the way to interpret the politically relevant sense of equality. People stand in a variety of relations to each other and to the state. We should not think that just one of these relations matters while the others do not. For instance, all people can be helped or harmed by the power of the state, and this matters when we design laws, institutions, policies, *etc.* However, some people have a feature that is of special importance with regard to their relations to the state. These people are capable of self-rule. Since political power is power to rule, the people who are capable of self-rule require special attention in considerations of the justification of political power. The reason is that state rule can, and probably will, interfere with self-rule for these people. This needs justification: under what conditions, if any, is this sort of public engagement with the *prima facie* legitimate jurisdiction of individuals morally permissible? Put more simply, when, if ever, should autonomous individuals think that the social collectives to which they belong have any legitimate say over how these individuals live their lives?

The political relevance of individual autonomy deserves more defence, so here are two *prima facie* arguments in support of using personal self-rule as a central way of interpreting the political commitment to equality. The first is a brief conceptual argument:

CA] Try to imagine a state made up completely of slaves. I mean 'completely' literally: every person who is a member of this state is denied self-rule. On its face, we cannot even imagine such a state. At least one person has to be free to rule, meaning that at least one person is not a slave. The ruler will have the psychological capacities for ruling a life (or else she will be replaced by someone else who has these capacities because she is literally incapable of ruling the state). Indeed, these capacities will be a central part of the reason that this person is the ruler, and hence free to rule her own life. However, others in the state will have these same capacities. The basic considerations of justice which we saw in Chapter 6 – treat equals equally and others unequally – demand (*prima facie,* at least) that these people have the same jurisdiction of self-rule as the leader. So, the very idea of political rule combined with the capacities that make this possible deliver at least the political relevance of autonomy and arguably its moral relevance too.

I mean this argument to be more suggestive than definitive. I have two related reasons for this. The first is that I am in general sceptical of the power of conceptual arguments. Perhaps I am wrong about what we can literally imagine, for instance. Second, whether a state can be made entirely of slaves strikes me as at least in part an empirical issue, yet I have no formal data to offer to support my assessment that such a state is impossible. My *a priori* assertion that this is impossible should be taken as provisional, not fully demonstrated.

The second argument for the political relevance of individual autonomy is a pragmatic one:

[PA] All actions pragmatically imply by their performance a *prima facie* right to such performance. By 'pragmatically imply' I mean that there is a claim to the legitimacy of the action made just by acting. The agent need not think of things in this way, and may even disavow any right to act as she does. Nevertheless, the mere fact that one acts involves a claim that this is, by some important standard, permissible. Now, consider Simon and Mark. Both are competent adults and hence, by both ordinary standards and those defended in Chapters 2 and 3, autonomous. Mark tries to exercise control over Simon's life. That is, Mark attempts various heteronomous actions regarding Simon. No special agreements about such control have previously been entered by Mark and Simon. Does Mark have a legitimate claim to authority over Simon's life? That is, does Mark have the right to exercise control over Simon regardless of what Simon thinks of this? This is implausible. For one thing, Simon has the ability to dictate the course of his life. For another, the consequences of present choices about his life will tend to impact him more than others. Because of this these consequences are likely to matter to him more than they matter to others, including Mark. So, since Simon is capable of living his life and since he has to live with it, so to speak, he has a very substantial claim to having ultimate authority over how his life will go. Moreover, even if Mark and Simon entered into arrangements about Mark having some sort of control over Simon, they would not erode this authority. We have already seen this line of thought in its most extreme form: selling oneself into slavery. The upshot is that Simon's authority over his life is greater than whatever claim Mark might have over Simon's life.

This is politically relevant for the following reason. The argument indicates that heteronomy needs autonomous endorsement in order for it to be legitimate. More specifically, for one autonomous agent to have a legitimate say over the life another autonomous agent, the second autonomous agent must somehow agree to the first agent's controlling role. But all political rule is heteronomy. It involves the authority of some people over others, and some of these others will be autonomous. In most contemporary states political rule involves the authority of state institutions over all members of the state, or practically all. This will bring with it indirect heteronomy – that is, indirect rather than direct control of some by others, for instance, of citizens by civil servants who run important state institutions. The present argument suggests that such control over autonomous agents requires the autonomous agreement of those agents in order to be legitimate.

Again, I mean this argument to be more suggestive than definitive. The premise about pragmatic implication of *prima facie* rights is offered on little more than an intuitive basis. Still, without this the argument for the political relevance of autonomy is even simpler. If attempts at heteronomy do not involve even an implicit claim to their legitimacy, then they offer nothing with which the authority of individuals over their own lives might conflict. Understood this way, since political power involves heteronomy, autonomy would be automatically politically relevant: autonomous people have authority over their lives while would-be political powers would have not even a *prima facie* claim to have any authority here.

These arguments about heteronomy and autonomy might seem, on the surface, to conflict with the discussion of paternalism in Chapter 6. I have just claimed that heteronomy needs autonomous endorsement in order for it to be legitimate, but in Chapter 6 I defended the possibility of justifiable paternalism, which seems to involve heteronomy without autonomous endorsement. There are a couple of reasons why there is not as much conflict here as there might appear. First, not all political rule is paternalistic. This is because it does not necessarily aim at the good of the lives of the people whose lives are interfered with. Justifiable public policy can be directly aimed at the good of subsets of a population even though everyone's abilities to rule their lives are affected. This is very clear when we consider policies aimed at addressing the good of clearly defined groups: women but not men, parents but not the childless, immigrants but not native citizens, *etc.*

The converse is also the case: not all paternalism involves heteronomy. I can aim at the good of another without or against that person's will without undermining or interfering in that person's capacities for or exercise of self-rule. For example, imagine that a parent has offered a young adult child a large amount of money to cover living expenses. The child rejects the offer: she wants to make her own way in the world, and she wants her parent to spend her own money on herself. Unbeknownst to the child, the parent puts the money in an account in the child's name to ensure that it is there should the child need or want it. This is paternalistic: it is for the good of the child and against the child's will. But it has no effect on the child's autonomy whatsoever – it neither undermines her capacities nor their exercise.

Still, some political power will be paternalistic, and in such cases the prior discussion applies. Instead of seeing this as in conflict with the present contention that heteronomy needs autonomous endorsement, let me suggest that justifiable state paternalism exemplifies one pole of the range of ways in which heteronomy can be suitably related to autonomy in order to be legitimate. The central part of the range involves more or less explicit endorsement of heteronomy by autonomy, and at one end there is the possibility of heteronomy that serves or respects citizens' autonomy without such endorsement. This exemplifies something of the spirit of the present line of thought without following it in letter. The notion of a range of ways in which state rule over citizens can be related to their autonomy will be important later in the chapter. Since I have already discussed paternalism, I shall put this issue aside and focus on non-paternalistic rule and the present claim that, since this involves heteronomy, it requires some sort of autonomous endorsement to be justifiable.

There is a feature of this line of thought about the justification of political authority that is worth noting, if only in passing. Most discussions of the justification of political power emphasize its coercive capabilities. For instance, consider the time of year during which you submit income tax reports. Whether or not we resent this practice, I take it that we all expect that there will be official forms of response in the event that we fail to submit our statements. It is reasonable to expect strongly worded letters from the civil servants who run the tax system, for instance. If we do not respond to these letters, then we can expect the police and judiciary to get involved, and for there to be court-imposed sequences of events and penalties. All of this is coercive. It might be legitimate, depending on a variety of things, but there can be no denying that this involves the coercion of citizens to comply with tax laws at least by reporting on their income and maybe also by paying money to the government. This calls out for justification, and, to generalize, it is not unreasonable to focus on state powers of coercion when addressing the legitimacy of political authority. However, such a focus is nevertheless unduly narrow. State power calls out for justification even when autonomous people are inclined to comply with it. We should understand why this is legitimate even if, for instance, the strongly worded letters are never written and the police are never deployed for reasons derived from taxation laws. All coercion involves heteronomy. This should be obvious upon reflection: to submit to force, or to its threat, is to 'allow' (in a certain sense) one to be controlled by another. But not all heteronomy involves coercion, or even its threat. I am inclined to think that political power necessarily involves heteronomy and only incidentally involves coercion. Hence to focus on heteronomy subsumes the more typical focal point while getting at the real nub of the issue.

All of this gives us a couple of reasons to take seriously the idea that we should interpret the political commitment to equality at least partly, but centrally, in terms of the autonomy of the individuals to be ruled. So, what are the implications of interpreting the foundations of political authority in terms of the capacities and rights to self-rule of the governed? This is a knotty question, but here are two suggestions.

First, it supports democracy as the general form of government that we should have. Here is a simple and direct argument linking autonomy with democracy via the heteronomy inherent in political power.

1 Political power necessarily involves heteronomy.

2 Some people are autonomous.

3 Heteronomy over autonomous people is legitimate only when these people autonomously authorize those others who would exercise control over them.

4 Democracy is the only form of government in which all autonomous citizens get to give political authority to those who would wield political power.

5 Democracy is the only form of government which can confer the required legitimacy to the heteronomy inherent to political power.

Once again, we should see this argument as more suggestive than final. Democracy comes in many forms, and it is reasonable to think that they do not do equally satisfactory jobs with regard to giving a voice to all autonomous citizens regarding the political authority of the government. Nevertheless, as a matter of definition, there is much to recommend this line of thought. Insofar as a form of government is designed in such a way to leave some autonomous agents who fall under its power out of the processes by which political power is conferred, that form of government falls short of the moral demands imposed by the nature of autonomy on heteronomy. Monarchy, tyranny, oligarchy, plutocracy, theocracy, *etc.* all fail by this standard.

The second thing that this line of thought implies is liberalism, to which I shall now turn in detail.

Autonomy and liberalism

Like all notions of political ideology – and perhaps like all of the other concepts that political philosophers discuss – just what 'liberalism' means is deeply contestable. Somehow liberalism involves a commitment to individual liberty as fundamental to just societies, but such a commitment has been articulated in importantly different ways – not to mention fought over – for centuries. Contemporary liberals arguably disagree just as much as they agree. Given all of this, let me suggest two tenets that are 'characteristic' (more on this word in a moment) of contemporary liberalism:

1   To be legitimate, political authority must derive – somehow – from the will of the governed.

2   The state should be neutral about how individuals choose to live their lives, within broad limits.

Let's call the first commitment the 'Authority' tenet and the second one the 'Neutrality' commitment. Why are these ideas merely 'characteristic' of contemporary liberalism, rather than definitive? For two interconnected reasons. First, not all contemporary liberals explicitly espouse both of these tenets. For example, Alan Ryan articulates classical and modern versions of liberalism in terms of freedom rather than these two commitments (1993, pp. 291–6). The

Neutrality commitment is particularly problematic. The issue, as we shall see, is whether the 'broad limits' within which states must be neutral are actually so narrow as to undermine the idea that the state really is neutral. Some critics of liberalism charge it with closet 'illiberalism' for precisely this worry: that the liberal state, rather than being neutral about how people live their lives, must privilege liberal ways of living over other ones. Conversely, some liberals argue that liberalism does not require such neutrality at all, despite the fact that this implies that state interference with people's lives would thereby be justified, which does not sound terribly liberal (e.g., Waldron 1987, p. 146). In between these options are liberals who are committed to state neutrality in some sense, while recognizing that there are legitimate limits to this. The challenges are to articulate the relevant senses of 'neutrality' and the broadest-yet-still-liberal limits.

Why should we be tempted by a political ideology characterized by the Authority and Neutrality commitments? My suggestion is that recognition of the value of personal autonomy makes these commitments rationally attractive. The Authority commitment consists merely in the deployment of the ideas about heteronomy and autonomy that have already been presented. The relevant 'governed' people, for the purposes of liberalism, are autonomous agents. Since political authority is the authority to rule others, it involves heteronomy. But, *prima facie* and *ceteris paribus*, if we value autonomy we should think that heteronomous control of autonomous agents needs endorsement by those autonomous agents for it to be legitimate. This applies to political authority just as much as it does to other kinds of heteronomy.

Less obviously, the Neutrality commitment is implied by the Authority tenet. Suppose that autonomous endorsement is needed for legitimate political power. This implies that such power cannot legitimately be used to promote some ways of life or understandings of the good over others, at least with regard to autonomous people. The reason is that doing so will involve attempts to control people's choices about how to live, perhaps even coercively. Whenever the state view of worthy ways of life conflicts with an autonomous individual's view, such controlling influence will lack the endorsement needed for it to be legitimate. It is reasonable to expect individuals to differ, perhaps greatly, about the nature of the good and the worthwhile ways to live lives. The state cannot hope to gain the endorsement of all affected citizens for some subset of these views. This means that, realistically, states cannot promote particular views of the good without infringing against the autonomy of some of their citizens. Hence, to live up to the value of autonomy, states should be neutral about the good and about the nature of lives worth living.

So much for why one might be attracted to a view defined by the Authority and Neutrality commitments. What sorts of views contrast with this characterization of liberalism? Contemporary liberal theorists tend neither to be radicals nor conservatives, and hence it is reasonable to place this sort of view between more and less conservative/radical alternatives. Liberals tend to see existing political arrangements as amenable to justification, albeit with the requisite liberal modifications, in terms compatible with the Authority and Neutrality commitments. Conservatives, broadly speaking, reject both of these commitments, at least insofar as they are committed to seeing political achievements as products of a slow process accomplished across generations. One implication of this is that, for at least some conservatives, political legitimacy is the result of processes of past political achievements, not of the endorsement of institutions by the presently governed. Another implication is the rejection of the Neutrality tenet: insofar as past processes have worked out desirable ways of living, they can be legitimately promoted by the state regardless of the will of present citizens.

On the more radical side (among other views), we find libertarians. Again speaking broadly, in one sense libertarians endorse the Authority and Neutrality commitments, and in another they reject them. Rather than autonomy, libertarians interpret these tenets in terms of freedom, and more specifically in terms of negative freedom – that is, freedom from constraints. So, libertarians certainly think that political authority is illegitimate if, in a sense, not rooted in the endorsement of the governed. But, strictly speaking, it is not out of a sense of the value of the autonomy of the governed that this is taken to be the case. Instead, libertarians (to put it crudely) hold that free choice is the root of obligation. As for the Neutrality requirement: insofar as the state must respect liberty, then libertarians endorse state neutrality regarding how to live. However, libertarians tend to be more sceptical than liberals about present political arrangements, and hence tend to think that present state institutions require modification, even rejection, because of a failure to respect freedom properly, regardless of the will of citizens. This amounts to a preference for certain state attitudes towards the way to live, rather than for state neutrality.

Although I will not belabour the point, liberalism stands in a different relation to democracy than conservatism and libertarianism. Again, this is implied by the relative degree of commitment to the Authority and Neutrality tenets. In principle, liberals have an expansive (but not unlimited) view of at least the potential range of topics for democratic discussion and decision. Likewise, in principle both conservatives and libertarians have a more restricted view. Since, at least to some extent, they reject the Authority tenet, conservatives tend to think that certain political arrangements should not be open to critical scrutiny or for democratic endorsement or rejection. Libertarians tend to see certain political arrangements as objectionable infringements of liberty even if arrived at through democratic processes. This brief characterization cannot help but obscure nuances with regard to both similarities and differences among these three positions. Still, it is worth emphasizing the relatively tighter link between democracy and liberalism compared to these other ideologies.

Suppose that we accept, at least provisionally, this characterization of liberalism in terms of the autonomy-based interpretations of the Authority and Neutrality commitments. It is reasonable to think that, at the same time, autonomy raises challenges, both practical and theoretical, for liberalism in the spirit of these very commitments. I shall conclude this section by briefly presenting these challenges. Fuller characterizations will be provided in subsequent sections along with consideration of prospects for liberal, autonomy-based responses to them.

The Authority commitment generates theoretical and, perhaps especially, practical challenges concerning the sorts of relations that are needed between political power and the will of governed for political authority really to be conferred. It is one thing to say that, in principle, political power is legitimate if and only if it suitably derives from the autonomy of the citizens subject to it. It is quite another thing to specify conditions and procedures which ensure that, in practice, legitimacy is indeed either conferred or withheld. Let's call this the *Authority Problem*.

The Neutrality commitment likewise generates problems that are both practical and theoretical in nature. Liberal states, it seems, somehow need to emphasize the importance of the autonomy of citizens within them. This is, on its face, implied by the Authority commitment. But not all ways of living are liberal. Some views of the good life downplay or altogether reject the importance of the capacities of self-rule of at least some of their members. Some social groups which are found in otherwise liberal societies have evolved around such views. Illiberal attitudes can take a variety of forms. It might be critical reflection on how to live that is rejected. It might, instead or as well, be practical participation in collective governance that is rejected, rather than critical reflection. Either way, the effect is that at least some views of how to live reject the role given to individual autonomy by liberalism. Liberal societies hence face a problem. On one hand, they can take a hands-off, putatively liberal stance towards these groups, as seems to be required by the Neutrality commitment. But this implies that particular autonomous individuals will be shut out of the processes by which political legitimacy is conferred on the state, thereby violating the Authority commitment. On the other hand, liberal states can interfere with these groups to help to ensure that all autonomous citizens have some sort of protected access to political participation, in apparent accordance with the Authority tenet. However, such measures appear to involve privileging liberal views of the nature of the good life over non-liberal ones, in violation of the Neutrality commitment.

The neutrality problem: Liberalism and pluralism about how to live

Broadly speaking, liberals have developed three approaches to the Neutrality problem. As already mentioned, some deny that it is a problem. Others acknowledge that it is a problem and try to answer it. Of particular note, although I will not discuss them in detail, are attempts by autonomy theorists to answer this problem explicitly in terms of autonomy – for example, Friedman 2003, chs. 8–9, Christman 2009, chs. 10, and Colburn 2010, chs 4–5. Still others try to distinguish specific ways in which liberal states must be neutral if they are to remain liberal and in other senses of 'neutral' which are not required of liberal states. For instance, some theorists distinguish between the *effects* of state policies and actions on one hand and, on the other hand, the terms of *justification* of these policies and of state authority in general (e.g., Rawls 1988, sec. 5; Kymlicka 1989, pp. 883–4; De Marneffe 1990, pp. 253–5; Mason 1990, p. 434). Although some people reject both senses (e.g., Raz 1986, pp. 114–24), others think that a specific sense of neutrality can be isolated as the one to which liberal states must be committed. John Rawls, for instance, argues that neutrality of effect is impossible – illiberal practices must be rejected – but that neutrality of justification is possible and desirable. Given that Rawls' position is so influential, it is worth a little attention in order to assess the prospects of strategies based on the distinction between justification and effects.

In his later work, Rawls distinguishes 'political' liberalism from 'comprehensive' liberalism. The latter notion gets its name from the related idea of a 'comprehensive doctrine', which is, to put it roughly, a substantial view of what the good life consists in. Comprehensive liberalism builds its liberalism on such a comprehensive doctrine. For instance, the argument presented above that generates liberalism out of thoughts about the value of individual autonomy is a comprehensive version of liberalism, by Rawls' standards. By contrast, political liberalism is a more specialized notion. It is a political notion designed for citizens in broadly liberal and complex states. Such states have an important characteristic: their citizens will inevitably have a plurality of comprehensive doctrines, at least some of which are incommensurable. These citizens have to live together, which means that they must, in some way, discuss and design state policies. Given that they do not share comprehensive doctrines, the terms that are used to justify particular policies cannot be drawn from such views. The reason is as much practical as it is theoretical: grounding public discussion in non-shared comprehensive doctrines is doomed to fail because citizens will not agree with which each other about the reasons why something should or should not be done. For instance, atheists will reject all attempts to ground state policies in religious ideas. What is needed is a new understanding of the nature of public discourse in such a pluralistic society. This is what political liberalism aims to offer. It is composed of a political, rather than a metaphysical, notion of citizens as free, equal and 'reasonable', in the particular sense of being committed to aiming at some degree of consensus about the reasons that support state activities. The implication of this view of political discourse is that the terms of justification of state actions, policies, *etc.* must be neutral regarding views of how to live one's life. Citizens, whether or not they are state officials, who reject such neutrality in political discourse are not 'reasonable' in Rawls' sense, as they are not committed to aiming at the right sort of consensus. Rawls presents his view in much more detail than I can discuss, of course, and there has been much discussion about it to which I cannot hope to do justice. Nevertheless, here are three lines of thought that give us reason to be suspicious of it, and of the use of the distinction between justifications and effects of state policies, as a response to the Neutrality problem. First, it seems to fail, if not by its own standards then by standards very close to them. Political liberals hope to make space, both theoretical and practical, for the justification of state policies in terms independent from comprehensive doctrines. But the very notion of citizens as free, equal and reasonable (in the special political sense presented above) appears to draw on at least egalitarian views of what is desirable in public life, thereby rejecting non-egalitarian ones at the very outset. Insisting that people think of citizens as politically reasonable – that is, as committed to aiming at neutral justifications of state actions – appears even more specifically substantially liberal. This is just to say that this insistence looks comprehensively liberal. While it may be the case that the particular justifications that are offered using this political conception of citizens and public discourse are independent of comprehensive doctrines, the political conception of justification itself is arguably not neutral. Justificatory neutrality perhaps can only be had within specifically circumscribed discursive spheres. Depending on just what is shut out of these discursive domains, we might have great doubts about the neutrality and hence the liberalism of this political approach.

The first line of objection is fairly specific to Rawls' political liberalism. The other two sources of worry apply more widely. Here is the second issue: this sort of approach is only as good as the distinction between neutrality of effect and neutrality of justification is. This is a practical distinction to make, but at its base it is not a rigid one, and hence it cannot really do the work of differentiating varieties of neutrality to which liberals might or might not be committed. The reason that this is a distinction with some practical merit should be clear: there are ways in which state institutions bring about effects that are independent of the terms in which these institutions and their activities are justified. For instance, a taxation policy reasonably justified in terms of fairness might have the short-term effect of reducing the quality of life of members of geographically specific ethno-cultural communities and the longer-term effect of eroding the integrity of these communities as their members move away in search of better-paying work. Hence it can make sense to pay separate attention to effects and to the terms of justification of policies. However, this practical point does not imply that justification and effect are completely divorced from each other. Offering public justifications of policies is itself a way of bringing about certain effects and even of promoting certain values. Such promotion can be implicit – that is, it need not be deliberate. It can be a side-effect of the perfectly justifiable and desirable practice of states engaging citizens in public decisions by making state justifications public. However, this implies that the effect/justification distinction is not so rigid as to be suitable to function as the foundation of an account of liberal neutrality in terms of the latter but not the former.

Here is an example to put some flesh on these rather abstract bones. Suppose that a religious community, located in a complex, broadly liberal state, has a tradition of preventing its members from learning about other ways of life. The Amish in North America are an example of such a community. Alternatively, imagine a religious community, located in a complex, broadly liberal state, that disallows its members from owning property, and that takes steps to prevent its members from thinking that they should be allowed to own property. Hutterites in Canada have such a tradition. Now consider public state justifications of any policy whatsoever. The policies themselves need not be about either property or diverse ways of living. However, suppose that the justifications deploy these ideas. That is, imagine state justifications, of any policy whatsoever, that deploy ideas about citizens legitimately owning property or legitimately being exposed to diverse ways of living. We should expect that such justifications will not be welcome to the members of these religious communities, or at least not to their satisfied members. The reason will be that these justifications, regardless of the policies in question, will themselves seem to promote these ideas. If the members of these communities are exposed to these justifications, this can be expected to have effects on them which are independent of the aims of the policy in question. Crucially, it is implausible to think that the members of these communities will receive these justifications as neutral with regard to desirability of ways of living. On the contrary, these communities can reasonably be expected to see themselves as not just geographically but culturally and politically isolated precisely because they would reject these terms of justification.

Finally, we should ask why we should be political liberals in the bare sense of being committed to discursive solutions to diversity about comprehensive doctrines. Uniformity of ways of living, or at least reduced plurality, can be accomplished through forceful use of law. Why should we seek political engagement and discursive consensus rather than enforced compliance with a particular way of living? This might seem like an unrealistic thing to consider in the eyes of readers in peaceful, twenty-first century multicultural states, but it is worth remembering the extent to which both the law and forceful means of enforcing it have actually been deployed to make people live in particular ways. Such measures might be expensive, but that is not much of a moral objection to this strategy, and I expect that most readers think that there is something more deeply morally objectionable to such an approach to diversity of ideas about how to live. A political solution is morally desirable, it seems to me, precisely because we recognize moral demands placed upon us by the nature of both ourselves and other people. In the political domain, the demands imposed by our autonomy are particularly important. In a nutshell, trying to cooperate through mutually respectful conversation seems, on its face, more respectful of our respective capacities and rights to direct the course of our own lives than the use of law and force to accomplish some sort of social unity. The demands grounded in our autonomy are not the only relevant consideration here, of course. For instance, insofar as the measures that might be taken to force compliance bring suffering with them, we have reasons rooted in considerations of well-being to seek more peaceful methods of living together. Nevertheless, the autonomy of many citizens provides moral support for seeking means of living together that involve some sort of sharing of rule, at least through opportunities to participate in discussion of public policy. This line of thought, however, amounts to the offering of a metaphysical justification of liberalism –it grounds the desirability of liberalism in a view of the nature and consequent importance of competent adults. This is precisely the sort of thing that Rawls tries to avoid with his political conception of liberalism, so it is a line of thought which is at least not straight-forwardly available as a defence of political liberalism, and it might not be plausibly available at all.

So, let's put both specifically political liberalism and the distinction between justifications and effects of state actions behind us. What are the prospects for finding an autonomy-oriented resolution of the Neutrality problem? To answer this, let's (finally) use the conceptual resources developed earlier in this book. The first issue to address is the kind of autonomy (if either) that has primary relevance to the Neutrality problem. Just what is it about autonomy that the state should be neutral about? The general answer is that the state should respect the capacity and hence the rights of people to lead their own lives. This should be taken in quite an active sense: citizens should be allowed *to direct* the courses of their lives, should they wish to. This suggests that it is autonomy of personhood that matters for the Neutrality problem, not, at least primarily, autonomy of choice. Whereas we can autonomously choose about anything whatsoever, autonomy of personhood is exercised more specifically over ourselves. In principle anything can fall within the domain of autonomy of personhood, but to do so it must be somehow integrated into someone's life.

The second question to ask is just how autonomy of persons matters when thinking of state neutrality. Should it be a constraint on state policies, or should it be a goal of them, or both? Alternatively, should a liberal state be concerned merely that its citizens have the capacity to direct their lives (in the ways discussed in Chapter 3), or should it take steps to encourage and perhaps even to ensure that its citizens exercise these capacities?

To get a grip on this question, consider once again an illiberal ethno-cultural group within a liberal state. Should this state take steps to encourage, and maybe even to ensure, that the members of this group actually exercise self-rule over their lives? That they have access to, find out about and use information about the various facets of their very nature to determine the course of their lives? Or, alternatively, should a liberal state have a more constrained approach, ensuring that these people are not prevented from exercising their autonomy if they so choose it, but refraining from encouraging them to do so? It seems to me that, other things being equal, a liberal state should be committed to the second option but not the first. The first approach – treating autonomy of persons as a goal of state activities – requires a great deal of state intervention in the activities of the social groups that fall within its jurisdiction. Recall that, by the standards of the account offered in Chapter 3, the capacities that constitute autonomy of persons include those for egocentric autonomy of choice, self-understanding and self-shaping. That it, to have the capacity to be an autonomous person one must have the capacity to use knowledge about oneself, including one's place in the wider world, to make decisions about both how it is worthwhile to live one's life and how to accomplish this for oneself. It is one thing for a state to ensure that the citizens who have these capacities are neither prevented from exercising them nor have these capacities undermined by state activities. This might require more than the steps needed to ensure negative liberty with regard to these capacities, but then again it might not. But to encourage and, especially, to ensure the exercise of these capacities would require much more state interference in both the lives of its citizens and the groups with which some of them identify.

To get a sense of the necessary measures, consider individuals alone. The state would have to design education and testing measures not just for general understanding of the world but for the more specific matter of self-understanding and self-shaping. Testing would be particularly intrusive. How could we assess whether someone had exercised their capacities for self-understanding and self-shaping without doing extensive individual interviewing? After all, each test would need to be tailored to the individual, to get a sense of (a) their understanding not just of their generic nature but of their specific tastes and opportunities, and (b) not just the steps they had taken to achieve their goals but also the steps that they could take. Besides being intrusive, such steps would be practically impossible. When we add the complexities due to the organization of people within a state into religious and/or ethno-cultural groups, we get another degree of state interference in the lives of its citizens if the state is to treat autonomy of persons as a goal. So, on both theoretical and practical grounds, we have reason to think that liberal states should treat autonomy of persons as a constraint, not as a goal.

It is worth emphasizing that this line of thought holds for the relationships of the state to citizens who already have the capacity for autonomy. We are currently considering autonomy and state-to-citizen relations, and from this perspective there is no particular reason for the state to aim at the development of the capacities for autonomy, either of choice or of personhood. This implies that, from this particular perspective, it is acceptable for illiberal groups to take steps to prevent these capacities from developing in their members. After all, these people would not be currently autonomous, so there could be no autonomy-based reason for the state to object to such measures. For instance, Kymlicka discusses the American court case *Yoder v. Wisconsin* (2002, p. 238). This concerned the desires of a Wisconsin Amish community to be able to withdraw their children from public schooling before they turned 16. The reason is that the members of this religious community want to limit both their members' understanding of the world beyond the bounds of their particular community and their abilities to deal with it. The American Supreme Court upheld the legal right of the Amish to do this, and, from the perspective of the significance of autonomy and state-to-citizen relations, this is an appropriate judgement. Since, presumably, children under 16 are more non-autonomous than autonomous, there can be no autonomy-based constraint on the state that licenses the use of legal measures to keep them in school. Bluntly put, they have no autonomy to do such constraining. Perhaps if it were legitimate for the state to aim at autonomy of persons as a goal a different legal decision would be warranted. But this is illegitimate, given the considerations so far examined, and so we have autonomy-based reason to think that the Court made the correct decision.

Generally speaking, to value autonomy of persons as a constraint, the state must (a) refrain from doing things that undermine the relevant capacities in its citizens, and (b) allow citizens the opportunity to exercise these capacities, at least with regard to things that fall within the state's jurisdiction, should they wish to do so. Living up to the demands of the first requirement is easier than living up to the second. For instance, consider laws which prohibit the wearing of religious symbols in such places as state-run schools and offices. This is acceptable by the standards of (a), but not, by the standards of autonomy, of (b). This sort of policy interferes with citizens' exercise of their capacities to direct the courses of their lives. Unless there is a compelling non-autonomy-based reason to interfere in this way, such laws are unacceptable by liberal standards.

Although this way of representing the political significance of the capacities for personal self-rule calls for the state to allow people to have a lot of elbow-room to run their lives, and hence to work out various ways in which to live, it is not as 'hands-off' a view as it might seem. The word 'allow' in the second clause is misleading: the state can be quite active in living up to this demand. When, for instance, illiberal ethno-cultural groups interfere with the activities of autonomous members of these communities against their will, the state has autonomy-based reason to step in and to interfere, in order to ensure precisely that these people get to exercise their capacities for self-rule. To allow these groups to interfere with the exercise of their members' autonomy would be to fail to allow some citizens the requisite opportunity to be autonomous persons, in the active sense. Official state actions, and maybe even policy, would violate a constraint imposed by the autonomy of its citizens by taking such a hands-off approach. We can put this in another way: since responsibility can be shared, the state can share in responsibility for the undermining of the capacities for and/or exercise of autonomy of personhood by allowing others to undermine these capacities. We need not understand 'constraint' to imply inactivity in order to value autonomy of persons as a constraint.

The bottom line is that, from the perspective of state-to-citizen relations, the Neutrality problem is solved so long as the state respects its citizens' capacities for autonomy of personhood as a constraint on its activities and policies. If this were the only perspective to take on the political relevance of autonomy, this would be the end of the story. However, things are more complex because we must also consider citizen-to-state relations. This is the domain of the Authority problem.

The authority problem: Liberalism and political legitimacy

The Authority problem is the challenge of designing measures by which political authority is given to rulers by the governed. This is required because all political rule involves heteronomy, and such control over autonomous agents requires authorization by those agents in order for it to be legitimate. Instead of the effects of state decisions and policies on citizens, this problem concerns the measures that must be taken for the governed to provide a morally legitimate foundation for those who would govern. The remarks about democracy presented above should put in mind some familiar procedures by which citizens confer authority on their leaders – that is, by voting in suitably arranged elections. This is a reasonable procedure to have in mind, and it is one to which I will return. However, when we start to think about political power, it should be clear that the business of government involves more decisions than can be settled through democratic elections. Instead of delivering political legitimacy directly to particular policies by discussing and voting on them, the citizens of large, complex liberal democracies vote for governments, and then the elected representatives go on to make decisions for the citizens without much formal consultation with them, perhaps for years. There can be multiple levels of government, giving citizens multiple opportunities to vote as time goes by. For instance, I live under the jurisdiction of municipal, provincial and federal governments, so there are three levels of democratic process in which I regularly participate as a citizen. But of course, many decisions are made by these various levels of government in which I play no active role, despite being, as an autonomous person, a vital part of the foundation of the legitimacy of such decision-making power. The general question, then, is how to understand political legitimacy that must derive from the autonomous will of the governed but which cannot, often, be actually solicited from the governed.

Liberal political philosophy has wrestled with this question for a long time. 'Voluntarists' insist on the importance of actual consent from citizens in order for political power to be legitimate. Jeremy Waldron offers Jean-Jacques Rousseau as a famous example because, in *The Social Contract,* Rousseau insists on the expression of the will of the people (1987, p. 140). Opposed to voluntarists are various theorists who, for both practical and theoretical purposes, offer the hypothetical consent of the governed as crucial to political legitimacy. Immanuel Kant and, most famously, Rawls fall into this tradition (Waldron 1987, pp. 141–2; Rawls 1971). For lack of a better name, I shall call this the 'hypotheticalist' option. How should we choose between 'voluntarism' and 'hypotheticalism'?

The distinction between valuing autonomy as a goal and valuing it as a constraint is useful here. Voluntarists emphasize the actual exercise of autonomy. This is just to say that the voluntarist option thinks that political legitimacy is conferred by processes that value autonomy as a goal. By contrast, hypotheticalists value autonomy as a constraint. That is, they do so insofar as they are concerned with autonomy. Much hypotheticalist work is put in terms of rationality, not autonomy. Hypotheticalists argue that, once we specify certain hypothetical conditions of discussion and agreement, certain things either would not be chosen by rational agents, should not be chosen by them,˙or, most strongly, could not be chosen by rational agents. These ideas constrain what sorts of state decisions can be made by rulers on behalf of the governed. The reason is that to choose these options would not be what these agents would choose for themselves if they were rational. Their presumed rationality is the foundation of the legitimacy of state decisions.

Very briefly, here is a specific example of hypotheticalism. In *A Theory of Justice*, Rawls argues against using utilitarian principles to determine the basic structure of society (1971, pp. 11–33). The reason for this is explained by considering a hypothetical situation in which citizens make a social contract – the 'Original Position'. The people operating in the Original Position are rational agents, but not much else. We are to imagine these people as standing behind a 'Veil of Ignorance' – they do not know specific facts about the real-world social positions that they will occupy after they leave the Original Position. They do not know whether they are male or female, rich or poor, sick or healthy, *etc.* These people are to choose principles to structure their social co-existence in ways that cannot privilege particular ways of living. Utilitarianism is rejected because it can require the subjection of some to serve the happiness of others. Rawls thinks that this is an unacceptable risk to the people in the Original Position. The Veil of Ignorance implies that these people don't know whether they would be part of the exploited group or of the happy one. Instead, rational agents choosing under these conditions would choose other principles to constitute the basic structure of society. By Rawls' standards, it is unjust for society to have a different basic structure, as it is inconsistent with what rational agents would choose in a fair contract-making situation. Since the actual citizens of actual countries are presumed to be rational, to respect the results of such a hypothetical choosing procedure is to respect the rational nature of actual citizens regardless of what they want or try to choose in actuality. If we assume that an unjust social structure cannot be legitimately chosen through democratic processes, Rawls' hypotheticalism delivers an account of political authority: it is delivered by the hypothetical consent of rational agents, not by the actual consent of actual agents.

Which way of valuing autonomy should we prefer when considering the Authority Problem? Let's agree that political power in the absence of both actual and hypothetical consent is illegitimate. After all, citizens in such a state are 'unfree' in a very important sense. On the other side, citizens who participate in a wide variety of opportunities for public discourse and decision-making are pretty clearly optimally placed to pass authority to their rulers via this participation. In between is the hypotheticalist option: citizens in a state in which they do not exercise their autonomy politically but which is so arranged as to be in accordance with what they would hypothetically consent to under certain important conditions. We should see this as second best, meaning that voluntarism is the best option overall. As Waldron puts it, 'Though a social order not legitimated by actual consent may be unfree, that unfreedom can be mitigated by our recognition that it is at least possible to imagine people giving it their consent.' (1987, pp. 140–1)

This can be made clearer when we consider the possible clash between a policy or institution justified on hypotheticalist grounds and the actual will of the citizens. Suppose that citizens reject such a policy. Which sort of political authority should we prefer – that conferred by actual consent or that conferred by hypothetical consent? The particular details will matter, at least to the confidence with which we make our judgement, but *ceteris paribus* it should be clear that the expressed autonomy of the citizens should matter more than their merely hypothetical and contrary endorsement. After all, these people have to live under the power of this policy or institution, and, by normal standards, they are capable of running their own lives. To prefer the rejected option to the chosen one would involve a significant degree of interference in the lives of autonomous people.

As a rough analogy, consider a medical example: Pierre is an autonomous person who rarely but occasionally exercises his autonomy. He ends up needing extensive, time-consuming medical care, but his capacity to control his life is still intact. His doctors respect him as an autonomous person, making medical decisions for him but doing nothing to undermine his capacity to do so for himself and preserving the option for him to do just this. The doctors try to imagine the treatment options that Pierre would make for himself, with some success. Occasionally, as with his life in general, Pierre intervenes in his medical treatment and participates in medical decision-making. When he does so, he sometimes chooses options that the doctors would not have chosen for him. Which should we privilege – the decisions that Pierre actually makes, or the different ones that his doctors would make for him if they choose for him? It should be clear, it seems to me, that Pierre has authority over his body, even when he chooses sub-optimal choices for himself, so his actual decisions matter more than the ones that the doctors imagine he would hypothetically make under other circumstances. Likewise, citizens have authority over the body-politic, and hence we should privilege their actual decisions over the ones we imagine they would make under important conditions. We should be voluntarists about both medical and political interpersonal authority, and we should see hypotheticalism as a legitimate but second-best option.

Moreover, suppose that Pierre's doctors are considering treatments that would undermine Pierre's autonomy. In Chapter 5 I argued that, in precisely this sort of case, it must be insisted that the patient autonomously participate in decision-making. This is implied even by valuing autonomy as a constraint – this is exactly one of the ways in which patient autonomy constrains what doctors can do. Now consider political decisions. These can regularly be autonomy-limiting, with regard at least to the options for citizen self-rule, and even regarding the very capacities for this. In such cases we have good reason to insist that citizens actually endorse the autonomy-limiting decisions. This holds, ideally, even for decisions that merely raise the risk of undermining citizen autonomy.

We should not, however, be voluntarists about any and every possible topic of political discussion and decision. Perhaps ironically, this is ruled out if the state is going to value autonomy as a goal. Suppose that we are going to try to preserve and encourage the exercise of individual autonomy about political decisions. A state that allows citizens to undermine this through these very decisions is actually failing to value autonomy as a goal. There must be official limits in place to preserve the possibility of autonomous citizens being free, equal decision-makers. This is the kind of thing that, for example, the Canadian Charter of Rights does – it ensures at least the possibility of a voluntarist basis for political authority in Canada by ensuring that Canadian citizens cannot vote to undermine the free, equal participation in public affairs of some subset of Canadians.

For political power to be legitimate, states should value autonomy as a goal; to value it as a constraint is a second-best option that invites both practical and theoretical problems. Now let's get more specific about just what notion of autonomy is relevant here. What sort of autonomy should be expressed through the democratic processes that confer political authority? Should a state value autonomy of choice as a goal, or autonomy of persons? The short answer is that a state should value autonomy of choice of its citizens as a goal in order to ensure the legitimacy of its political authority. The reason is that the issues that require the attention and decisions of citizens are ones about the actions and nature of the state. These topics need not have much to do with the lives of particular citizens; many of them in actuality will not, at least from the perspective of these citizens themselves. This is just to say that, strictly speaking, the issues that require the attention and decisions of citizens will be, strictly speaking and in the first place, allocentrically represented. Autonomy of persons, by contrast, involves topics that are of direct relevance to how people conceive of and direct their lives, and hence these topics will be egocentrically represented. Moreover, the state has no obvious interest in ensuring that citizens pursue self-knowledge and then use this knowledge to shape the course of their lives. Since these are the capacities constitutive of autonomous personhood, it should be clear that to answer the Authority problem in terms of autonomy of persons would be to divert the state's attention and resources to things that are not obviously its legitimate concern.

To value the autonomy of choice of citizens as a goal, with regard to issues concerning the activities and nature of the state, means that the state must promote and preserve the exercise of individual choice about these topics. This will involve more than giving citizens adequate opportunity to participate in discursive and democratic processes concerning (directly or indirectly) these topics. To live up to the demands of valuing citizen autonomy of choice as a goal, the state must also educate its citizens about both their democratic opportunities and the topics about which they can, and arguably should, be making decisions. More generally, the state must have pro-democracy policies – that is, it cannot legitimately take steps to limit or even prevent citizen chances to exercise their choice about issues of public import. Ideally, in a practical sense, the state should have policies that encourage participating in political processes. For a rather rigid example consider Australia, which has a law that requires citizens to vote in elections. While we might have concerns about the legitimacy of the authority conferred by votes cast without any understanding of the relevant issues, which is all but ensured by such a law, as a measure for connecting political authority to the expressed will of citizens such a law is the best that we can do.

One thing must be emphasized about the state's prospects for ensuring that its citizens make autonomous choices about matters of public import: the state can only put citizens in a good place to make such decisions, through educational and democratic institutions. The state cannot, literally, ensure that its citizens make autonomous choices because the state cannot directly bring about the psychological integration that is the hallmark of autonomous choice. So, even in a state that is maximally concerned to preserve and promote the exercise of the capacities that constitute autonomy of choice, some citizens will make non-autonomous choices about the relevant issues. Perhaps they will be controlled by others; perhaps they will be under no control whatsoever, making contributions to public discursive and democratic processes as whims take them. This is unavoidable; so be it. A state that gives its citizens ample chances to learn and think about issues of public significance and to make choices about how these issues will be handled by public institutions has lived up to the demands placed upon it by individual autonomy.

I said earlier that to answer the Authority problem in terms of autonomous choosing is the short answer. It is fundamentally correct, but it is not, however, complete. First, many issues of public import will dovetail with the concerns of particular citizens. This might even be why they are of public significance at all. For these issues and these people, state efforts at ensuring some understanding of these issues and some degree of autonomy of choice regarding how to handle them will amount to promotion of egocentric rather than allocentric autonomy of choice. But egocentric autonomy of choice is at the core of autonomy of personhood, which means that these state efforts will, as a matter of fact if not of intention, promote autonomy of persons and not just autonomy of choices.

The second line of thought to be added cuts more deeply. I have spoken of the legitimacy of state power, but, in general, legitimacy comes in degrees. The legitimacy of political power stems from individual autonomy, and this also comes in degrees. Both choices and persons can be more or less autonomous. Presumably, the authority of state power is more legitimate when it stems from more rather than less autonomous choices. Choices are more rather than less autonomous when they arise from the perspective of an individual life plan, rather than being detached from such a perspective. Recall Nicholas and Olivia in the food court: in the original case, Nicholas is an autonomous person but chooses the fries non-autonomously. Olivia is a non-autonomous person who acts autonomously regarding the French fries. Suppose that we change the case: Olivia chooses autonomously without being an autonomous person, whereas Nicholas' choice about the fries stems from his overall understanding of himself and from the plans about how to live that have been developed on the basis of this understanding. Now both choices about the French fries are autonomous, but, it seems to me, Nicholas' choice is more autonomous because he exercises relatively more control over it. This is because he has formed a life plan, whereas Olivia has not, and the place of this particular decision in his plan or his life involves greater psychological integration than we find in the case of Olivia. If this is correct, then a lesson follows for political authority: the legitimacy of political power is greater when it derives from more rather than less autonomous choices made by the people subject to this power. More autonomous choice are likely – but not necessarily – to be made when people form and act upon life plans, which means that the choices stem from and fit within a psychological background comprised of self-knowledge and self-shaping. In a nutshell, the highest possible degree of legitimacy of political authority is most likely to be delivered by citizens who are autonomous persons, rather than non-autonomous persons who nevertheless make autonomous choices about matters of public significance. More subtly, the more citizens are autonomous persons, the more likely it is that the choices they make about issues of public significance will be more rather than less autonomous, and hence the legitimacy conferred to the state by their choices will tend to be deeper than that conferred by less autonomous people.

So, despite it being the case that legitimate political power is most directly delivered when citizens make autonomous choices regarding the state and its policies, it is both likely and desirable, from the perspective of the Authority problem, that state measures promote autonomy of persons, not just autonomy of choices. Is this practically feasible? It is hard to see how it could be. Consideration of the difficulties found here helps to explain why hypotheticalists focus on rational persons. To be an autonomous person, one must cultivate an understanding of oneself and then form some plan about how to live. This will vary from person to person insofar as tastes and abilities vary between people. It is impossible for the state to take into account such interpersonal variety. However, our nature is not entirely interpersonally variable. The focus on rationality is a practical shortcut forced by the practical difficulties of living up to the interpersonally particular demands of autonomy of personhood. This should be a sobering lesson regarding autonomy of persons: even if the deepest political legitimacy is delivered by choices made by autonomous persons, interpersonal variety of life plans cannot be reasonably expected to be promoted by the state. As a consequence, the state can only be reasonably expected to promote autonomy of choices regarding issues of public import, not autonomy of personhood.

That said, there might still be a role for considerations of rationality in a liberal account of political authority. Suppose that a state is committed to fostering autonomy of choices in its citizens, at least with regard to topics of public significance. How should the state act? In particular, just what sorts and amounts of information should it convey to its citizens? Rationality can act as a guide to answering this question, albeit just a rough one. A suggestive guide is found in Canadian medical law. In *Reibl V. Hughes*, the Supreme Court of Canada ruled on the standard of disclosure of information from physicians to patients. They decided that physicians must be held to a rational person standard, which means that physicians must tell patients what rational persons would want to know about their conditions and options in their particular circumstances. If we extrapolate from this, on the basis that the right to participate in the body-politic is at least somewhat like the right to control what happens to one's body, then the lesson is that the state should inform citizens about matters of public significance to the degree that rational persons would want to be informed about these matters in their particular circumstances. The qualification 'in their particular circumstances' cannot be met by the state, given that such informing must be done for large groups of people rather than for citizens on a one-by-one basis. So, if we abstract from the details of particular people's lives, it seems that there is some reason to think that the state should inform people about matters of public import, for the purposes of getting those people to think about and decide regarding the same issues, to the extent that rational persons would want to know about these issues. To the extent that this is a practical guide, rationality can function as part of an answer to the Authority problem, not as part of the very foundation of political authority but instead as an important part of the yardstick for measuring the adequacy of measures taken by the state to include its citizens in discursive and democratic processes.

Conclusion: Pessimism and optimism

Liberalism's foundation of individual autonomy gave rise to two challenges, the Neutrality problem and the Authority problem. To answer the Neutrality problem, liberal states must design themselves so as to value autonomy of persons as a constraint on their activities. To answer the Authority problem, liberal states must, other things being equal, design themselves especially to value the exercise of their citizens' capacities to make autonomous choices regarding topics of public significance, and maybe also to promote the exercise of their citizens' capacities for acquiring self-knowledge and for designing their lives in the light of this knowledge, at least with regard to issues that are clearly of import with regard to the concerns of the state. It seems that the means of answering the Authority problem risk requiring liberals to relinquish the Neutrality commitment. On the other side, the worry is that to respect neutrality liberals must design states that fail by the standards of the Authority commitment. There are pessimistic and optimistic ways to read these results. I am inclined to be optimistic, but I shall let readers judge the prospects for themselves.

I shall start with the pessimistic interpretation. According to this view, things are as bad as they seem. On one hand, the state should respect the autonomy of personhood of its citizens as a constraint on its activities. On the other hand, states should value their citizens' autonomy of choice regarding public issues as a goal of state policies. This combination is incoherent. It amounts to an inconsistent directive to the state: you must and cannot promote individual autonomy. If this is implied by liberalism, then this ideology is incoherent and must be rethought or given up altogether.

However, maybe these results regarding autonomy indicate not a deep and insurmountable structural incoherence in liberalism but instead an unavoidable practical challenge. In practice, liberal societies must constantly strive to approach an ideal of respect for individual autonomy. At the same time, they must retract from the danger of infringing against it. Given the nuances of the workings of personal self-rule, state policies that live up to the demands of autonomy in one respect can violate it in another respect. The practical challenge is to develop increasingly better ways of doing the former while avoiding the pitfalls that involve the latter. Particular societies will face particular challenges and opportunities with regard to the autonomy of their citizens. Perhaps a perfectly liberal society is impossible, when seen from the complex perspective of the value of the capacities for self-rule of citizens. Nonetheless, awareness of both the ideal and of the dangers that lie in this territory paves the way for more rather than less liberal societies.

Reading guide

Political philosophy is a vast and deep domain. Worthy introductions include *A Companion to Contemporary Political Philosophy*, edited by Robert E. Goodin and Philip Pettit (Blackwell Publishers Ltd, 1993) and Will Kymlicka's *Contemporary Political Philosophy: An Introduction, 2nd Edition* (Oxford University Press, 2002). Kymlicka's book is particularly good for the light shone on the egalitarian foundation of contemporary political theories and for bringing out concerns relevant to individual autonomy.

For the vagaries and essentially contestable nature of the concepts that comprise contemporary thought about democracy, I recommend Anthony H. Birch's *The Concepts and Theories of Modern Democracy* (Routledge, 1993).

Ronald Dworkin's thought about equality as the foundation of modern political theories is found in *Taking Rights Seriously* (Duckworth, 1977).

Much has been written explicitly on liberalism. Some useful examples: 1) Ronald Dworkin, 'Liberalism' in S. Hampshire (edited), *Public and Private Morality* (Cambridge University Press, 1978), pp. 113–43; 2); Jeremy Waldron, 'Theoretical foundations of liberalism', *The Philosophical Quarterly*, Vol. 37, No. 147 (April

1987), 127–50; 3); Alan Ryan, 'Liberalism,' in Goodin and Pettit (edited), *A Companion to Contemporary Political Philosophy* (Blackwell Publishers Ltd, 1993), pp. 291–311. The papers, chapters and books on more specific topics noted elsewhere in this guide also contain statements about the nature of liberalism.

Readers interested in ideologies other than liberalism will have to do most of the work themselves. The relevant chapters in Kymlicka (2002) are a good place to start. For a writer working from a non-liberal starting point, I have used Anthony Quinton, 'Conservativism', in Goodin and Pettit (eds), *A Companion to Contemporary Political Philosophy* (Blackwell Publishers Ltd, 1993), pp. 244–68.

The Neutrality problem features prominently in contemporary liberal theorizing. Besides the works on liberalism already noted, see 1) Joseph Raz, *The Morality of Freedom* (Oxford University Press, 1986), pp. 114–24; 2); Will Kymlicka, 'Liberal individualism and liberal neutrality', *Ethics*, Vol. 99, No, 4, 883–905; 3); Peter de Marneffe, 'Liberalism, liberty, and neutrality', *Philosophy & Public Affairs*, Vol. 19, No. 3 (Summer 1990), 253–74; 4); Andrew D. Mason, 'Liberalism and state neutrality', *The Philosophical Quarterly*, Vol. 40, No. 161 (October 1990), 433–52. For discussions in work explicitly about individual autonomy, see 5) Marilyn Friedman, *Autonomy, Gender, Politics* (Oxford University Press, 2003), chs 8–9; 6) John Christman, *The Politics of Persons: Individual Autonomy and Socio-historical Selves* (Cambridge University Press, 2009), ch. 10; 7) Ben Colburn, *Autonomy and Liberalism* (Routledge, 2010), chs 4–5.

John Rawls has written much that is important and influential, and hence there is a vast literature that either builds on or criticizes his positions. Much that is already noted here discusses Rawls; beyond this, readers are left to themselves to find commentators. Primary texts relevant to the present discussion include 1) *A Theory of Justice* (Harvard University Press, 1971); 2) 'The priority of right and ideas of the good', *Philosophy & Public Affairs*, Vol. 17, No. 4 (Autumn 1988), 251–76; 3) *Political Liberalism* (Columbia University Press, 1993); 4) 'The idea of public reason revisited', *University of Chicago Law Review*, Vol. 64, No. 3 (Summer 1997), 765–807.

Waldron offers the following works by Rousseau and Kant as relevant to what I have called the Authority Problem: 1) Jean-Jacques

Rousseau, *The Social Contract and Discourses* (J.M. Dent, 1973), especially III, Chs XI–XV; 2) Immanuel Kant, 'On the common saying' This may be true in theory but it does not apply in practice"' in H. Reiss (edited.), *Kant's Political Writings* (Cambridge University Press, 1970), pp. 61–92, especially p. 77.

The now-classic source for thought about the moral irrelevance of species membership is Peter Singer's, *Animal Liberation* (Harper Collins, 1975). For discussions of the nature of species see 1) Marc Ereshefsky (edited.), *The Units of Evolution* (MIT University Press, 1991); 2) Robert A. Wilson (edited.), *Species: New Interdisciplinary Essays* (MIT University Press, 1999).

The Canadian Charter of Rights and Freedoms is available online: http://publications.gc.ca/collections/Collection/CH37-4-3-2002E.pdf

Reibl V. Hughes [1980] 2 S.C.R. 880 is summarized in an accessible manner at http://en.wikipedia.org/wiki/Reibl_v._Hughes. This entry contains a link to the complete text.

CHAPTER EIGHT

Is autonomy omnirelevant?

Gerald Dworkin ends an article about autonomy in political philosophy with this observation: 'So we end our tour having seen how autonomy enters into every part of contemporary political philosophy theory from the theory of justice to the theory of value.' (1993, p. 364) We should not think of political philosophy as hermetically sealed. Far from it: the concerns of political philosophers are, ultimately, the concerns of anyone interested in the nature of the good for humans. Given that political thought is shot through with concerns about individual rule, and given the relations between political philosophy and evaluative concerns more generally, we should ask about the extent of the evaluative significance of autonomy. For just what issues and in just what ways does autonomy matter? Is personal self-rule *always* relevant when we are faced with questions about what is good for us and how we ought to act? Is autonomy, to coin a term, 'omnirelevant'?

I cannot definitively answer this question. The reason should be obvious: this is not the place to look at all possible ethical questions and to assess whether or not individual autonomy is relevant to answering them. I am not convinced that this is a task that can be accomplished anywhere, never mind here. Instead, I can make only a partial and tentative case for the omnirelevance of autonomy. Part of the job has already been done: the last couple of chapters have looked at the significance of autonomy in interpersonal relations. More specifically, they are about autonomy in relations between an agent and other persons *qua* persons. In the present chapter, I shall supplement this with two other perspectives on interpersonal relations. First I shall look at autonomy in interpersonal relations that are mediated by information found in the world at large. Then I shall look at autonomy in interpersonal relations with special focus on agents as embodied. Don't worry; these rather abstract characterizations will be tied to very familiar ethical questions. Given the brevity of these discussions, readers are reminded that I shall be presenting autonomy-based assessments and that comprehensive treatments of these issues would require attention to other values. To begin, however, the notion of 'omnirelevance' needs some attention.

Two sorts of omnirelevance

There are two things that we might mean when we speak of some value being relevant everywhere. First, we might strictly mean that this value is relevant to all particular moral issues. Less strictly, we might mean that it is widely relevant without being, literally, applicable to all issues. For lack of a better term, let's give the name 'issue-omnirelevance' to this first notion. The idea is that, for whatever moral issue you consider, the value in question is relevant to it. That is, it is not beside the point to examine the significance of this value for this issue, and it might even be decisive to do so. Examples of failures of issue-omnirelevance – of issue-irrelevance instead – are not difficult to imagine. For instance, it is difficult to see what could be gained by adding considerations of beauty to contemporary debate about abortion. For a more clearly moral value, take honesty and, well, moral issues that seem not to turn on considerations of honesty, such as worries about the moral significance of ecosystems, or whether and, if so, under what conditions it is justifiable to harm non-combatants in the course of a war. Given that specific values can clearly be irrelevant with regard to particular issues, in the sense of being beside the point when examining them, a claim that a particular value is issue-omnirelevant is in need of significant defence.

Second, we might mean that the value in question is relevant to understanding what is meant when we speak of seemingly distinct values. In this sense, the first value is at least partly constitutive of the other values. Let's call this 'constitutive omnirelevance'. The idea is that, in order to understand the nature and significance of some particular value, you must understand the nature and significance of at least one other particular value because the second value, at least partly, makes up the nature of the first one.

As already stated, I cannot make a definitive case for either sense of omnirelevance with regard to autonomy. I cannot survey comprehensively the role of autonomy in all moral issues or all seemingly distinct moral values. With regard to issue-omnirelevance, the best that I can do is to add some thoughts about the role of autonomy in understanding moral issues that I have not yet examined. As for constitutive omnirelevance, I shall present some considerations that suggest that personal self-rule is part of the nature of values that appear to be distinct from autonomy.

Constitutive omnirelevance is particularly worth a second thought. In the last few chapters I have spoken, at least in passing, of possible conflict between autonomy and other values. But if autonomy is constitutively omnirelevant, then I must have spoken in error, or at least too quickly. If, for example, autonomy is at least partly constitutive of the value of happiness, then they cannot, strictly speaking, conflict. Or, if they do conflict, the nature of such conflict must be demonstrated rather than being taken to be conceptually possible from the outset. In short, the impression that autonomy can conflict with other values will have to be earned and explained rather than being taken for granted. Even though all of this requires some detailed discussion, the idea that we should question whether values which appear to conflict *really* conflict is one worth considering regardless of the arguments to come in this chapter.

So much for the conceptual outlines; let's get to the details.

Advertising as a model for autonomy and information-mediated interpersonal relations

We all know that the early twenty-first century world differs from that of the late twentieth century. There is one such difference that I have in mind: the proliferation of information and of devices for accessing such information. I do not mean that the world has more objects, or more types of objects, than it used to; it probably does, but not, to my eye, to any particularly striking extent. I mean instead that we interact with more representations – more words and pictures, both moving and still – than we used to. These representations engage our minds – that is, after all, their point – and since autonomy is a psychological phenomenon, it is worth asking whether the oceans of information in which we find ourselves might pose problems and/or opportunities from the perspective of individual self-rule. What sorts of effects, if any, do the representations we encounter all the time have on autonomy of choice? On the acquisition of self-knowledge? On our capacities for designing lives for ourselves? On pursuit of such lives?

Two things can be said at the outset. First, it is reasonable to expect there to be various effects on the psychology of autonomy from our wealth of information. Some will be good, in the sense of supporting and even encouraging self-rule. Some will be undesirable. Blanket assessments of the effects of these representations on individual autonomy are too simplistic to be taken seriously. Second, we can reasonably expect clusters within this variety: some technologies will tend to be autonomy-supporting, some autonomy-undermining; some representational media will undermine self-knowledge, some will foster it. Some technologies and forms of information could be good in one way and bad in another. Getting a grip on all of these details will require the combined efforts of multiple disciplines, not a portion of a chapter in a single book by one philosopher.

All of that said, some suggestions can be made. Long before the current information age, philosophers were wondering about the implications for autonomy – as well as other ethical issues – posed by the widespread presence of a particular family of representations in our environment: advertisements. Advertising is interesting when thinking about autonomy for various reasons. It is overtly persuasive, meaning that it is aimed at having effects on our thought and, particularly, our behaviour. Bluntly put, commercial advertising is for separating us from our money. It comes in a great number of forms – we hear advertisements on the radio, see them on television, have them pop-up on our computers, flip by them in magazines and newspapers, drive by them on billboards, benches and bus-stops, stare at them in cabs, buses, trains, *etc*. We encounter some advertisements willingly, others quite unwillingly, and sometimes – perhaps quite often – we barely notice that we are encountering them at all. This plethora of forms of representation and of interaction with them makes advertising a good place to look to get a sense of some possible effects that living in a sea of information has on our prospects for being autonomous. So, let's look at advertising and autonomy as a way of dipping our toes into the vast pool of ethical issues offered by our information-rich world. I shall restrict my focus to commercial advertising, rather than, for example, political or public-service advertisements. The reason is that commercial advertisements form the overwhelmingly vast majority of the advertisements to which we are exposed, and since they are so clearly aimed at persuading us to do something, their links to self-rule are particularly worth thinking about.

For our purposes, we can divide the moral concerns that philosophers have had about commercial advertising into two groups: those explicitly having to do with autonomy, and those overtly having to do with other issues. For just one example of the first kind of concern, in the 1980s Robert Arrington and Roger Crisp had a debate about autonomy and advertising. Crisp argued that advertising was problematic for individual autonomy, whereas Arrington defended it. For an example of the second kind of discussion, there has been a simultaneous discussion among theorists who turn away from autonomy and towards the ideological aspects of advertising. Barbara Phillips and John Waide are good examples. Phillips turns explicitly from the individual to the collective effects of advertising and its corresponding capitalist ideology. Waide claims to be turning away from autonomy altogether – he has been persuaded by Arrington on this front (1987, p. 73). Instead, he wants to look at the kinds of people the ideology of consumerism produces.

It is a shame, for a variety of reasons, that these discussions have tended to be divorced from each other. On one hand, the autonomy theorists have been inclined to focus on autonomous choice. This is reasonable, from a practical point of view: advertising is aimed at getting us to make purchasing choices that are favourable to the people paying for the advertising. But, as we have seen throughout this book, choice is not all that there is to autonomy. Moreover, our own lives provide us with some reason not to worry about advertisements compromising our autonomous control of our choices. The paradigmatic example of the manipulation of autonomous choice by advertisers is subliminal advertising. Attention was once often given to the well-known (but probably apocryphal) example of movie-theatre patrons who flock to the concession stand for ice cream after being exposed to a subliminal suggestion on the movie screen. Now attention is paid to subconscious priming using images which are not consciously noticed by viewers but which nevertheless are detected by our sensory apparatus. However, whether subconscious priming has effects on our thought and behaviour is deeply contested; regardless, the purported effects seem to be very minor. Moreover, there is the phenomenology of being a consumer: it typically does not feel like one is being jerked around and parted from one's money like a puppet. Although far from being conclusive on its own, this point is usefully combined with more objective considerations. In the movie theatre case, the patrons are exposed to the advertisement once, and the subsequent action is described as happening in the very near future, during the same visit to the theatre. But this does not seem to be what happens to people who are exposed, for example, to many television commercials during an evening at home. Typically, they do not get up and go to the mall to buy something they have just seen in an advertisement. To suggest that the supposed push-button effects of subliminal advertising have much wider application should strike us as a cartoonish representation of our own experience with modern commercial media.

On the other side, it can be difficult to see what the ideological problem is supposed to be. Suppose that a person does not feel uncomfortable with their exposure to consumerist values, or with their character, or with their participation in capitalist culture. Discussion of commercial advertising because of its links to these things is likely to leave this person unmoved. Moreover, if the purported problems do not show up in consumer choice or conduct, as the disavowal of interest in autonomous choice suggests, then the debate at least seems to be about aspects of the world around us that just do not make a difference to our thought and behaviour. Why should we care about this?

I think both strands of thought about advertising are on to something. There are problems posed by advertising to individual self-rule, but this is best put in terms of autonomy of persons, not autonomy of choices. Since the other strand of debate concerns the kinds of persons advertising produces, it can, despite what the authors think, be put in terms of autonomy after all, so long as we focus on autonomy of persons.

Recall that autonomy of persons has three components: autonomy of choice about oneself, self-knowledge and self-shaping. Strictly speaking, self-shaping relies on both autonomy of choices and self-knowledge. Consequently self-shaping is at the heart of autonomy of personhood. I shall focus of self-shaping to suggest the problems that commercial advertising poses to autonomy.

In Chapter 3 I argued that, to shape ourselves, we must reflect upon and choose with regard to two things:

A our lower-order mental states, especially first-order ones, in the light of our values, and

B our values themselves.

I used the work of Charles Taylor on strong evaluation to explain (A) and (B). To be performed well, strong evaluation requires conceptual richness, especially regarding the background of standards of significance against which we can judge the structure of our own lives. This conceptual richness requires language. Since our concepts and language skills are rooted in the social context(s) in which we live and develop, and since we define ourselves through the deployment of these concepts and skills in strong evaluation, out of sheer self-interest we have a reason to be concerned with the moral tone of the context(s) in which we live. Moreover, strong evaluation requires openness to possible ways of living. Without this, we are poorly positioned to think about our values. These two components of strong evaluation – openness to possible ways of living and conceptual richness – are threatened by the amount of commercial advertising to which we are exposed.

(1) Being open to a background of values and possibilities from which to choose and evaluate our own life requires (at least) three things: (a) knowledge of such values and possibilities, (b) a willingness on the part of the agent to examine both her own life and this background of values and possibilities and (c) the mere existence of such horizons of ways of being. Exposure to large amounts of commercial advertising, however, compromises all three of these things.

First, for people to know of, for example, ways of living other than their own, they have to be exposed to them in some way. One way this happens is through exposure to representations of these ways of living (as opposed to actual instantiations of them).

However, advertising works against this, in two ways. Particular advertisements encourage homogeneity. Since the purpose of an advertisement is to sell a product, the advertisement works if it can get large groups of people to act in one way. The more people actually act in essentially one way, we can reasonably speculate (but not more than that at this point) that the easier the advertiser's job becomes. Once some homogeneity is brought about, advertisers have a background of similarity to appeal to. Instead of portraying ways of living significantly different from those being lived by the people exposed to advertising, advertisers will be rewarded by tapping into what already appeals to people living these sorts of life.

An obvious rejoinder to this aspect of the problem of knowledge is to point to the competition between advertisements. Particular advertisements encourage homogeneity, but various advertisements are selling different products, and hence are providing consumers with a variety of models of ways of living. Competition leads to exposure to variety; competition will naturally lead to the spread of the sort of information that fosters strong evaluation. This answer has some point, but we have reason to think that its application is very limited. The sorts of models of ways of living people are exposed to through advertising are best seen a part of just one over-arching way of living.

Turning from particular advertisements to advertising as a whole reveals the reinforcement of a deeper sort of homogeneity. Barbara Phillips argues that advertising as a whole is a powerful institution that instals and reinforces the values of capitalism (Phillips 1997, p. 109). As such, it works against exposure to non-capitalist and non-consumerist values and ways of living. But human history has been characterized by many sorts of non-consumerist societies: various forms of socialist, agricultural and hunter-gatherer ways of living come to mind very quickly. While these ways of living may not be viable candidates for twenty-first century westerners to take up completely, it is reasonable to think that we can still learn from them. These ways of living involve values that many people might find enriching if they knew about them. Advertising, as an institution devoted to the strengthening of one way of living, works against having knowledge of other ways of living.

In a similar vein, John Waide characterizes advertising as embodying an ideology. Waide argues that associative advertising encourages people to think that they are what they own (Waide,

1987, p. 75). With this message comes suppression (not necessarily conscious or deliberate) of ideas which suggest that we can form our identities in ways that do not involve the market.

Second, commercial advertising also works against the willingness of people to examine their lives against a rich background of values and possibilities. Insofar as commercial advertising is an institution devoted to perpetuating one consumerist way of being (Phillips 1997) or inculcating an ideology that encourages us to form our identities through consumption of goods available through markets (Waide 1987), it addresses and shapes our desires fairly directly. Part of the ideology of advertising is the notion, so deeply embedded that it is hard for us to articulate, that whenever we want something or feel some dissatisfaction, the market can satisfy our desires. Even more deeply, the effect of nearly constant exposure to commercial advertising is the spread of the idea that we should want the things that the market can provide. The institution of advertising embodies a normative standard that is very powerful. Exposure to this standard erodes willingness to resist it.

Waide usefully defends and develops these ideas. He discusses what we can call 'internal' and 'external' effects of advertising on the will. This is the closest Waide comes to discussing autonomy of persons. The external influence on the will to explore oneself and alternative ways of being comes from pressure from other people. The ideology of advertising embodies a standard of being by which we can measure ourselves and others. When someone deviates – when one does not own the right things, or tries to define oneself in ways that do not turn on consumption – one invites response from people who have embraced the norm offered by advertising. Waide calls this sneer group pressure (Waide 1987, p. 76); its effect is to penalize people who stray.

More deeply, Waide notes that constant exposure to the ideology of commercial advertising influences our self-perception (Waide 1987, p. 76); this is an internal effect. We can come to see ourselves as defined as consumers (as opposed to thinkers, builders, community members – choose your own alternative), and this can further incline us to desire as consumers, and to look askance on the possibility of defining ourselves in other ways. This is, perhaps, acceptable if it is the result of a process of strong evaluation. If, however, it stands in the way of the exercise of autonomy of personhood, then it is a moral problem.

Phillips makes the same point in terms of values. According to Phillips, 'Advertising, as the mouthpiece for capitalism, presents values and assumptions that color consumers' perceptions of reality.' (Phillips 1997, p. 112) There are two reasonable inferences we can make from this point. One is that of the value of capitalism itself – it is presented as a way of living which embodies or presents a route to the good. Second, it is reasonable to think that our values can influence our desires. Combining these ideas leads to the possibility that inculcating the ideas and practices of capitalism is self-perpetuating. This can work against the willingness of people to consider ways of life that are different, perhaps incommensurably so. Yet if we are to shape our identities and the course of our lives, we have to perform this sort of strong evaluation.

Waide gathers concerns about knowledge of ways of living and willingness to reflect on one's life into one line of thought. Associative advertising, according to Waide, leads one to seek market solutions to desires/interests which can really only be satisfied in non-market ways (Waide 1987, pp. 73–4). Associative advertising works by linking products with deep needs or desires, such as for friendship, self-esteem, and the like. These are non-market goods because they cannot be directly bought or sold. Attaining these non-market goods probably involves developing skills and character traits that also cannot be bought or sold (Waide 1987, p. 75). For instance, developing friendships involves developing the traits required to be close to others. These include compassion and trustworthiness, among others. Developing self-esteem might well involve developing the skills required to undertake meaningful projects. These traits and skills take work to acquire. The ideology of advertising works against the development of these skills and traits by encouraging us to spend our time and resources buying things, but non-market goods and skills cannot be bought. The points about knowledge and willingness to examine oneself and others in the light of that knowledge are specific but very important versions of the skills and traits Waide is discussing.

Third, not only does advertising compromise both the knowledge of ways of living and the willingness to pursue and use this knowledge, it also compromises the existence of the objects of such knowledge. This point is an implication of the previous two. Advertising is a powerful tool for the spread of a certain ideology. This ideology brings with it values including a particular conception of the human good – (something like) you are better off if you buy things. As we have seen, the current extent of commercial advertising poses a threat to one's ability to think of alternatives to this ideology. But taking up a way of living requires being exposed to it, so far as I can tell. Moreover, incorporating aspects of one way of living into a life previously structured by a different set of values takes effort. Since advertising works against such exposure and effort, it presents an obstacle to the living of the sorts of life incommensurate with capitalism or consumerism. The recent history of the world suggests that capitalism is a very powerful idea. Its existence, along with the use of advertising to reinforce and spread its values, poses a very powerful threat to non-capitalist ways of living. Not only does advertising limit epistemic access to the horizons of significance emphasized by Taylor; it also impoverishes them. The homogenization of the world under the influence of capitalism and its primary tool, advertising, relegates some ways of life to history books. This is appropriate for some ways of living, but not for all. (a), (b) and (c) are significant on their own, but they are especially problematic when one phenomenon accomplishes them all together, as advertising does.

(2) The seeds of the exposition of the manner in which advertising threatens linguistically rooted conceptual richness necessary for autonomy of persons have already been sown, so I will discuss this very briefly. First, in the process of threatening the existence of the ways of living which constitute the background against which examination of a life takes place, advertising might be reducing the number of things we have to think about. At the very least, it makes such phenomena harder to think about. In other words, either advertising directly impoverishes our conceptual horizons, or it practically does so by making certain ideas harder to think about. Either way, advertising is a threat to strong evaluation via its influence on the concepts needed for such an endeavour.

Second, let's return to Waide. Among the non-market goods which advertising co-opts but actually threatens is friendship. This can be broadened to include mere fellow-feeling, or even the general sense of community or togetherness. Commercial advertising threatens these ways of being together by encouraging us to spend our time and money buying things rather than investing them in the development of the skills and character traits necessary for these sorts of relationship. Language is one of the skills threatened in the process. We learn language from other people, we develop our linguistic skills in dialogue with others, we acquire and refine concepts in such dialogue, and we articulate our senses of ourselves and the rest of the world in the process. This latter articulation benefits from the acquisition of new ways of seeing ourselves and the world in complex, attentive conversation. If advertising works against the development of the sorts of relationships in which such conversation takes place, then advertising makes it much more difficult to acquire and refine concepts. It also makes it much more difficult to put concepts to use in articulation of our views of ourselves and the world. Instead of enriching our lives, which is the superficial message of capitalism, advertising poses a direct threat to the conceptual resources necessary for the process of strong evaluation and hence threatens our capacities to shape our lives.

So much for autonomy and advertising; briefly, let's consider whether these considerations apply to other aspects of our information-rich environment. Advertising threatens autonomy of persons by undermining our capacity to shape our lives. It does this in a variety of ways, but at base the threat is that our opportunities and ability to think about how we wish to live will be diminished by the volume of commercial advertising to which we are exposed. This is a threat posed in principle by any sort of representation; whether it is a realistic or clear and present threat will depend on the details of the contexts in which one finds oneself. However, this threat can, also in principle, be alleviated through representations – that is, they can support and even increase our opportunities and capacity to think about how we would like to live. A diet rich in a variety of kinds of information is conducive to being able to exercise greater control rather than less over one's identity. Depending both on one's taste and on the content of these representations, this might even prompt more extensive self-shaping. Since the details matter, nothing more specific can be said about autonomy within the twenty-first century ocean of information. It should be clear, however, that it is a mistake to think that our informational context is ethically innocuous.

This medium-length look at advertising and the exceedingly brief considerations of other encounters with information adds a plank to the view that autonomy is issue-omnirelevant. It also makes a minor contribution to the idea that it is constitutively omnirelevant. The literature about advertising had developed a tendency to separate ideology from autonomy. One of the lessons of the discussion of advertising is that this is a false dichotomy. The moral relevance of ideology, at least with regard to advertising, is interwoven with that of autonomy of personhood. Arguably we cannot understand either value, when considering advertising, without paying attention to the other.

With an eye on both sorts of omnirelevance, let's turn to a different type of issue.

Autonomy, embodiment and abortion

Much of my discussion of the value of autonomy in the past few chapters has drawn on medical ethics. This has been very useful. At the same time, something is conspicuously absent. When we are patients, as virtually all of us will be at some time, we have some sort of bodily concern that we must entrust to others, in part, for care. My prior discussions of autonomy and medical ethics have taken no particular note of our embodiment, although it has come up in passing. This topic is worth more attention. What can be said about interpersonal relations mediated by our bodies?

As with informationally mediated relations, this is too vast a question to be answered thoroughly in this brief section. Nevertheless, I think that important suggestions can be made even in this brief context. My strategy shall be twofold. First, I shall draw attention to the significance of a general feature of our embodiment within interpersonal contexts. Second, I shall show this feature at work with regard to a particular moral issue: the question of the moral permissibility of abortion.

When we think about human bodies in interpersonal contexts, one general thing should be clear: we stand in different relations to our own bodies than we do to the bodies of others. Others' bodies are, it seems to me, primarily potential resources to us. My body is a potential resource of many kinds to other people. It could be food – cannibals use human bodies as resources of this kind. It could be the physical material for making something. Human skin is useful in the same way that the skins of other animals are. The same goes for fat, which can be used, infamously, to make candles and soap, for example. Less grotesquely, my body can be used to make other people. Depending on how I die, I hope that something like this happens to my organs – I hope that they are used to reconstruct other people whose own organs have in one way or another failed them. My body could be an energy source. It could be burned for heat, for instance. More subtly and more infamously, it could be used for work. It is, in fact: my employer and students use me this way, with my consent, which requires that my body be in particular places at specific times and, more locally, which requires that I use my body to do such things as speak. Others' bodies have been used less agreeably for work, by making them into slaves. My body can serve others as a source of pleasure. Sexual pleasure is the most obvious kind, but we can add other kinds. Bodies are a famous source of aesthetic pleasure, and this is not necessarily sexual, although the two are often intertwined. Pleasure can be taken in the use of my body as, primarily, a different sort of resource. Cannibals might not only be nourished by human flesh, they might also be pleased by it. This pleasure, and others like it, can have intellectual dimensions. I'm not sure that there has ever been one, but the idea of a cannibalistic gourmand is not incoherent. With enough time and imagination we could, no doubt, enumerate other ways in which our bodies are resources to each other, but enough has been said to make the point clear.

One might quibble with this view of others' bodies. Surely we see some people as embodied and yet simultaneously not necessarily as potential resources. Consider our relations to our loved ones. It might be thought that there is something wrong with seeing these people in terms of resources. Yet we might also be conscious of properties of their bodies. Put aside my earlier invocation of sexual and aesthetic resources. We might, instead, be attuned to Deborah's hair as part of what makes her *her*, the individual for which one cares. There is Daein's smile, Robert's long arms, and so on, all seen and responded to as parts of individuals, not as things to be used. Fair enough, but this does not undermine the general view of others' bodies as potential resources. The present view should not be confused with the more contentious view that other people are primarily resources for each other. The present point is specifically about others' bodies. Perhaps the bodies of others are not necessarily *primarily* potential resources to us. Still, the general view of bodies as resources is not contestable. Even those individuals with whom we have particular relations stand as potential resources to us, as do we to them. Think of organ transplants between blood relatives as an example: the mother who donates a kidney to a child does not thereby cease to stand in an interpersonal relation to that child, including to that child as embodied, but her body has clearly functioned as a medical resource to the child.

Our relations to resources, including potential resources, are aptly thought of in terms of property, including property rights. To put it crudely, to have a legitimate claim to a resource is to have a property right. To acquire such a claim is to acquire such a right, and to infringe against such a claim is to violate someone else's right. After all, property rights are (whatever else they might be) rights to use something as we see fit, within certain limits (such as refraining from harming others through such use). For something to be fit for use is just what it is for something to be a resource, however. Moreover, to have a legitimate claim to something is at least part of what it is to have a right to that thing. So, insofar as bodies are resources, they are apt for discussion in terms of property and property rights.

All of this holds for our relations to the bodies of other people. Our relations to our own bodies are different. Let there be no mistake: our own bodies do present us with resources. The example of organ transplantation makes this particularly clear. We can dispossess ourselves of some of our parts, which is one of the very important things that we do with property. We can make use of substitute parts for ones that have gone missing or that have started to malfunction due to disease or injury. This is, in central ways, the same thing that we do with the parts of automobiles, which are clearly property. Consequently, the vocabulary that is used to discuss the ethics of organ transplantation uses terms that can be used for exchanges of other kinds of property: for example, donation, markets, sales, harvesting. With enough effort, we can imagine and describe other ways in which our bodies are our resources, and hence in which it is appropriate to think of them as our property. However, our own bodies are not only our resources. They are us, at least in part. Recall my use of Diana Tietjen Meyers' five-fold taxonomy of aspects of selves in Chapter 3. One of these is the embodied self. I am inclined to think that we should take this seriously and literally: among the various ways in which we are ourselves, one is by being embodied, or, to speak more simply, by being bodies. For example, my fingers are not merely resources for me, conceived of as a self distinct from them, to use to accomplish things. They are part of me. When I use them to do things, it is me that is directly doing the things that they do. This is different from the way I use mere resources to do things. When I use a knife or a pencil or a hammer or a laptop, my experience is of me using something distinct from me to, for example, cut a mango. But when I use my fingers to eat the mango, I do not experience them as distinct from me. If you do not share this relation to your fingers, think about your relation to other body parts – for example, your eyes, your tongue. If you share this relation with none of your body parts, then you stand in a very different relation to your body than the one I enjoy with mine. However, I take my case to be typical, not special, given what I see around me. Crucially, I take it that our relation to our bodies as parts of ourselves is typically a more important relationship than our relation to our bodies as resources.

The conceptual framework of property rights that suits bodies when we think of them, legitimately, as resources does not fit bodies when we see them as components of selves. To own property is for, let's say, a person to own something that is, in principle, distinct from that person. But intra-self relations, as between a self as a whole and the embodied self that is a part of it, are different. It is difficult to pin down the nature of this relationship exactly. On one hand it seems like identity: I just am my body, in some way. But the qualification 'in some way' works against seeing the relation as, strictly, identity. The reason is that there are, arguably, properties that bodies have that are not properties of selves. When two things have different properties, they are not identical to each other, although they might stand in other, very intimate relations. For instance, bodies have mass; does it make sense to speak of selves having mass? Is this implied by taking talk of 'embodied selves' seriously? I am not sure. Short of identity, other possibilities are part-whole relations and realization relations. Perhaps our bodies are parts of us, and thereby not distinct. Perhaps we stand to our bodies in the same relation that Michelangelo's *David* stands to the piece of marble that realizes its form. Thankfully we do not need to pin down the precise nature of self-body relations for present purposes. All that is required is the idea we are our bodies in a more intimate way than we are related to the things that are our mere property.

If we accept this, then there are two possible reactions that we might have. On one hand, we might think that this implies that, conceived of as parts of selves, we cannot have distinct sorts of rights over our bodies. This would derive from an assumption that property rights are the only sorts of rights there are. On this assumption, we can only have property rights regarding our bodies. This general assumption, however, is unwarranted. It certainly is not part of the way in which people normally speak of rights. Rights to, as examples, privacy or life are not naturally taken to be special kinds of property rights. A special case must be made for seeing them in this way, and I know of no such case. This leaves the other possibility: to think that we can and do have rights over our bodies as parts of our selves, rights which are not property rights. We have property rights to our bodies as well, but this does not exhaust the nature of the sorts of legitimate claim we have over our bodies. We have other sorts of claim that constitute our general authority over our selves, and this non-property sort of right that we have over our bodies derives from these. For lack of a better term, let's call these 'self-rights'. According to this line of thought, we can have, and arguably do have, self-rights over our bodies as well as property rights.

Suppose that the value of autonomy is construed in terms of rights. Are these self-rights or property rights, or rights of some other kind? I see no reason to think that one category exhausts the rights that come with the capacities for autonomy. However, insofar as autonomy is self-rule, we should see self-rights as particularly important to the value of autonomy. If autonomy gives one authority over anything, it is over oneself, whatever might be meant by 'self'. To my eye, it is reasonable to construe such authority in terms of rights, and self-rights are the most natural candidate for autonomy-based rights. Moreover, to the extent that it is correct to think of us as, at least partly, embodied selves, then autonomy brings with it self-rights over our bodies, or at least over those parts of our bodies that are, at the same time, ourselves. Bluntly put: if one is going to respect another person as autonomous, that is, as having the right to rule herself, then one must respect that person's authority over her body. The less clearly things are parts of oneself, the less compelling is the extension of autonomy-based rights, especially self-rights, to them.

All of this becomes practically important when we consider interpersonal situations. Let's assume that we are talking about autonomous persons, unless otherwise specified. The crucial issue is more specific: the interplay of property-based and self-based rights. I shall focus on rights as a way of shedding light on the more specific sorts of claims that should structure relations between embodied autonomous persons. I have one sort of potential claim to others' bodies – property claims to the use of their bodies as some sort of resource – but I have two sorts of potential claims to my own body – property claims and self-based claims. Other people sit, asymmetrically, in the same relations to their bodies and to me and my body. Getting clear about this framework can be helpful in cases of conflict – that is, in cases where (let's say) two people make practically conflicting claims about the use of and authority over part of one of these persons' bodies. Such conflict can, in principle, take a variety of forms, but we can say a few things in general. First, very often the respective property claims will suffice to settle the issue. It will be clear that one person should be thought of as owning the body or body part in question and that the other person should be thought of as having no legitimate say over its use. This is such a common state of affairs that we are perhaps blind to it. This way of thinking, for instance, instantly settles the potential claims I might have to the use of the bodies of the people that live in my neighbourhood: there is no reason to think that I have legitimate property claims over their bodies, just as I have no such claims to their other kinds of property, and so any practical questions there might be, as things stand today, are instantly settled in favour of their authority over their bodies, purely considered as property.

The second thing to say concerns a much rarer situation: one in which the property-based claims of two people to the use of at least part of one their bodies seem to tie. That this should be thought to be rare is implied by the commonness of the situation discussed in the first paragraph. Let's acknowledge the conceptual possibility of such a tie in general without attending to the particular details that would have to be the case for such a tie actually to occur. These details don't matter, it seems to me, because of the asymmetrical relations people stand in with regard to bodies. When two people have equal property-based claims to the use of one of their bodies, the person whose body it is has a second sort of claim to it that breaks the tie. Putting aside the even rarer and more difficult case of conjoined twins, only one person can have a self-claim over a particular body or body part. In these cases, the tie is automatically broken in favour of the person whose body it is. The property-based claims can be factored out of the picture because, by hypothesis, they are equal. The only remaining claim is the self-based one.

The third sort of situation to consider is one in which one person has a property-claim to the use of another person's body that is greater than that person's own property-based claims. This might seem even rarer than the last case, but we should give this a second thought. Cases in which property-claims are equally balanced are likely to be rarer than cases in which one claim outweighs the other. Moreover, property rights are not free-floating. They are generated by more fundamental considerations, and when we turn to these we find the possible grounds for this sort of situation. This is not the place to discuss the details of a well-developed theory of property rights. Instead, consider two possible parts of a foundation for such rights. On one hand, we tend to think that legitimate property-claims are generated by labour: people are entitled to things that they earn through work. Besides this, we sometimes speak as if need generates legitimate property-claims. The idea of 'basic rights' reflects, in part, this foundation: need arguably generates legitimate claims to such things as food and shelter. Where one person's labour-generated property right conflicts with another person's need-generated right, we might well think that the second claim outweighs the first. Perhaps it is, for instance, legitimate for the coercive powers of the state to be used to take a portion of wealthy citizens' income through taxation in order to provide food and shelter for other people.

These lines of thought present the following possibility with regard to bodies: one person's property-based claim to a second person's body could, in principle, outweigh the second person's property-based claim to their own body when the first claim is generated by need and the second is not (at least in the immediate circumstances). This is arguably what is found in many cases of pregnancy: the fetus needs the mother's body to survive, but the mother's sharing of her body with the fetus does not compromise any needs of her own. The qualification 'arguably' is very important here: this way of framing the situation presupposes many controversial things. For instance, it assumes that fetuses can have rights, including (to make it explicit) a right to life. I do not think that this is the case, but there are two reasons for making this assumption here. First, the grounds of such rights are sufficiently contestable to require extensive discussion to settle definitively, and this is not the place for such discussion.

More importantly, it is illuminating to see what follows if we allow this assumption, both theoretically and practically. So I shall make this assumption for the sake of argument. Even in such a case, we have reason to think that the second person's self-based claims to the body – in the case of pregnancy, the mother's self-based claims to her body – decide the case in favour of this person's authority over the body in question. At the very least it is a very important consideration that should not be thought to be automatically over-ridden by property-based claims.

Why might this be the case? To dispossess someone of a piece of their property is one thing; to violate that person's very self is quite another, calling out for more justification, and perhaps even justification of a different kind. A line of thought that supports the body-owner's authority over her body even in cases where the other person has a greater property-based claim than her own to her body is found when we turn to the question of the foundation of a right to life. This right famously needs interpretation as to its limits. What should be included – protection against mortal harm? Must others merely refrain from killing us, or must they also give us aid when we face such peril? Does this right bring with it access to basic resources? If so, is it only when these are easily provided, or also when they cost a lot and take great effort to provide? The grounds of the right to life can reasonably be thought to aid us in answering these questions. We do not have a right to life due to life itself, lest we think dandelions and viruses share this right with us, which I find implausible. Nor is it due to being a member of particular species, such as *homo sapiens*: the moral irrelevance of species membership was brought up in Chapter 7, and it implies that this cannot be the foundation of a right to life. Here is my suggestion: the right to life is derived from the value of selfhood. The psychology that is required to be a self should be seen as a necessary condition of having a right to life. Perhaps it is not sufficient –perhaps only particular kinds of selves have rights to life – but let's put this aside for present purposes and give any self a right to life. If this is at all correct, then we should think of the right to life as in place to defend selves. This in turn suggests limits to the right to life: one person's self-based right to life generates potentially legitimate claims within limits: it is constrained by other people's self-based rights.

This view of the foundation of the right to life strongly suggests the solution to the practical problem we are currently considering.

When one person's need generates a property-claim to another person's body that is greater than the second person's own property-based claims, the second person's self-based authority nevertheless is decisive. It is not that the self-rights that one has to one's body are more important than the other person's property-claims. We need not think that the value of a self is more important than, and hence outweighs, the value of life, although we should take the value of selves seriously. This is the wrong way to think of the conflict between these sorts of value. It is instead that the legitimate domain of property-claims generated by considerations of the value of selves does not include other selves. Strictly speaking, when we consider our bodies as parts of autonomous selves, other people can have no over-riding claim here at all. Self-rights are not necessarily more important claims; they are instead prior claims, and this priority suffices to make them decisive. Because of this priority, questions of balancing and of which is more important do not arise at all. The legitimacy of others' use of our bodies derives from our autonomous consent to this; when such consent is withdrawn, others have no legitimate grounds on which to make an overriding appeal.

Two qualifications are worth noting. First, we tend to think that rights can be overridden once the stakes are high enough. Presumably, this applies to self-rights just as much as to property rights. If we combine this with the present focus on need-generated property claims, then we get the possibility that, if enough lives could be saved by the use of one autonomous person's body, this can be justified even if the person in question does not consent. This is probably true, even if it is arguably tragic. The question of the extent of the threshold that must be passed for such use to be legitimate will have to be addressed somewhere else. Second, the present line of thought applies specifically to property-rights that are generated by need. Perhaps there can be a distinct ground of property rights which delivers greater property-based claims for one person to another person's body than the second person has. The specific details of such a case require direct attention for a satisfactory treatment. That being said, we should nevertheless think that the present line of thought makes it very unlikely that self-rights over bodies will be somehow outweighed by such other grounds of rights. Need, after all, is a very important consideration, and it fails to deliver to others overriding authority over our bodies.

The implications for thinking about pregnancy and abortion are worth making more explicit. Even if we make very generous assumptions and think of the fetus as having both a self and a right to life, this does not mean that abortion is impermissible. The reason is that a fetal right to life does not deliver to the fetus authority over the mother's body. The mother retains this, not because her body is her property but because it is part of her 'self', and self-rights limit the legitimate domain of others' property rights. At the very least, the mother acts within her rights by removing bodily support for the fetus's life, which, in practical terms, requires removal of the fetus from her body. The details about how this should be done will depend on our practical and technological abilities and limitations, as well as on further details about fetal rights, none of which can be pursued here.

The present line of thought about abortion is very much in the spirit of Judith Jarvis Thomson's famous argument in 'A Defense of Abortion'. The difference lies in the details. Thomson does not explicitly address the underlying nature of the right to life, but she speaks as if it at least involves property rights, and it is common for people to interpret her case in terms of property rights (e.g., Mackenzie 1992, p. 150). Thomson makes her case by considering a series of cases that are not themselves about pregnancy or abortion, but which instead concern the right to life and other rights. The one that gives the strongest impression of the right to control one's body as a property right concerns a coat: two people are at risk of freezing to death, and there is only one coat available to keep them warm. Thomson writes, 'If Jones has found and fastened on a certain coat, which he needs to keep him from freezing, but which Smith also needs to keep him from freezing, then it is not impartiality that says "I cannot choose between you" when Smith owns the coat. Women have said again and again "This body is my body!" and they have reason to feel angry, reason to feel that it has been like shouting into the wind.' (1971, p. 53) The line of thought presented in this chapter suggests that it is not incorrect to speak of our bodies as our property – they are. But it is certainly incomplete to do so, and with regard to the ethics of abortion it is arguably misleading, if not beside the point. Ultimately it is not property rights that ground women's authority over their bodies, it is self-rights.

Presumably it is not surprising that autonomy is relevant to the question of the moral permissibility of abortion. Many philosophers discuss abortion in terms of autonomy. Moreover, given that this question belongs to the broader category of medical ethics, the centrality of autonomy generally to ethical issues in medicine applies to this more specific issue. The direct contribution of this discussion to considerations of the issue-omnirelevance of autonomy is minor. But the indirect contribution is more significant, and it comes via contributions to our view of the potential constitutive omnirelevance of autonomy. At the very least, the ideas in this section suggest that it is necessary to consider autonomy in order to understand the value our bodies have. More tentatively, the present discussion points towards the relevance of autonomy to the right to life and even to property rights. These values show up in many diverse moral issues. If the present case does indeed contribute this much to our view of the constitutive relevance of autonomy, it thereby contributes a great deal to our sense of the extent of its issue-relevance.

Some concluding reflections about constitutive omnirelevance

I think that enough has been said to constitute a presumptive case in favour of seeing autonomy as issue-omnirelevant. In Chapters 6 and 7 I addressed some ways in which autonomy shows up as significant in interpersonal relations. Some of these were specific, but others were abstract and hence of wide application. In this chapter, I have briefly looked at autonomy in interpersonal relations mediated by representations, on one hand, and by our embodiment on the other. Autonomy is showing up as relevant, and perhaps even as decisive, in a lot of places. However, more should be said about whether autonomy is constitutively omnirelevant. Does autonomy show up in a lot of places just because self-rule happens to be relevant to so many of the situations in which we find ourselves? Or is this constant presence due, instead, to a more fundamental role for autonomy in our evaluative concerns?

As with issue-omnirelevance, a presumptive case has already been growing in favour of seeing autonomy as constitutively omnirelevant. Further planks could be added to this case by considering the role of autonomy in still more values. The discussions of advertising and embodiment concern individual autonomy as a limit on others' behaviour. Further contributions could be made by finding cases in which autonomy seems to function as a goal. For instance, Onora O'Neill makes a Kantian case for interpreting the demands of justice and benevolence in terms of the autonomy of the people with whom one is interacting, and particularly in terms of their ability to endorse or reject the things that you want to do with them (1986). The capacity for and performance of such endorsing and rejecting is just what the present account offers as the nature of autonomous choice. More specifically (but translated into the terminology of the present book), O'Neill contends that justice requires that we treat the autonomy of others as a constraint on our behaviour with them, whereas benevolence requires that we make their autonomy a goal for ourselves. For another example, Mihaly Csikszentmihalyi argues, on an empirical basis, for a constitutive role for autonomy in happiness (1991). Csikszentmihalyi used beeper technology to interrupt subjects at all times of the day; subjects were to report at that moment what they were doing and how happy they were. On the basis of these studies, Csikszentmihalyi claims that a particularly deep form of happiness is associated with being immersed in activities that require us to perform near the limits (but not past them) of our abilities. Another way of putting this is to say that we are significantly happy when we get a chance to exercise control in challenging ways over the things that we do. To exercise such control, to my ear, is part of what we mean when we speak of being autonomous. On its face, Csikszentmihalyi's research seems to support a case for seeing our own autonomy as a goal for ourselves.

I will not pursue the details of these cases any further, nor will I add any more planks to the case for the constitutive omnirelevance of autonomy. Readers can pursue the details of these projects on their own. Instead, I shall conclude with two questions. Suppose that autonomy turns out to be constitutively omnirelevant. Why might this be the case, and what should we do about it?

Here are two merely suggestive lines of thought to explain the (hypothetical) constitutive omnirelevance of autonomy. The first is an ancient line of thought about values in general which has been put in an influential way by John McDowell (1979). The ancient line of thought, including McDowell's, is put in terms of virtues rather than values, and can be thought of as a 'unity of virtues' thesis in its traditional form. Consider a hypothetically just person.

This person has the virtue 'justice' and is thereby sensitive to justice-based claims. However, for this to be the case, this person must be sensitive to claims of indefinitely many kinds. The reason is that, due to particular details of specific cases, the claims of justice are interwoven with claims based on other values. For instance, the just person must also be sensitive to the things to which the benevolent person is sensitive. The reason is that, sometimes, claims of justice are tempered and even outweighed by claims based on benevolence. One cannot really understand justice without understanding how it works in connection with benevolence. This point can be repeated for any value and any virtue. The implication is that it is misleading to speak of virtues and values on a one-to-one basis. Instead, we should think of virtues and values as deeply unified. Rather than people who are individually sensitive either to the demands of benevolence or to the demands of justice, we should think of the overall outlook of virtuous people, sensitive to various interwoven demands. Although it is traditional to speak of the purported unity of virtues, we can just as well call this a 'unity of value' thesis, as it implies that the demands of, for example, justice are deeply interwoven with those presented by other values, such that for an agent to be sensitive to one value, she must be sensitive to all of them. The unity of virtue/value thesis is contentious, to the extent of being a live topic, subject to reasonable debate, among contemporary ethicists. We cannot assume that it is either true or false. If it turns out to be vindicated, however, then it provides an explanation for why autonomy is omnirelevant. Although the unity of value thesis is dramatic, its implications for autonomy are not uniquely striking. The reason is that, by the standards of a general unity of value thesis, *any* particular value is constitutively omnirelevant. There is no such thing as a value that is not deeply interwoven with other values. Given this, there is no surprise that autonomy is constitutively omnirelevant; every value is.

The second line of thought that I shall offer as a possible explanation of the (hypothetical) constitutive omnirelevance of autonomy is more specific. However, it is arguably even more tentative than the argument based on the unity of values. The very notion of 'autonomy' concerns, somehow, our control of our actions. This is arguably the key to understanding the constitutive value of autonomy. The reason is that values, whatever else they are and whatever else they do, regulate our conduct. That is, they are, by definition, relevant to questions of how we ought to act. Autonomy of action, however, is, for practical purposes, action with a certain sort of psychological source. That is, just as values concern how we act, so does the very notion of autonomy. Wherever questions of how to act arise, this line of thought goes, so do questions of autonomy. Since these questions arise wherever it makes sense to speak of values, autonomy is omnirelevant with regard to questions of value.

As suggestive as this line of thought is, I think that we should not take it as definitive. The reason is that we speak ambiguously when we speak of 'how to act'. Sometimes we mean to refer to our manner of acting when we use this terminology. By 'manner of acting' I mean to direct attention to the thoughts from which action proceeds. For example, sometimes we act habitually, at other times quite self-consciously and deliberately. Sometimes we act thoughtlessly, sometimes not, and so on. This is the sense to which autonomy is, by definition, relevant, for autonomy, with regard to choice and action, is a matter of the manner by which we choose and act. However, when we ask about how to act, sometimes – arguably often – we are interested in finding out what we should do, regardless of how we think about these things. For instance, one might hold that people should give a certain percentage of their income to charity regardless of whether they like this idea. The value of giving this percentage need not be affected by how people feel about giving this amount. Maybe the people who like giving this amount should be admired, whereas the people who resent it should be admonished. Regardless, the value of their giving need not be sensitive to their attitudes: it is what is owed, let's say, and it is good because of its nature and effects, not because of its psychological roots. On this understanding of questions about how we should act, autonomy is not automatically relevant. Since autonomy pertains to the origins of action, to the extent that values are not determined by considerations of the origins of action, autonomy will be constitutively irrelevant.

Let's turn to the implications of the (hypothetical) constitutive omnirelevance of the value of autonomy. These pertain to our theoretical and practical concerns about conflict between values. We typically think that values can, and do, conflict. For example, justice might require that wealth is taken away from a particular person, but benevolence might require that this person be allowed to keep this money. But if autonomy is constitutively omnirelevant, then it helps to make apparently other values what they are. This at least complicates our understanding of whether and how autonomy can conflict with other values.

There are stronger and weaker interpretations of the challenge that would be raised in this event. I shall start with the stronger one: although I have spoken, at least in passing, of autonomy clashing with other values, this is not possible. If autonomy is constitutively omnirelevant, then such conflict among values is impossible. This poses the following theoretical and practical challenge: instead of trying to settle conflicts between autonomy and other values, we must work to understand what is generating the appearance of such conflict. This should throw details on how autonomy and merely-apparently-distinct values fit together, and, hopefully, these details will illuminate how we should act.

A weaker interpretation of the implications of constitutive omnirelevance preserves the possibility of genuine conflict among values. However, this approach requires us to rethink the nature and implications of such conflict. Suppose that autonomy is omnirelevant by being a part of other values. Distinct parts of wholes can conflict. Suppose that we seem to be faced by a conflict between autonomy and happiness, but that we also think that autonomy is constitutively interwoven with happiness. That is, we think that individual self-rule is a component of human happiness. This seems to rule out a conflict between autonomy and happiness, but it doesn't rule out conflict between autonomy and other components of human happiness. The challenge, then, when faced with apparent conflict between autonomy and other values is to ensure that we have a clear grasp of the details. What seems like conflict between autonomy and some other generally compelling value might turn out to be more specific, more tractable, and less tragic.

Two worries should be raised about the weaker interpretation. First, when pressed, it might turn out to be unstable. Suppose that autonomy is a value and is, at the same time, a component of other values. These other values have other components, and presumably some of these are also values, just like autonomy. If autonomy is literally constitutively omnirelevant, then it seems to be a constituent of these other components as well. But this now calls into question the possibility of conflict after all. So, the weaker interpretation, when pushed, might turn out not to be an alternative to the stronger interpretation. Conflict between autonomy and other values might be ruled out either way.

The first worry calls into question whether the weaker interpretation is weak at all. The second worry wonders whether it isn't even weaker than it seems. The details to which this interpretation draws our attention are of at least two kinds. On one hand there are the details about the content of particular values. This book is about the nature and significance of autonomy in general; in particular situations there will be specific details about particular lives and particular opportunities and challenges to self-rule. Similar details will be needed for the other values of which autonomy is a part and with which it interacts to compose these values, as well as about the particular situations in which these values function at particular times. On the other hand, more abstract details about such things as part-whole relations are also needed. The weak interpretation assumes that parts cannot conflict with wholes, but perhaps this is not true. If parts can conflict with wholes, then the constitutive omnirelevance of autonomy does not call into question the possibility of conflict with values after all. Presumably, particular conditions must be satisfied for there to be conflict between parts and wholes, and this implies that when autonomy seems to clash with another value, we must still attend to the details to ascertain whether this appearance is genuine or misleading.

It might seem that both the weak and strong interpretations of the (hypothetical) constitutive omnirelevance of autonomy make thought about autonomy and other values hopelessly difficult, by turning our attention to lots of details about diverse issues. This worry, however, is born only of the abstract nature of these concluding remarks. The discussions of autonomy and related issues presented in this book, and in books like it, stand as examples of the sorts of work that are required. Moreover, this sort of work has to be done, and will be performed, even if autonomy is not constitutively omnirelevant. Regardless of this particular issue, I hope that the preceding chapters convey the sense that this work is worthwhile.

Reading guide

Gerald Dworkin's remark about autonomy in political philosophy is found in his 'Autonomy' in Goodin and Pettit (eds), *A Companion to Contemporary Political Philosophy* (Blackwell Publishers Ltd, 1993), pp. 359–65.

My treatment of advertising is drawn from Andrew Sneddon's 'Advertising and deep autonomy', *Journal of Business Ethics*, Vol. 33, No. 1 (September 2001), 15–28, but it is modified to use the terminology that I have used throughout this book. The relevant papers that I discuss are: 1] Robert L. Arrington, 'Advertising and behavior control', *Journal of Business Ethics*, Vol. 1 (1982); 3–12. 2] Roger Crisp, 'Persuasive advertising, autonomy, and the creation of desire', *Journal of Business Ethics*, Vol. 6 (1987), 413–18; 3] Barbara J. Phillips, 'In defense of advertising: a social perspective', *Journal of Business Ethics*, Vol. 16 (1997), 109–18 and 4] John Waide, 'The making of self and world in advertising', *Journal of Business Ethics*, Vol. 6 (1987), 73–9. Much has been written on advertising and autonomy since these papers, as well as on advertising and other ethical issues, but I am not convinced that the treatments of issues of basic concern have improved. There is also a lot to be read about subliminal persuasion and indeed, about subconscious aspects of our thought in general, and here I am confident that our understanding is improving steadily. For an accessible entry point, see Wikipedia: http://en.wikipedia.org/wiki/Subliminal_stimuli.

Judith Jarvis Thomson's famous paper on abortion is 'A defense of abortion', *Philosophy & Public Affairs*, Vol. 1, No. 1 (Autumn 1971), 47–66. It has been widely reprinted and discussed. Notable responses are too numerous to list. I refer to Catriona Mackenzie, 'Abortion and embodiment', *Australasian Journal of Philosophy*, Vol. 70, No. 2 (1992), 136–55, because it is so clearly related to the concerns of this chapter.

The Formula of the 'End In Itself' comes from Immanuel Kant, *Grounding for the Metaphysics of Morals* (widely available from various publishers and in anthologies). Onora O'Neill presents her widely read interpretation in 'A simplified version of Kant's ethics: perplexities of famine and world hunger', in Tom Regan (edited.), *Matters of Life and Death: New Introductory Essays in Moral Philosophy*, *2nd Edition* (Random House, 1986), pp. 319–29.

Mihaly Csikszentmihalyi's work on happiness can found in the relatively new edition of his *Flow: The Psychology of Optimal Experience* (Harper Perennial, 2008).

John McDowell's famous treatment of the unity of virtue thesis is in his 'Virtue and reason', *The Monist*, Vol. 62, No. 3, The Concept of a Person in Ethical Theory (July 1979), 331–50. McDowell attributes this thesis to Socrates.

BIBLIOGRAPHY

Adams, F. and Aizawa, K. (2010), *The Bounds of Cognition*. Oxford: Wiley-Blackwell.

Aristotle (1962), *Nicomachean Ethics*. New York: Macmillan.

Arrington, R. L. (1982), 'Advertising and behavior control', *Journal of Business Ethics* 1, 3–12.

Benson, P. (2005), 'Feminist intuitions and the normative substance of autonomy', in J. S. Taylor (ed.), *Personal Autonomy: New Essays on Personal Autonomy and Its Role in Contemporary Moral Philosophy*. Cambridge: Cambridge University Press, pp. 124–42.

Berlin, I. (2002), 'Two concepts of liberty', reprinted in H. Hardy (ed.), *Liberty*. Oxford: Oxford University Press.

Berofsky, B. (1995), *Liberation from Self: A Theory of Personal Autonomy*. Cambridge: Cambridge University Press.

—(2005), 'Autonomy without free will', in J. S. Taylor (ed.), *Personal Autonomy: New Essays on Personal Autonomy and Its Role in Contemporary Moral Philosophy*. Cambridge: Cambridge University Press, pp. 58–86.

Bickenbach, J. (1998), 'Disability and life-ending decisions', in M. Battin, R. Rhodes and A. Silvers (eds), *Physician-Assisted Suicide: Expanding the Debate*. London: Routledge, pp. 123–32.

Birch, A. H. (1993), *The Concepts and Theories of Modern Democracy*. London: Routledge.

The Canadian Charter of Rights and Freedoms: http://publications.gc.ca/collections/Collection/CH37-4-3-2002E.pdf

Childress, J. F. (1983), *Who Should Decide? Paternalism in Health Care*. Oxford: Oxford University Press.

Childress, J. F. and Siegler, M. (1984), 'Metaphors and models of doctor-patient relationships: their implications for autonomy', *Theoretical Medicine and Bioethics* 5, 17–30.

Christman, J. (1991), 'Autonomy and personal history', *Canadian Journal of Philosophy*, 21, 1, 1–24.

—(1993), 'Defending historical autonomy: a reply to Professor Mele', *Canadian Journal of Philosophy*, 23, 281–90.

—(2009), *The Politics of Persons: Individual Autonomy and Socio-historical Selves*. Cambridge: Cambridge University Press.

Christman, J. and Anderson, J. (eds) (2005), *Autonomy and the Challenges to Liberalism*. Cambridge: Cambridge University Press.

Clark, A. (2008), *Supersizing the Mind*. Oxford: Oxford University Press.

Clark, A. and Chalmers, D. (1998), 'The extended mind', *Analysis*, 58, 10–23 (reprinted in Clark's *Supersizing the Mind*).

Colburn, B. (2010), *Autonomy and Liberalism*. New York: Routledge.

Crisp, R. (1987), 'Persuasive advertising, autonomy, and the creation of desire', *Journal of Business Ethics*, 6, 413–18.

Csikszentmihalyi, M. (2008), *Flow: The Psychology of Optimal Experience*. New York: Harper Perennial.

Dancy, J. (1991), *Introduction to Contemporary Epistemology*. Oxford: Wiley-Blackwell.

Davidson, D. (2001), 'Knowing one's own mind', in his *Subjective, Intersubjective, Objective*. Oxford: Oxford University Press, pp. 15–38.

de Marneffe, P. (1990), 'Liberalism, liberty, and neutrality', *Philosophy & Public Affairs*, 19, 3 (Summer), 253–74.

Dennett, D. (1992), *Consciousness Explained*. London: Penguin Books.

—(2003), *Freedom Evolves*. New York: Penguin Books.

Doris, J. (2002), *Lack of Character*. Cambridge: Cambridge University Press.

Dworkin, G. (1972), 'Paternalism', *The Monist*, 56, 64–84.

—(1988), *The Theory and Practice of Autonomy*. Cambridge: Cambridge University Press.

—(1993), 'Autonomy', in R. E. Goodin and P. Pettit (eds), *A Companion to Contemporary Political Philosophy*. Oxford: Blackwell, pp. 359–65.

—(2010), 'Paternalism', *Stanford Encyclopedia of Philosophy*: http://stanford.library.usyd.edu.au/entries/paternalism/

Dworkin, R. (1977), *Taking Rights Seriously*. London: Duckworth.

—(1978), 'Liberalism', in S. Hampshire (ed.), *Public and Private Morality*. Cambridge: Cambridge University Press, pp. 113–43.

Ekstrom, L. W. (1993), 'A coherence theory of autonomy', *Philosophy and Phenomenological Research*, 53, 3 (September), 599–616.

—(1999), 'Keystone preferences and autonomy', *Philosophy and Phenomenological Research*, 59, 4 (December), 1057–63.

—(2005), 'Autonomy and personal integration', in J. S. Taylor (ed.), *Personal Autonomy: New Essays on Personal Autonomy and Its Role in Contemporary Moral Philosophy*. Cambridge: Cambridge University Press, pp. 143–61.

Ereshefsky, M. (ed.) (1991), *The Units of Evolution*. Cambridge, MA: MIT University Press.

Fischer, J. M. (2006), *My Way: Essays on Moral Responsibility*. Oxford: Oxford University Press.

Fischer, J. M. and Ravizza, M. (eds) (1993), *Perspectives on Moral Responsibility*. Ithaca, NY: Cornell University Press.

—(1998), *Responsibility and Control: A Theory of Moral Responsibility*. Cambridge: Cambridge University Press.

Frankfurt, H. (1969), 'Alternate possibilities and moral responsibility', *Journal of Philosophy*, 66, 3 (December 4), 829–39.

—(1971), 'Freedom of the will and the concept of a person', *Journal of Philosophy*, 68, 1 (January 14), 5–20.

—(1988), *The Importance of What We Care About*. Cambridge: Cambridge University Press.

Friedman, M. (2003), *Autonomy, Gender, Politics*. Oxford: Oxford University Press.

Funder, D. C. (1999), *Personality Judgment*. Washington: Academic Press.

Garren, D. (2006), 'Paternalism, part I', *Philosophical Books*, 47, 4 (October), 334–41.

—(2007), 'Paternalism, part II', *Philosophical Books*, 48, 1 (January), 50–9.

Glannon, W. (2005), *Biomedical Ethics*. Oxford: Oxford University Press.

Goldberg, L. R. (1993), 'The structure of phenotypic personality traits', *American Psychologist*, 48, 26–34.

Goodin, R. E. and Pettit, P. (eds) (1993), *A Companion to Contemporary Political Philosophy*. Oxford: Blackwell.

Greene, J. and Cohen, J. (2004), 'For the law, neuroscience changes nothing and everything', *Phil. Trans. R. Soc. Lond. B*, 359, 1775–85.

Guyer, P. (2003), 'Kant on the theory and practice of autonomy', in E. Frankel Paul, F. D. Miller, Jr. and J. Paul (eds), *Autonomy*. Cambridge: Cambridge University Press, pp. 70–98.

Haji, I. (2005), 'Alternative possibilities, personal autonomy, and moral responsibility', in J. S. Taylor (ed.), *Personal Autonomy: New Essays on Personal Autonomy and Its Role in Contemporary Moral Philosophy*. Cambridge: Cambridge University Press, 235–57.

Hartshorne, H. and May, M. A. (1928), *Studies in the Nature of Character I: Studies in Deceit*. New York: MacMillan.

Hoefer, C. (2010), 'Causal determinism', *Stanford Encyclopedia of Philosophy*: http://plato.stanford.edu/entries/determinism-causal/

Hurley, S. (2011), 'The public ecology of responsibility', in C. Knight and Z. Stemplowska (eds), *Responsibility and Distributive Justice*. Oxford: Oxford University Press, pp. 187–215.

Hurka, T. (1987), 'Why value autonomy?', *Social Theory and Practice*, 13, 3, 361–82.

Isen, A. M. and Levin, P. F. (1972), 'Effect of feeling good on helping: cookies and kindness', *Journal of Personality and Social Psychology*, 21, 384–8.

Kant, I. (1970), 'On the common saying "This may be true in theory but it does not apply in practice"', in H. Reiss (ed.), *Kant's Political Writings*. Cambridge: Cambridge University Press, pp. 61–92.

——(1993), *Grounding for the Metaphysics of Morals*, J. W. Ellington (trans). Indianapolis: Hackett Publishing Company.

Kymlicka, W. (1989), 'Liberal individualism and liberal neutrality', *Ethics*, 99, 4, 883–905.

——(2002), *Contemporary Political Philosophy: An Introduction, 2nd Edition*. Oxford: Oxford University Press.

Libet, B., Gleason, C. A., Wright, E. W. and Pearl, D. K. (1983), 'Time of conscious intention to act in relation to onset of cerebral activity (readiness-rotential)', *Brain*, 106, 623–42.

Mackenzie, C. (1992), 'Abortion and embodiment', *Australasian Journal of Philosophy*, 70, 2, 136–55.

MacKenzie, C. and Stoljar, N. (eds) (2000), *Relational Autonomy: Feminist Perspectives on Autonomy, Agency and the Social Self*. New York: Oxford University Press.

Mason, A. D. (1990), 'Liberalism and state neutrality', *The Philosophical Quarterly*, 40, 161 (October), 433–52.

McCrae, R. R. and Costa, Jr., P. T. (1996), 'Toward a new generation of personality theories: theoretical contexts for the five-factor model', in J. S. Wiggins (ed.), *The Five-Factor Model of Personality: Theoretical Perspectives*. New York: Guilford, pp. 51–87.

McDowell, J. (1979), 'Virtue and reason', *The Monist*, 62, 3, *The Concept of a Person in Ethical Theory* (July), 331–50.

McKenna, M. (2005), 'The relationship between autonomous and morally responsible agency', in J. S. Taylor (ed.), *Personal Autonomy: New Essays on Personal Autonomy and Its Role in Contemporary Moral Philosophy*. Cambridge: Cambridge University Press, pp. 205–34.

Mele, A. (1991), 'History and personal autonomy', *Canadian Journal of Philosophy*, 23, 271–80.

——(1995), *Autonomous Agents: From Self-Control to Autonomy*. Oxford: Oxford University Press.

——(2006), *Free Will and Luck*. Oxford: Oxford University Press.

——(2009), *Effective Intentions: The Power of Conscious Will*. Oxford: Oxford University Press.

Meyers, D. T. (1989), *Self, Society, and Personal Choice*. New York: Columbia University Press.

——(2004), *Being Yourself: Essays on Identity, Action, and Social Life*. Lanham, MD: Rowman and Littlefield Publishers.

—(2005), 'Decentralizing autonomy: five faces of selfhood', in
J. Christman and J. Anderson (eds), *Autonomy and the Challenges to
Liberalism*. Cambridge: Cambridge University Press, pp. 27–55.

Milgram, S. (1963), 'Behavioral study of obedience', *Journal of Abnormal
and Social Psychology*, 67, 371–8.

Mischel, W. (1968), *Personality and Assessment*. New York: John Wiley
and Sons.

Nozick, R. (1974), *Anarchy, State, and Utopia*. New York: Basic Books.

O'Neill, O. (1986), 'A simplified version of Kant's ethics: perplexities
of famine and world hunger', in T. Regan (ed.), *Matters of Life and
Death: New Introductory Essays in Moral Philosophy, 2nd Edition*.
New York: Random House, pp. 319–29.

Oshana, M. (2005), 'Autonomy and free agency', in J. S. Taylor (ed.),
*Personal Autonomy: New Essays on Personal Autonomy and Its Role
in Contemporary Moral Philosophy*. Cambridge: Cambridge University
Press, pp. 183–204.

—(2006), *Personal Autonomy in Society*. Aldershot, UK: Ashgate.

Phillips, B. J. (1997), 'In defense of advertising: a social perspective',
Journal of Business Ethics, 16, 109–18.

Quinton, A. (1993), 'Conservativism', in R. E. Goodin and P. Pettit
(eds), *A Companion to Contemporary Political Philosophy*. Oxford:
Blackwell, pp. 244–68.

Rawls, J. (1971), *A Theory of Justice*. Cambridge, MA: Harvard
University Press.

—(1988), 'The priority of right and ideas of the good', *Philosophy &
Public Affairs*, 17, 4 (Autumn), 251–76.

—(1993), *Political Liberalism*. New York: Columbia University Press.

—(1997), 'The idea of public reason revisited', *University of Chicago Law
Review*, 64, 3 (Summer), 765–807.

Raz, J. (1986), *The Morality of Freedom*. Oxford: Oxford University Press.

Reibl V. Hughes (1980), 2 S.C.R. 880; http://en.wikipedia.org/wiki/
Reibl_v._Hughes.

Robbins, P. and Aydede, M. (eds) (2008), *The Cambridge Handbook of
Situated Cognition*. Cambridge: Cambridge University Press.

Ross, L. and Nisbett, R. E. (1991), *The Person and the Situation:
Perspectives of Social Psychology*. Philadelphia: Temple University Press.

Rousseau, J.-J. (1973), *The Social Contract and Discourses*. London:
J.M. Dent.

Ryan, A. (1993), 'Liberalism', in R. E. Goodin and P. Pettit (eds), *A
Companion to Contemporary Political Philosophy*. Oxford: Blackwell,
pp. 291–311.

Sartre, J.-P. (2007), *Existentialism as a Humanism*. New Haven: Yale
University Press.

Singer, P. (1975), *Animal Liberation*. New York: Harper Collins.

Sneddon, A. (2001a), 'What's wrong with selling yourself into slavery? Paternalism and deep autonomy', *Criticá*, 33, 98 (August), 97–121.

—(2001b), 'Advertising and deep autonomy', *Journal of Business Ethics*, 33, 1 (September), 15–28.

—(2006), 'Equality, justice, and paternalism: recentering debate about physician-assisted suicide', *Journal of Applied Philosophy*, 23, 4, 387–404.

—(2011), *Like-Minded: Externalism and Moral Psychology*. Cambridge, MA: MIT Press.

Soon, C. S., Brass, M., Heinze, H.-J. and Haynes, J. D. (2008), 'Unconscious determinants of free decisions in the human brain', *Nature Neuroscience*, 11, 5 (May), 543–5.

Stoljar, N. (2000), 'Autonomy and the feminist intuition', in C. MacKenzie and N. Stoljar (eds), *Relational Autonomy: Feminist Perspectives on Autonomy, Agency and the Social Self*. New York: Oxford University Press, pp. 94–111.

Strawson, P. F. (1962), 'Freedom and resentment', *Proceedings of the British Academy*, 48, 1–25.

Subliminal Stimuli: http://en.wikipedia.org/wiki/Subliminal_stimuli

Taylor, C. (1985a), 'Self-interpreting animals', in his *Human Agency and Language: Philosophical Papers 1*. Cambridge: Cambridge University Press, pp. 45–76.

—(1985b), 'What is Human Agency?', in his *Human Agency and Language: Philosophical Papers 1*. Cambridge: Cambridge University Press, pp. 15–44.

—(1985c), 'Atomism', in his *Philosophy and the Human Sciences: Philosophical Papers 2*. Cambridge: Cambridge University Press, pp. 187–210.

—(1989), *Sources of the Self: The Making of the Modern Identity*. Cambridge, MA: Harvard University Press.

—(1991), *The Ethics of Authenticity*. Cambridge, MA: Harvard University Press.

Taylor, J. S. (ed.) (2005), *Personal Autonomy: New Essays on Personal Autonomy and Its Role in Contemporary Moral Philosophy*. Cambridge: Cambridge University Press.

—(2009), *Practical Autonomy and Bioethics*. New York: Routledge.

Thomson, J. J. (1971), 'A defense of abortion', *Philosophy & Public Affairs*, 1, 1 (Autumn), 47–66.

van Inwagen, P. (1978), 'Ability and responsibility', *The Philosophical Review*, 87, 2 (April), 201–24.

Veatch, R. (1972), 'Models for ethical medicine in a revolutionary age', *Hastings Center Report*, 2 (June), 5–7.

—(2012), *The Basics of Bioethics, 3rd Edition*. Boston, MA: Pearson Education, Inc.

Velleman, D. (2005), 'The self as narrator', in J. Christman and J. Anderson (eds), *Autonomy and the Challenges to Liberalism*. Cambridge: Cambridge University Press, pp. 56–76.

Waide, J. (1987), 'The making of self and world in advertising', *Journal of Business Ethics*, 6, 73–9.

Waldron, J. (1987), 'Theoretical foundations of liberalism', *The Philosophical Quarterly*, 37, 147 (April), 127–50.

Wegner, D. (2002), *The Illusion of Conscious Will*. Cambridge, MA: MIT Press.

Wilson, R. A. (ed.) (1999), *Species: New Interdisciplinary Essays*. Cambridge, MA: MIT Press.

Wolf, S. (2005), 'Freedom within reason', in J. S. Taylor (ed.), *Personal Autonomy: New Essays on Personal Autonomy and Its Role in Contemporary Moral Philosophy*. Cambridge: Cambridge University Press, pp. 258–76.

INDEX